Ultimate Natural Language Processing with spaCy and Hugging Face

Master the End-To-End Journey of NLP by Using Foundational Methods, Building Projects with spaCy, and Fine-Tuning Transformer Models with Hugging Face

Abhinaba Banerjee

www.orangeava.com

First Published: October 2025

Published By: Orange Education Pvt Ltd, AVA®

Address: 9, Daryaganj, Delhi, 110002, India

275 New North Road Islington Suite 1314 London,
N1 7AA, United Kingdom

ISBN (PBK): 978-93-49888-63-0
ISBN (E-BOOK): 978-93-49888-46-3

Scan the QR code to explore our entire catalogue

www.orangeava.com

Dedicated To

My Beloved Mom and Dad,

Dipti Banerjee and Ajoy Kumar Banerjee-

My Strength and Support System.

About the Author

Abhinaba Banerjee holds a Master of Science in Big Data Analytics for Business from IESEG School of Management, Lille, France, and a Bachelor of Technology and Master of Technology in Electronics and Communication Engineering from MAKAUT (formerly West Bengal University of Technology), Kolkata, India. He has experience working with Fintech and social media startups in France and is currently employed as a Data Analyst with the Government of Andhra Pradesh. In this role, he works with real-world government data, focusing on data extraction, cleaning, and insight generation.

He has published several research papers in the field of Communication Engineering and signal processing.

Abhinaba frequently shares blogs on Medium, creates projects on MLOps, NLP, and AI, and actively posts on social media platforms such as Twitter.

In his free time, he likes listening to podcasts about history, technology, and horror.

About the Technical Reviewer

Karun Thankachan is a Senior Data Scientist at Walmart E-Commerce, specializing in Recommender Systems and Information Retrieval. His work focuses on leveraging data science to enhance item selection and availability for millions of customers. Karun's extensive career spans high-impact sectors, including E-Commerce, FinTech, and EdTech, where he has consistently contributed to complex data science and engineering projects. His technical leadership is evidenced by his numerous academic publications and his two patents in Machine Learning.

Beyond his professional role, Karun is deeply committed to nurturing the next generation of data scientists. He mentors extensively on platforms such as Topmate, where he has been recognized as a Top 50 Topmate Creator in North America (2024) and a Top 10 Data Mentor in the USA (2025).

He is highly active in the data science community, serving on the editorial boards of the *International Journal of Data, Knowledge and Process Management* (IJDKP) and the *Journal of Data Science* (JDS). He is also the co-founder of BuildML, a community that hosts weekly research discussions, and shares his insights with over 75,000 followers on LinkedIn.

Acknowledgments

Starting on the journey of writing *Ultimate Natural Language Processing with spaCy and Hugging Face* has been the most challenging task, blended with rigorous learning and testing my writing to the best potential. I am very thankful to the communities, the tool creators, and other fellow bloggers, article writers, course creators, and book writers, without whom I could not have completed the book as I wanted it to be.

To begin with, many thanks goes to the Data, NLP community and the wonderful professionals, without whom I could not have gotten the knowledge level, and foundation to write the book.

Especially, the Hugging Face LLM course, Transformers GitHub repositories, various NLP, LLM, and AI blogs by data camp, the various NLP and Deep Learning notebooks from Kaggle, and some real-life use cases that I created as part of the book curriculum that helped me understand the inside outs of the contents of the book. Moreover, the technical reviewers' careful attention to technical details and exhaustive theory-based explanations were the best inputs I got. Their dedication and expertise have been an asset, when it comes to improving the contents of the chapters, and maintaining the quality. Additionally, the inclusion of recent AI trends such as AI Agents, updated LLM models, and AI safety and ethics has made the book competitive in the market.

I thank my family for their unwavering support. Specifically, I want to express my deep appreciation to my mother, Dipti Banerjee, whose constant encouragement has been a real saver throughout the writing journey. I would also like to thank my father, Ajoy Kumar Banerjee, for his anchoring support throughout this endeavor.

I would also like to thank everyone at the publication house, *Orange Education Pvt Ltd* who have contributed in various capacities. Their collective efforts have just made things perfect by the day! I appreciate the collaborative spirit that has helped create *Ultimate Natural Language Processing with spaCy and Hugging Face*.

Finally, to the readers, thank you for choosing this book as your go-to book for learning. May it be a valuable companion on your journey to mastering NLP, using spaCy and Hugging Face.

Preface

The world of NLP is evolving faster than ever before, with the introduction of the *Attention is all you need* paper forming the bedrock of modern-day LLMs such as GPT, Llama, Grok, Claude, Deep Seek, and so on. With the most used supporting libraries such as nltk, spaCy, and Hugging Face, there are a lot of projects and real-life use cases on text summarization, text-to-text generation, question answering, text classification, and translation that are being created these days.

So, let us embark upon *Ultimate Natural Language Processing with spaCy and Hugging Face* – where you, the readers, will learn about NLP in depth, using theory and real-life use cases and thus, applying them in your workplace to stay ahead in the field of NLP and build projects.

This book comprises 12 chapters that will help you learn about the NLP concepts, and solve problems with them. You will know the theory, and be exposed to real-life use cases and projects. Python programming will be used, and the relevant libraries such as Hugging Face transformers, spaCy, and nltk, as well as related tools are also covered. You will have a hands-on exposure to NLP from scratch which will include basic NLP such as POS tagging, NER, word embeddings, and more recent models such as BERT, transformers, and GPT. Moreover, you will also be exposed to the recent trendy LLMs such as GPT, Llama, Claude, Grok, Deep Seek, Gemini, and so on.

Hence, whether you are a professional developer looking to expand your skills by building projects, or a fresher willing to learn and apply your knowledge in NLP, this book has something for everyone.

Chapter 1: Introduction to NLP and the Essential Libraries

The chapter lays the foundation for exploring NLP, introducing the important concepts and tools. The building blocks of NLP such as tokenization, stemming, lemmatization, and handling stop words, are also explained step by step. Also, the recently used powerful Python libraries such as spaCy, Hugging Face Transformers, and NLTK are introduced to the readers for preprocessing text, extracting information, and building our first NLP models.

Chapter 2: Building Blocks and Techniques for NLP Algorithms

This chapter dives deep into the building blocks of NLP algorithms. Techniques like the Bag-of-Words model, n-grams, and TF-IDF are being explored. Moreover, concepts such as word embeddings, sentence embeddings, and word sense disambiguation are introduced. Additionally, Parts-of-Speech (POS) tagging and Named Entity Recognition (NER) are also explained with examples, along with NLP evaluation metrics, coreference resolution, and dependency parsing.

Chapter 3: Sentiment Analysis Using NLP

This chapter has real-life use cases on sentiment analysis, topic classification, and text classification. Techniques such as bag-of-words, TF-IDF, word embeddings, POS tagging, NER, and sentence embeddings are used.

Chapter 4: Deep Learning in NLP

This chapter explains Deep Learning in NLP, where neural networks and their application to language tasks are explored. Concepts such as CNNs and RNNs are explained with hands-on Python coding from scratch.

Chapter 5: Working with CNN

This chapter has engaging projects leveraging CNN models. It has data understanding and exploration, data preparation, CNN model preparation and training, as well as model evaluation.

Chapter 6: Building NLP Pipelines Using spaCy

This chapter explains the concept of spaCy pipelines in detail, creates and customizes pipelines, and gives real-life NLP tasks, using pipelines such as tokenization and lemmatization, POS tagging, Named Entity Recognition, and Sentiment Analysis.

Chapter 7: Building a spaCy Pipeline for Extracting Information

This chapter builds spaCy pipelines to extract events and dates from news articles, extract customer and transaction information from business emails, and perform legal document analysis for entity and relationship extraction. These are real-life use cases that showcase the application side of spaCy.

Chapter 8: Building a Transformer Using Hugging Face

This chapter introduces the novel transformers architecture, the Hugging Face transformers library overview, training a custom transformer with code implementation, and exploring case studies with Python implementation such as medical text summarization for health records, personalized product recommendations, and fraud detection in credit card transactions.

Chapter 9: Training Language Models

This chapter explains the fundamentals of training language models, types of language models, fine-tuning a pre-trained model, training a custom model from scratch, and building a question-answering system.

Chapter 10: Importance of Large Language Models and their Applications

The chapter introduces Large Language Models (LLMs), their differences from traditional NLP models, the latest LLMs such as GPT-5, Claude-4 (Anthropic), Llama 3, Deep Seek R1, and Grok 3, the architecture and training methods, efficient training techniques such as LoRA, Mixture of Experts, and Distillation. This chapter also covers the capabilities and applications of LLMs such as content generation, Natural Language Understanding, chatbots, code generation, and search and information retrieval. Lastly, this chapter has information on the ethical considerations and responsible AI such as bias and fairness in LLMs, misinformation and hallucinations.

Chapter 11: Fine-Tuning LLMs and Building Text-Powered Tools

This chapter explains fine-tuning and different types of fine-tuning. Then, a text summarizer is fine-tuned as a case study. A code completion assistant and text generation system are built. Retrieval Augmented Generation is explored, and a pipeline is created. Then the fine-tuned models are evaluated, using Perplexity, BLEU, and F1 scores.

Chapter 12: Best Practices and Future Trends of NLP

This chapter shows the best practices in NLP, ethical and responsible AI, the five most influential research papers in NLP, an introduction to AI Agents, tools to build AI Agents, real-life use cases of AI Agents, and some future trends of NLP.

Get a Free eBook

We hope you are enjoying your recently purchased book! Your feedback is incredibly valuable to us, and to all other readers looking for great books.

If you found this book helpful or enjoyable, we would truly appreciate it, if you could take a moment to leave a short review with a 5 star rating on Amazon. It helps us grow, and lets other readers discover our books.

As a thank you, we would love to send you a free digital copy of this book, and a **30%** discount code on your next cart value on our official websites:

www.orangeava.com

www.orangeava.in (For Indian Subcontinent)

☑ **Here's how:**

Leave a review for the book on Amazon.

Take a screenshot of your review, and send an email to **info@orangeava.com** (it can be just the confirmation screen).

Once, we receive your screenshot, we will send you the digital file, within 24 hours.

Thank you so much for your support – it means a lot to us!

Downloading the code bundles and colored images

Please follow the links or scan the QR codes to download the ***Code Bundles and Images*** of the book:

https://github.com/ava-orange-education/Ultimate-Natural-Language-Processing-with-spaCy-and-Hugging-Face

The code bundles and images of the book are also hosted on ***https://rebrand.ly/2zyh9yh***

In case there's an update to the code, it will be updated on the existing GitHub repository.

Errata

We take immense pride in our work at **Orange Education Pvt Ltd,** and follow best practices to ensure the accuracy of our content to provide an indulging reading experience to our subscribers. Our readers are our mirrors, and we use their inputs to reflect and improve upon human errors, if any, that may have occurred during the publishing processes involved. To let us maintain the quality and help us reach out to any readers who might be having difficulties due to any unforeseen errors, please write to us at :

errata@orangeava.com

Your support, suggestions, and feedback are highly appreciated.

DID YOU KNOW

Did you know that Orange Education Pvt Ltd offers eBook versions of every book published, with PDF and ePub files available? You can upgrade to the eBook version at **www.orangeava.com** and as a print book customer, you are entitled to a discount on the eBook copy. Get in touch with us at: **info@orangeava.com** for more details.

At **www.orangeava.com**, you can also read a collection of free technical articles, sign up for a range of free newsletters, and receive exclusive discounts and offers on Print Books and eBooks.

PIRACY

If you come across any illegal copies of our works in any form on the internet, we would be grateful if you would provide us with the location address or website name. Please contact us at **info@orangeava.com** with a link to the material.

ARE YOU INTERESTED IN AUTHORING WITH US?

If there is a topic that you have expertise in, and you are interested in either writing or contributing to a book, please write to us at **business@orangeava.com**. We are on a journey to help developers and tech professionals to gain insights on the present technological advancements and innovations happening across the globe and build a community that believes Knowledge is best acquired by sharing and learning with others. Please reach out to us to learn what our audience demands and how you can be part of this educational reform. We also welcome ideas from tech experts and help them build learning and development content for their domains.

REVIEWS

Please leave a review. Once you have read and used this book, why not leave a review on the site that you purchased it from? Potential readers can then see and use your unbiased opinion to make purchase decisions. We at Orange Education would love to know what you think about our products, and our authors can learn from your feedback. Thank you!

For more information about Orange Education, please visit **www.orangeava.com**.

Table of Contents

CHAPTER 1
Introduction to NLP and the Essential Libraries

Introduction

We are in an era where computers can understand human language using the technology of **Natural Language Processing (NLP)**. NLP is a branch of Artificial Intelligence. In this chapter, we will slowly understand NLP and its real-life applications from search engines and chatbots to sentiment analysis and machine translation. We will understand the significance of using Python as the most significant programming language while solving NLP problems. We will learn about the fundamentals of text processing, such as tokenization, lemmatization, stemming, stop word removal, and so on. These are the basic building blocks of dealing with texts and understanding their significance, for example, extracting the sentiment of Amazon product reviews (positive, neutral, or negative), classifying topics into various categories such as news, sports, business, and so on. Finally, we will briefly explore relevant Python libraries such as Hugging Face Transformers and spaCy that will support us in building real-life NLP applications. Brace yourself and leverage NLP to its best to solve problems.

Structure

In this chapter, we will cover the following topics:

- Introduction to NLP
- Why is Python Used for NLP?
- NLP Fundamentals
    - Text Preprocessing

- Essential NLP Libraries
    - spaCy
    - Hugging Face Transformers
    - NLTK
- Projects and Further Exploration

Introduction to NLP

We are all aware of Siri, Cortana, Alexa, and even Jarvis (from the Iron Man movies). Siri, Cortana, Alexa, and Google Assistant are very good assistants when it comes to answering questions accurately. NLP is the technology that runs them. In the conventional era, the programming capabilities were not as flexible as present-day NLP algorithms that can easily comprehend human-level questions and answer them accurately.

NLP can tap into the unstructured texts from emails, documents, social media posts, news articles, and more for further analysis.

NLP utilizes these steps to understand and generate human-level responses:

1. **Decoding the meaning of texts:** NLP not only recognizes sentences, but it can also analyze the context, grammar, and sentiment to extract the intended meaning from a sentence or document exactly like a human does.
2. **Breaking the text into smaller chunks:** NLP leverages techniques such as tokenization that divide a text into smaller units, such as words or sentences, making it easier for the computers to perform further processing.
3. **Identify key elements:** NLP can recognize named entities (for example, people, places, organizations, and also specific tags such as dates, industry names, and landmarks), parts of speech (nouns, verbs, adjectives, pronouns), and relationships between the words, identifying the dependencies between them, providing valuable information about the meaning of the text.
4. **Generate intelligible texts:** NLP advancements can also generate texts on top of understanding them. This helps us to develop daily applications such as chatbots that can hold real-life conversations or generate texts as per the requirement.

Various applications of NLP help companies and individuals improve their businesses and ease their daily activities. Some of them are as follows.

- **Information Retrieval:** Search engines utilize NLP to detect and comprehend various user queries and deliver the right results with the best accuracy, making information retrieval faster and more efficient.

- **Sentiment Analysis:** NLP helps analyze the sentiment of the text data (as in Amazon product reviews, YouTube comment reviews, Twitter reviews, and so on), providing valuable insights into customer satisfaction and the mindset of the audience.
- **Machine Translation:** NLP minimizes language barriers by translating text from one language to another, thus improving communication and understanding across diverse cultures (Google Translate, Deepl, Reverso, to name a few). There are also dedicated devices that translate the original language to the target language in real time without switching on the application.
- **Chatbots and Virtual Assistants:** NLP is used to develop chatbots that understand user intent and respond in a natural way (customer service is heavily automated using chatbots, and humans are not doing the mundane tasks of talking to people and understanding queries; only complicated queries are being transferred to humans to be answerable).
- **Text Summarization:** NLP can generate summaries of large-sized documents, saving users time and effort, while also having the users get the most important topics from the documents.

The applications of NLP extend far beyond these use cases, thus being utilized in diverse sectors such as healthcare, finance, e-commerce, supply chain, and legal services, to name a few.

These days, NLP has evolved into something more revolutionary, where large texts can be generated from queries, codes, poems, short stories, and novels, and can be written using tools such as ChatGPT, Google Gemini, Microsoft Bing AI, Perplexity-AI, and Claude, to name a few.

Importance of Python in NLP

Natural Language Processing (NLP) is a fast-growing field that enables computers to understand human language and simplify tasks for people. Python is the ideal programming language for NLP developers due to its supportive features and conditions.

- **Readability and Simplicity:** One of Python's greatest strengths is its simple-to-understand syntax. This makes it easier to learn for anyone without a programming background. This user-friendly nature allows NLP practitioners to focus on building language processing applications rather than getting involved in the complexities of the programming language itself. Moreover, Python is a free tool, so anyone can start learning it without any fuss.
- **Diverse and Powerful Libraries:** Python is very well equipped with built-in libraries that provide a plethora of features and functionalities. Libraries such as spaCy have robust pipelines for tasks such as Named Entity Recognition (NER)

to identify people, places, dates, organizations, and so on, and Parts of Speech Tagging (POS) for identifying nouns, pronouns, verbs, adjectives, conjunctions, and so on. There is the Natural Language Toolkit (NLTK) library that forms the foundations of NLP and offers functionalities such as tokenization, stemming, lemmatization, stopword removal, and so on. Moreover, there is Hugging Face Transformers, which provides state-of-the-art pre-trained models such as BERT and GPT-3, to more recent text generation models such as MistralAI, Llama3 from Meta, and Phi-3 from Microsoft. However, Hugging Face also has categories of Computer Vision models, Audio (text-to-speech and speech-to-text), Reinforcement learning, and so on.

- **Smoother Development:** From the previous point on various powerful libraries, the developers can leverage them, and build their NLP applications quickly, test, add features, iterate, and repeat without doing a lot of coding in the background. The overall time and effort are saved with maximum efficiency.
- **Seamless usage:** NLP Applications or models written in Python can easily be run and reused on Linux and Mac systems (if they are written on the Windows Operating System). This way, collaboration among teams is smooth and flexible with easy deployment.
- **Active Community and Extensive Resources:** Python has a very large and active community. As of February 2024, the Python programming language community is estimated to have 8.2 million developers worldwide, which is 44.6% of all software developers. Python is the second most-used programming language on GitHub, with over four million developers using it in 2022. The language's popularity has grown due to the rise of data science and machine learning, and it is used to build websites and software, automate tasks, and conduct data analysis. Moreover, there are various online resources, tutorials, courses, blogs, and books that are a major help in solving NLP-based problems.

Overall, Python's ease of usage, being an open-source tool, having powerful libraries, smoother development, ease of seamless usage, and a large and active community of developers make it the number 1 choice for developers who are building NLP models and applications. Python can be used by any inexperienced programmer who is just starting to learn NLP or a highly experienced developer who has seen it all, in terms of text analysis to generating texts from queries.

NLP Fundamentals

Each of the fundamental techniques for text analysis is included in this part. Tokenization breaks down text into meaningful units, such as words or sentences. Stemming and lemmatization reduce words to their base forms, but with key distinctions. Stemming chops off suffixes without considering grammatical context, while lemmatization identifies the dictionary form (lemma) based on the language model's understanding. Stop word removal eliminates common words (for example, "*the*," "*a*") that carry little meaning on their own to make the analysis more efficient and focused.

Text Preprocessing

When NLP is performed, the machine must understand raw text data and prepare it for the next analysis step. This is known as text preprocessing, which involves breaking down texts into smaller chunks and removing irrelevant information. Several important steps make up Text Preprocessing. These are primarily the NLP fundamentals that every NLP practitioner needs to know: tokenization, stop word removal, stemming versus lemmatization, and (optional) normalization.

Tokenization

Sentences can be long or short depending on the number of words present. In tokenization, the sentence is divided into words, punctuation, emoticons, or even phrases called tokens. There are different types of tokenization.

- **Word tokenization:** Splitting the sentence into words.
- **Sentence tokenization:** Splitting a set of sentences into individual sentences.
- **N-gram Tokenization:** Creates sequences of n consecutive words (for example, bigrams, trigrams).

The type of tokenization depends on the specific NLP task that is needed for the user to perform. Word tokenization is most frequently used, but sentence tokenization is also useful when doing sentiment analysis at the sentence level, and n-grams are helpful for language modeling tasks.

We will see a Python code below to understand the process of tokenization using the spaCy library.

```
import spacy

nlp = spacy.load("en_core_web_sm")

text = "The best video game is Call of Duty, World War 2."
tokens = nlp(text)

for token in tokens:
    print(token.text)
```

spaCy is a library for advanced Natural Language Processing in Python. It has pre-trained pipelines and has functionalities for 70+ languages. We need to install the library and then import it. There are 4 trained pipelines for the English language.

One of them is "`en_core_web_sm`" which we are using in the above code snippet. The "`en_core_web_sm`" refers to a specific model size, with "`sm`" indicating a smaller, faster model. The **`tokens = nlp(text)`** processes the text using the loaded spaCy model, and the result is stored in the tokens variable. In the for loop, we have individual words that are printed using the **token.text** operation. This is called tokenization, and the individual words are the tokens.

```
The
best
video
game
is
Call
of
Duty
,
World
War
2
.
```

Figure 1.1: *Tokenization result*

The above screenshot shows the result of the tokenization, where we have the words and punctuations.

Stemming vs Lemmatization

Both stemming and lemmatization reduce words to their base form. However, there are important differences between the two:

Stemming: This process reduces suffixes to the base form.

For example, stemming might convert "**`running`**," "**`runs`**," and "**`ran`**" to a common base such as "**`run`**." There can be situations where words such as "**`universal`**", "**`university`**", and "**`universe`**" are reduced to the same base word (by Porter Stemmer algorithm in **`nltk`**), so, in that case, it is wrong since they are completely different in a contextual sense. This is also called **Overstemming**. In some cases, the words "*alumnus*," "alumnae," and "alumni" are reduced to the same word stem, but they should be synonyms. This is called **Understemming**. Also, words can be reduced to meaningless base forms that disturb the context of the sentence.

Let us take the example of a famous and most used Stemmer Algorithm known as the **`PorterStemmer`** using Python code. However, there are other Stemmers such as

Lancaster Stemmer, Lovins Stemmer, Dawson Stemmer, Krovetz Stemmer, Xerox Stemmer, N-Gram Stemmer, Snowball Stemmer, to name a few.

```
from nltk.stem import PorterStemmer
stemmer = PorterStemmer()
# Example words for stemming
words = ["running", "jumps", "happily", "running", "happily"]
# Apply stemming to each word
stemmed_words = [stemmer.stem(word) for word in words]
# Print the results
print("Original words:", words)
print("Stemmed words:", stemmed_words)
```

In the above code, we are using **nltk** (Natural Language Toolkit) as the library and **PorterStemmer** as the function. We have selected some words to understand the stemming process. We have the output as the main words and the final base words after stemming.

```
Original words: ['running', 'jumps', 'happily', 'borrow', 'begin']
Stemmed words: ['run', 'jump', 'happili', 'borrow', 'begin']
```

Figure 1.2: *Stemming result*

From the above result, we can see that the stemmed words are fine in all the cases except for happily.

Lemmatization: This process uses a dictionary and morphological analysis to identify the dictionary form (lemma) of a word. Thus, the base form of any word is meaningful.

For example, lemmatization would correctly identify the lemma for "**running**," "**runs**," and "**ran**" as "**run**." Lemmatization is generally more accurate but computationally expensive compared to stemming.

For lemmatization, we will see the Python code.

```
import nltk
from nltk.stem import WordNetLemmatizer
nltk.download('punkt')
lemmatizer = WordNetLemmatizer()
print("boxes :", lemmatizer.lemmatize("rocks"))
print("universal :", lemmatizer.lemmatize("corpora"))
# a denotes adjective in "pos"
print("anger :", lemmatizer.lemmatize("angry", pos="a"))
```

In the above code, we are using the function **WordNetLemmatizer** from the **nltk** library. There is the resource package "**punkt**" that needs to be done for sentence tokenization before lemmatization. We are creating a **lemmatizer** object from **WordNetLemmatizer** and using the **lemmatize()** function on the words. In the last example, we use the **pos = "a"** (Part of speech as an adjective, so the result will be an adjective form of the main example).

```
boxes : box
universal : universal
anger : angry
```

Figure 1.3: *Lemmatization result*

In the above result, we observe that lemmatization is done successfully on the words with meaningful results. For the last example of "**anger**", we are getting the result in the form of an adjective, that is, "**angry**".

Stemming is faster and more efficient, but can be affected by Understemming, Overstemming, and context-less words. On the other hand, Lemmatization is more focused on the context of the words; thus, accuracy is maintained when it is done. Moreover, it also produced meaningful words. However, Lemmatization is more time-consuming in comparison to Stemming since it performs morphological analysis and derives the meaning of words from a dictionary.

Stopwords

Natural languages have a lot of common words, such as "**the**", "**a**", "**an**", "**you**", "**he**", "**him**", "**she**", "**her**", and so on, which are essential when forming sentences. These are called stop words. They are important for the languages, but they also add disruptions during the process of text analysis. So, it is imperative that stop words are removed from the texts. We can understand the process of stop word removal using a custom function in spaCy. It will check whether a token is present in spaCy built-in vocabulary. The code is as follows.

```
import spacy
nlp = spacy.load("en_core_web_sm")
def remove_stopwords(text):
    stop_words = spacy.lang.en.stop_words.STOP_WORDS
    doc = nlp(text)
    filtered_tokens = [token.text for token in doc if token.text
not in                    stop_words]
    return " ".join(filtered_tokens)

text = "Natural Language Processing is a very important sub-field
in data landscape."
filtered_text = remove_stopwords(text)
print(filtered_text)
Output:
Natural Language Processing important sub-field data landscape.
```

In the above code.

- A **remove_stopwords** function is defined that takes text as input.
- The spaCy stop words list is accessed that is **spacy.lang.en.stop_words.STOP_WORDS**.
- The text is processed with spaCy's nlp object.
- The tokens are iterated through, and only those that are present in the stop words list are filtered out.
- The remaining tokens are joined back into a string.

The spaCy doc attribute is used to identify and remove the stopwords. The code is given as follows.

```
import spacy

nlp = spacy.load("en_core_web_sm")

text = "Natural Language Processing is a very important sub-field
in data landscape."
doc = nlp(text)

filtered_tokens = [token.text for token in doc if not token.is_
stop]
filtered_text = " ".join(filtered_tokens)
print(filtered_text)
```

Output:

```
Natural Language Processing important sub-field data landscape.
```

In the above code.

- The text is processed with spaCy's nlp object.
- Then list comprehension is used to iterate through tokens.
- Then the **token.is_stop** attribute is used to check if a token is a stop word (returns True if it is).
- The stop words are finally filtered out, and the remaining tokens are joined back into a string.

Normalization

Normalization refers to various techniques used to standardize text data. This can include:

- **Lowercasing:** The process of converting all text to lowercase for case-insensitive analysis.

- **Punctuation Removal:** Removing the punctuation marks such as commas, periods, and so on.
- **Accent Removal:** Removing all accents from characters (for example, converting "**café**" to "**cafe**").

```
import spacy
import string
from unidecode import unidecode
# Load spaCy model
nlp = spacy.load("en_core_web_sm")
# Sample text
text = "Café, Coffee, and More!"
# Process text
doc = nlp(text)
# Lowercasing, punctuation removal, and accent removal
cleaned_text = " ".join(unidecode(token.text.lower()) for token
in doc if token.text not in string.punctuation)
print(cleaned_text)
```

Output:

```
cafe coffee and more
```

Lowercasing: Applied using **`.lower()`**.

Punctuation Removal: Uses **`string.punctuation`** to filter out punctuation marks.

Accent Removal: The unidecode library converts accented characters (e.g., "**é**" to "**e**"). Installed with pip install unidecode.

Normalization can improve consistency in the texts and help improve further text processing. However, we need to keep the information in the text intact when dealing with them, so it is better to consult the stakeholders before removing punctuations, accents, or even lower casing.

Essential NLP libraries

In NLP, there are various powerful tools to make computers understand human language. There are primarily three very important Python libraries that help us build real-world NLP applications: spaCy, Hugging Face Transformers, and NLTK.

spaCy

spaCy is an open-source library that is commonly used for performing NLP tasks. It has a user-friendly interface and a set of pre-trained statistical models for various NLP applications. Apart from the tasks of tokenization, lemmatization, stemming, and stop word removal, there are also tasks such as Named Entity Recognition (NER), Part of

Speech (POS) tagging, dependency parsing, and others that make it a crucial tool for learning NLP and building NLP applications.

Moreover, these are some of the features that make spaCy stand out. Some of them are as follows.

- It supports 70+ human languages such as Chinese, Spanish, Portuguese, French, German, Russian, Romanian, Italian, Japanese, Korean, Dutch, and so on. It also supports Indian languages such as Bengali, Hindi, Tamil, Telugu, Marathi, and so on.
- It does multi-task learning with pre-trained transformers such as BERT.
- There is support for pre-trained word vectors and embeddings.
- It is fast.
- It provides support for custom models in PyTorch, TensorFlow, and other frameworks.
- Built-in visualizers for syntax and NER.
- Production-ready training system.

spaCy also provides end-to-end NLP workflows from prototype to production and orchestrates training, packaging, and serving the custom pipelines. spaCy projects also make it easy to integrate with many other **awesome tools** (DVC, prodigy, Streamlit, FastAPI, and Weights and Biases) in the data science and machine learning ecosystem to track and manage the data and experiments, iterate on demos and prototypes, and ship the models into production.

Hugging Face Transformers

Hugging Face Transformers is the go-to library these days when one is building an NLP application. It is built on top of frameworks such as PyTorch and TensorFlow. It has a user-friendly interface for working with pre-trained transformer models and a powerful deep-learning architecture. It has various models in the lines of text-to-text generation, text-to-image generation, question answering, text classification, summarization, feature extraction, sentence similarity, video classification, image classification, object detection, image-to-video, automatic speech recognition, audio classification, text-to-speech, text-to-audio, time series forecasting, reinforcement learning, and so on.

Transformers provides APIs to download and use pre-trained models (the ones mentioned above, but not limited to them) on text and fine-tune them on the dataset. We can easily create our applications within a few hours with readymade models. Transformers have models with lower compute costs, thus with a smaller carbon footprint. Moreover, the models can be customized as per the requirements.

There are a few example models that are already hosted on the Hugging Face site.

- Masked word completion with BERT (https://huggingface.co/google-bert/bert-base-uncased?text=Paris+is+the+%5BMASK%5D+of+France)
- NER with Electra (https://huggingface.co/dbmdz/electra-large-discriminator-finetuned-conll03-english?text=My+name+is+Wolfgang+and+I+live+in+Berlin)
- Text generation with Mistral (https://huggingface.co/mistralai/Mistral-7B-Instruct-v0.2)

The above are some of the models that solve problems such as word completion by predicting the word (Masked word completion). Named Entity Recognition (NER) helps to tag the words accordingly, such as whether it is a person, location, organization, date, and so on. The Text Generation model by Mistral (https://news.crunchbase.com/) generates text as asked by the user. It answers an asked question.

There are also a few brilliant projects that are built with Transformers.

- Gpt4all (https://github.com/nomic-ai/gpt4all) is an ecosystem of open-source chatbots trained on massive collections of clean assistant data, including code, stories, and dialogue.
- IOPaint (https://github.com/Sanster/IOPaint) is an Image painting tool powered by the Stable Diffusion model.
- Llamaindex (https://github.com/run-llama/llama_index) is a project that provides a central interface to connect LLMs with external data.
- Sentence transformers (https://github.com/UKPLab/sentence-transformers) provide an easy method to compute dense vector representations for sentences, paragraphs, and images.

We can explore a concise Hugging Face notebook by installing the transformers, datasets, PyTorch, and TensorFlow libraries, then importing the pipeline function for sentiment analysis on example text to determine its positive, negative, or neutral score. Additionally, we can use automatic speech recognition to convert audio files into text and analyze non-English texts' sentiment with the BERT model.

We can just go through a simple Hugging Face notebook. We first install the transformers and datasets libraries. Then we install PyTorch and TensorFlow. Then, from the transformers library, the pipeline function is imported, which is being used for sentiment analysis.

We can use an example text to analyze the sentiment, whether it is positive, negative, or neutral, and observe its score.

We can also perform automatic speech recognition and use audio files to retrieve speech as text.

Moreover, it is also possible to handle non-English language texts using the BERT model and check its sentiment.

This is one of the notebooks with various functionalities by Transformers. We can always build our own NLP application or learn from these notebooks (https://huggingface.co/docs/transformers/notebooks).

There is also Hugging Face LLM course that provides details on topics such as Transformers, Datasets, Tokenizers, and Accelerate. It also demonstrates the use of Transformers in speech processing, computer vision, and building demos for production environments.

NLTK

The NLTK is a powerful library when it comes to dealing with comprehending human-level texts. It is widely used in academia and industry. It has the fundamental capabilities of tokenization, lemmatization, stemming, and stop-word removal, but it also does word replacement, synonym and antonym replacement, POS tagging, parsing, transforming chunks, transforming trees, and so on.

NLTK supports building and evaluating text classifiers. It works well with machine learning algorithms such as Naive Bayes, Decision Trees, Maximum Entropy, and more. Users can also create labeled datasets, perform feature extraction from texts, and train classifiers for sentiment analysis, spam detection, topic classification, text modeling, and summarization, to name a few.

NLTK has a diverse collection of corpora and lexical resources. They are the famous Brown Corpus, the Gutenberg Corpus, and the WordNet lexical database. These resources form the base for training models, linguistic analysis, and creating various language applications. The corpora largely involve diverse genres, languages, and styles, thus making it more flexible when it comes to experimenting with various texts.

NLTK also helps with parsing and syntactic analysis. It includes both dependency and constituency parsers that can be used to analyze grammatical sentence structures. This can be used to correlate different parts of the sentence, which can then be used for information extraction, machine translation, and question answering.

NLTK also helps identify and classify texts such as person names, organizations, locations, and dates. The process is called Named Entity Recognition (NER) and is also done by spaCy. NER makes it easier since some structured information is extracted from unstructured texts. NER has applications in various sectors such as legal, marketing, e-commerce, tech, social media, and more.

NLTK supports language models such as n-grams for text generation, speech recognition, and summarization by analyzing word sequence probabilities, while also identifying collocations to enhance understanding of word relationships and improve tasks such as keyword extraction. It provides tools to evaluate NLP model performance with metrics such as precision and recall, and offers visualization options such as tree diagrams and dispersion plots to interpret data effectively.

NLTK also supports various language models, such as the n-gram model. These models are helpful for text generation, speech recognition, predicting text input, and text summarization. By analyzing the probabilities of word sequences, language models help understand and generate human-level texts.

Collocations are pairs or groups of words that frequently appear together. NLTK can find collocations and word associations, which can be useful for understanding word relationships and improving language models. This analysis can reveal interesting patterns and help in tasks such as keyword extraction and text summarization.

NLTK has some tools for evaluating the performance of NLP models. This includes methods for calculating precision, recall, F1-score, and other metrics. Proper evaluation is crucial for understanding the effectiveness of models and making informed decisions about model improvements.

Visualization is an important aspect of NLP for understanding and interpreting data. NLTK offers various visualization tools, such as tree diagrams for syntactic parsing and dispersion plots for analyzing word usage over a text.

Comparative Analysis of NLTK, Hugging Face, and spaCy

We discussed the libraries of NLTK, spaCy, and Hugging Face Transformers briefly. However, we will have dedicated chapters and use cases using spaCy and Hugging Face Transformers in detail. We can do some comparison between the three libraries as follows.

- **NLTK**: It is best for traditional NLP tasks and educational purposes, with a steep learning curve and extensive documentation.
- **Hugging Face Transformers**: It is ideal for state-of-the-art NLP using transformer models, offering extensive pre-trained models and high performance, developing own NLP applications, but with a steeper learning curve.
- **spaCy**: Designed for production-ready user-friendly interfaces, robust pipelines, and efficient performance, suitable for both beginners and advanced users.

There are also other NLP libraries such as Textblob, CoreNLP, Gensim, polyglot, pattern, and scikit-learn.

Projects and Further Exploration

Now that we have scratched the surface of NLP and have explored the capabilities of spaCy, Hugging Face Transformers, and NLTK, we can explore various projects. This section will show us the variety of use cases and project ideas that showcase the application of the libraries. We will explore various kinds of ideas that can be used to build NLP solutions using libraries.

Unveiling the World with spaCy

spaCy's capabilities are often ideal when it comes to building NLP applications such as NER systems, Part of Speech taggers, building chatbots for sentiment analysis, and building spaCy pipelines. Here are some project ideas below to build on, though they are not limited to these:

- **Building a Named Entity Recognizer (NER) System:**
  - **Use Case:** Extract key entities such as people, locations, organizations, and dates from text data.
  - **Project Idea:** Develop a NER system for news articles, social media posts, legal contracts, open-source e-books, or historical documents. This system could be used to track trends, understand the legal details in contracts such as terms, conditions, exceptions, and so on, identify key events, or enrich historical data.
- **Creating a Chatbot with Sentiment Analysis:**
  - **Use Case:** Analyze the sentiment (positive, negative, or neutral) of user messages during chatbot interaction.
  - **Project Idea:** Build a customer service chatbot that understands the sentiment behind user queries so it can customize its responses accordingly. This could improve customer satisfaction and resolve the issues more effectively. This can be done for any domain, be it e-commerce, finance, tech, education, entertainment, manufacturing, and so on.
- **Constructing a Text Summarizer:**
  - **Use Case:** Generate concise summaries of lengthy documents or articles.
  - **Project Idea:** Develop a text summarizer for research papers, news articles, contracts, manuscripts, reviews, tweets, or product descriptions. This is very useful when it comes to shortening long texts or creating informative product summaries.
- **Implementing a Part-of-Speech (POS) Tagger and Dependency Parser:**
  - **Use Case:** Analyze the grammatical structure of sentences and understand the relationships between words.

  - **Project Idea:** Build a tool that identifies the part of speech for each word in a sentence and parses the sentence structure. This could be used for tasks such as text classification based on grammatical patterns or machine translation that requires understanding sentence structure.

- **Exploring Custom spaCy Pipelines:**
  - **Use Case:** Extend spaCy's capabilities by creating custom pipelines for specific NLP tasks.
  - **Project Idea:** Develop a custom pipeline for identifying specific jargon or technical terms relevant to a field. This could be used for tasks such as analyzing domain-specific documents or filtering social media content for relevant topics. This can also be done in various other languages (since spaCy supports 70+ languages).

By undertaking these spaCy projects, we will gain practical experience in real-world NLP applications. However, these are just one of many applications that can be developed. We can explore the spaCy documentation and community resources to discover even more possibilities!

Unveiling the Power of Hugging Face Transformers

Hugging Face Transformers leverages the potential of pre-trained transformer models for building complex NLP tasks. Here are some use cases and project ideas that we can build:

- **Building a Text Classification System:**
  - **Use Case:** Classify text data into predefined categories, such as sentiment analysis (positive/negative reviews) or topic classification (sports news versus entertainment news versus political news).
  - **Project Idea:** Develop a system to classify customer reviews on an e-commerce platform to identify positive or negative feedback. Alternatively, build a system to categorize news articles based on their topics.
- **Constructing a Question Answering System:**
  - **Use Case:** Provide answers to user questions based on a given context or dataset.
  - **Project Idea:** Develop a question-answering system for a specific domain, such as answering frequently asked questions about products on a website or providing historical information based on a real dataset.

- **Experimenting with Text Generation:**
  - **Use Case:** Generate human-quality text, such as creative writing, or translate languages while preserving meaning.
  - **Project Idea:** Develop a creative text generator that can produce different writing styles, such as poems, short stories, or code. Alternatively, explore building a simple machine translation system.
- **Fine-tuning Pre-trained Models for Specific Tasks:**
  - **Use Case:** Tailor a pre-trained model's capabilities to a specific NLP problem by fine-tuning it with our dataset.
  - **Project Idea:** Fine-tune a pre-trained model for sentiment analysis specific to a company's customer reviews. This could allow the model to better understand the nuances of the company's language and provide more accurate sentiment analysis.
- **Exploring Advanced Transformer Architectures:**
  - **Use Case:** Delve deeper into the world of transformers by experimenting with different architectures (for example, BERT, GPT-3) and understanding their strengths and weaknesses.
  - **Project Idea:** Compare the performance of different pre-trained models on a specific NLP task. This will help you compare the performance of different pre-trained models on a specific NLP task. This will help identify the best model for your needs and gain insights into the effectiveness of different transformer architectures.

Unveiling the Power of NLTK

NLTK's functionalities are mostly beginner-friendly and educational, with a lot of documentation. However, this does not stop us from building projects to solidify our understanding of NLP. Here are a few use cases and projects that can be solved using NLTK.

- **Constructing a Chatbot with Simple Pattern Matching:**
  - **Use Case:** Create a basic chatbot that can interact with users using predefined patterns and responses.
  - **Project Idea:** Build a simple chatbot that understands basic user queries and provides pre-programmed responses. Leverage NLTK's tokenization and pattern-matching capabilities to identify keywords in user input and respond accordingly.
- **Implementing a Text Preprocessing Pipeline:**
  - **Use Case:** Develop a comprehensive pipeline for cleaning and preparing text data for further analysis.

  - **Project Idea:** Build a text preprocessing pipeline that performs tasks such as tokenization, stop word removal, stemming/lemmatization, and normalization. This pipeline can be used as a foundation for various NLP projects, ensuring our data is ready for further processing by other NLP tools.
- **Experimenting with NLTK Corpora and Lexical Resources:**
  - **Use Case:** Utilize NLTK's built-in corpora (text collections) and lexical resources (for example, WordNet) for tasks such as named entity recognition or word similarity.
  - **Project Idea:** Develop a system that identifies named entities (people, locations) in text data using NLTK's named entity recognition capabilities and pre-trained corpora. Alternatively, explore building a tool that calculates word similarity using WordNet, allowing you to identify words with similar meanings.

While projects provide valuable hands-on experience, our NLP exploration does not end there. Here are some ways to further expand knowledge and stay at the forefront of this dynamic field:

- **Engage with the Hugging Face Community:** The Hugging Face community is a vibrant hub for NLP enthusiasts. Joining the forums, participating in discussions, and learning from other users help us gain significant knowledge and open a world of opportunities. We can share projects, ask questions, and gain valuable insights from experienced practitioners.
- **Contribute to Open-Source Projects:** Open-source projects are the backbone of NLP advancements. Considering code contributions, documentation, or bug fixes to existing projects on spaCy, NLTK, or Hugging Face Transformers. This is a brilliant way to give back to the community, learning from experienced developers, and deepening our understanding of the codebase.
- **Stay Updated with Research:** The field of NLP is constantly evolving. Subscribing to research blogs, following leading researchers on Twitter or LinkedIn, and attending conferences to stay updated on the latest advancements and breakthroughs. This will expose us to new ideas and inspire us to explore new avenues within NLP.
- **Exploring Advanced NLTK Functionalities:** NLTK offers functionalities beyond basic tasks. Dive into topics such as statistical language modeling, N-grams, or machine learning integration within NLTK to broaden our capabilities.

Conclusion

In this chapter, we understood the definition of NLP, its applications, the usage and the significance of using Python, and NLP fundamentals such as text preprocessing, consisting of tokenization, stemming, lemmatization, normalization, and stop-word removal using Python. Moreover, we also discussed the capabilities of spaCy, NLTK, and Hugging Face Transformers, and a range of use cases and project ideas to apply and build NLP applications.

So, let us embrace the journey, experiment with different approaches, and ask questions. As we dive deeper into this fascinating field, we will unlock the power of language and create innovative NLP solutions that transform how we interact with information.

In the next chapter, we will look more into the details of building blocks and techniques of NLP algorithms. We will learn about techniques such as the Bag-of-Words model, n-grams, and TF-IDF there. Moreover, we will also learn about word embeddings, one-hot encoding, and other relevant techniques.

References

- https://sunscrapers.com/blog/9-best-python-natural-language-processing-nlp/
- https://tjzhifei.github.io/resources/NLTK.pdf
- https://www.tutorialspoint.com/natural_language_toolkit/natural_language_toolkit_tutorial.pdf
- https://colab.research.google.com/github/huggingface/notebooks/blob/main/transformers_doc/en/quicktour.ipynb#scrollTo=zQ0Ff5lqau3h
- https://github.com/huggingface/transformers/blob/main/awesome-transformers.md
- https://github.com/huggingface/transformers
- https://huggingface.co/models
- https://gist.github.com/sebleier/554280
- https://www.datacamp.com/tutorial/stemming-lemmatization-python
- https://www.geeksforgeeks.org/introduction-to-stemming/
- https://www.geeksforgeeks.org/python-lemmatization-with-nltk/
- https://github.com/explosion/spaCy/tree/master
- https://spacy.io/models/en
- https://spacy.io/usage/projects
- https://explosion.ai/
- https://spacy.io/usage/training

- https://www.statista.com/statistics/1241923/worldwide-software-developer-programming-language-communities/#:~:text=According%20to%20the%20survey%2C%20the,with%2044.6%20percent%20of%20developers..
- https://www.statista.com/statistics/793628/worldwide-developer-survey-most-used-languages/
- https://blog.invgate.com/chatgpt-statistics#:~:text=ChatGPT%20general%20facts,-OpenAI's%20GPT%2D4&text=The%20chatbot%20was%20trained%20on,summarization%2C%20and%20question%2Danswering.
- https://iq.opengenus.org/nlp-project-ideas/
- https://www.geeksforgeeks.org/top-natural-language-processing-nlp-projects/
- https://www.datacamp.com/tutorial/nlp-project-ideas-for-all-levels
- https://neptune.ai/blog/10-nlp-projects

CHAPTER 2
Building Blocks and Techniques for NLP Algorithms

Introduction

We learned about NLP, its significance, applications, text preprocessing, and libraries (spaCy, NLTK, and Hugging Face) used to build applications. Continuing with that, this chapter will delve into the essential building blocks and techniques that form the building blocks of NLP algorithms. Here, we will investigate techniques such as Bag-of-Words, n-grams, and TF-IDF (Term Frequency-Inverse Document Frequency). We will also understand the power of word embeddings, which capture semantic relationships between words and transform them into vectors, thus assisting computers in understanding the context of languages.

We will also explore two fundamental NLP tasks: Part-of-Speech (POS) tagging and Named Entity Recognition (NER). POS tagging reveals the grammatical roles of words in a sentence, such as nouns, pronouns, verbs, adjectives, conjunctions, punctuations, and so on. At the same time, NER identifies and classifies named entities such as people, places, dates, and organizations. Additionally, the concept of Dependency Parsing will also be explored. Moreover, we will also understand the evaluation metrics of NLP.

Structure

In this chapter, we will discuss the following topics:

- Representing Text Data: From Words to Numbers
- Unveiling Meaning with Word Embeddings
- Word Sense Disambiguation
- Part of Speech (PoS) Tagging

- Named Entity Recognition (NER)
- Coreference Resolution
- NLP Evaluation Metrics
- Dependency Parsing

Representing Text Data: From Words to Numbers

Computers convert texts into numbers to understand human-level text data.

Representing text data as numbers is a fundamental step in natural language processing. This process involves converting words, phrases, or entire documents into numeric formats so that algorithms can perform mathematical operations on them. Previously, techniques such as **one-hot encoding** and **bag-of-words** transformed text into high-dimensional sparse vectors, while more advanced methods, such as **TF-IDF**, weigh the importance of words based on their frequency and distribution. Recently, continuous vector representations or word embeddings (for example, **Word2Vec and GloVe**) have gained popularity, as they capture semantic relationships between words by mapping them into dense, low-dimensional spaces.

This chapter will dig deep into these techniques: **Bag-of-Words (BoW)**, which treats documents as word collections, capturing word frequencies. **N-grams** capture sequences of words (such as bigrams or trigrams) as features, providing some context for the sentences using the bigrams or trigrams. There is also **TF-IDF (Term Frequency-Inverse Document Frequency)** that considers both the word's frequency within a document and its frequency across a collection of documents, thus providing a more detailed text analysis. These techniques are important for text analysis, therefore unlocking latent meaning within texts.

Bag-of-Words (BoW) Model

The Bag-of-Words (BoW) model is a fundamental technique in NLP that represents text documents as a collection of words, irrespective of their order or grammar. We can look at an example to understand the concept along with the step-by-step Python implementation. Let us consider the 3 documents.

Document1: "*I am a good man*"

Document2: "*You are a good man too*"

We can create a vocabulary of the unique words in the two documents. The Python code is as follows:

```
# Define the documents
documents = ["I am a good man", "You are a good man too"]
# Function to tokenize documents (using split())
def tokenize_documents(documents):
    all_tokens = []
    for document in documents:
        all_tokens.extend(document.split())  # Extend list with
split tokens
   return all_tokens
# Get all tokens
all_tokens = tokenize_documents(documents)
# Print all tokens
print("All Tokens:", all_tokens)
Output:
All Tokens: ['I', 'are', 'man', 'a', 'too', 'good', 'You', 'am']
```

In the above code, we have split each sentence to get the words and then used the **set()** function to get the unique words.

In the next step, we create a dictionary where there are words and their frequencies. The Python code is as follows.

```
# Function to create bag-of-words model
def create_bow_model(tokens):
    vocabulary = set(tokens)  # Create vocabulary (unique words)
    bow_model = {word: 0 for word in vocabulary}  # Initialize
dictionary
    for token in tokens:
        bow_model[token] += 1  # Count word occurrences
    return bow_model

# Get all tokens
all_tokens = tokenize_documents(documents)

# Create bag-of-words model
bow_model = create_bow_model(all_tokens)

# Print bag-of-words model (dictionary)
print("Bag-of-Words Model:", bow_model)
Output:
Bag-of-Words Model: {'I': 1, 'are': 1, 'man': 2, 'a': 2, 'too':
1, 'good': 2, 'You': 1, 'am': 1}
```

We reused the **tokenize_documents()** function for the tokens. We set the **create_bow_model()** function, and inside the function, we create a variable named **vocabulary** to have the unique tokens. We initialize an empty dictionary **`bow_model`** to represent the BoW model. This dictionary will map each word in the vocabulary to its frequency (count) within the combined tokens. We then iterate through each token in the tokens list. For each token, we check if it exists in the **`bow_model`** dictionary. If the token exists, we increment its count by 1. If the token does not exist, we add it to the dictionary with an initial count of 1. Finally, the function returns the completed **`bow_model`** dictionary.

We then call the **`tokenize_documents`** function to get all tokens and store them in **`all_tokens`**. Then we call the **`create_bow_model`** function with the **`all_tokens list`** and store the result in **`bow_model`**. Then print the **`bow_model`** dictionary, which represents the BoW model for both documents.

If we see the output, we can find the frequency of each word in a key-value format.

BoW models are applicable in **text classification** to represent input text for the classification model. The model can learn to predict the class label based on the presence or absence of certain words in the input text. In information retrieval, both documents and search queries are transformed into these vectors, which are then compared using similarity measures such as cosine similarity. This approach allows systems to efficiently index large corpora and rank documents according to their relevance to a given query. Despite its simplicity and scalability, BoW may overlook contextual nuances inherent in language. Text similarity is also another application where the BoW model is used, where two or more documents are compared by comparing the word frequencies. In machine translation, the BoW model can serve as a baseline by representing sentences as collections of word frequencies without considering order. This approach can help identify lexical similarities and inform initial word alignments between languages. However, because it disregards context and syntax, BoW is generally less effective than advanced models that capture sequential dependencies..

There are certain advantages and disadvantages of using BoW models.

Advantages

- **Simplicity of Usage:** BoW models are easy to understand and implement. They do not need high computational power in comparison to other complex NLP techniques.
- **Robustness:** BoW models are flexible when it comes to the order of words in text documents. This can be helpful while handling noisy or unstructured text data.
- **Ease of Feature Engineering:** The bag-of-words model is a simple representation of text data, which makes it easy to extract additional features from the data.

Disadvantages

- **Missing Word Order:** BoW does not take into consideration the word order; thus, contextual information is lost.
- **Unable to Capture the Semantic Relationships:** Adding to the previous disadvantage, since word order is not considered, BoW treats all words equally, thus the word relationship is lost. Words such as "`tall`" and "`short`" are the same for BoW since it does not capture the semantics.
- **Sensitivity to Stop Words**: BoW models can be highly sensitive to the inclusion or exclusion of stop words (common words such as "`the`" or "`a`").

  https://spotintelligence.com/2022/12/20/bag-of-words-python/

  https://web.stanford.edu/~jurafsky/slp3/slides/LM_4.pdf

  https://spotintelligence.com/2023/04/05/n-grams/

  https://spotintelligence.com/2022/11/28/tf-idf/

N-grams Model

The Bag-of-Words (BoW) model ignores the word order and word relationships. N-grams address this limitation by capturing sequences of n consecutive words. It can be 2-grams, where 2 consecutive words are captured, or 3-grams, where 3 consecutive words are captured, and so on. So, if we consider the sentence from the preceding section, "I *am a good man*", for 2-grams it will be "I *am*", "*am a*", "*a good*", and "*good man*". This way, we can get some contextual advantage over the BoW model. It is used in sentiment analysis, language modeling, and machine translation.

Contiguous word sequences that can provide local sentiment cues are captured using **N-grams**. For example, **bi-grams or tri-grams** can identify particular words such as "*not good*" or "*very happy*" that add to the text's overall mood. Their capacity to consider context in addition to individual words enhances sentiment classification models' accuracy.

N-grams offer a statistical framework for language modeling that predicts a word's likelihood based on its preceding words. Models that capture local word dependencies are created using this Markov assumption-based method, which is helpful for tasks such as speech recognition and text synthesis.

By modeling word sequences, n-grams capture local syntactic and semantic patterns that help select accurate translations, forming the basis for generating coherent and contextually appropriate translated text. N-grams are essential in machine translation, especially in phrase-based translation systems, where they help identify and align common phrases between source and target languages.

We can also investigate some advantages and disadvantages of the N-grams model.

Advantages

- **Context:** We observed from the previous example that since N-grams can pick up adjacent words, they can help us understand the words and phrases, thus providing some amount of context.
- **Flexible:** N-grams can be used with single characters and larger text paragraphs, thus making it easy to analyze the language in different ways.

Disadvantages

- **Not enough context:** N-grams do pick up context, but not on a higher level, thus losing out on having a big picture of the text chunks, such as the text's meaning.
- **Data Sparsity**: As the size of an n-gram grows, so does the number of possible combinations. This can lead to data sparsity and make it harder to get accurate information about all possible n-grams.
- **Lack of Understanding of Word Meanings:** N-grams do not have a semantic understanding of the language, which means they are unable to capture the meaning of the words or phrases, and thus can be inaccurate while giving results.
- **Overfitting**: Using n-grams as features in machine learning models can lead to overfitting, which occurs when a model is too complex and performs well on training data but poorly on new or unseen data.

Now, let us explore Python code for creating n-gram models.

```
from nltk.util import ngrams
# Example sentence
sentence = "Natural Language Processing is a powerful tool for
analyzing text data."
# Tokenize the sentence into words
words = sentence.split()
# Create 4-grams from the list of words
fourgrams = ngrams(words, 4)
# Print the bigrams
for fourgram in fourgrams:
    print(fourgram)
Output:
('Natural', 'Language', 'Processing', 'is')
('Language', 'Processing', 'is', 'a')
('Processing', 'is', 'a', 'powerful')
('is', 'a', 'powerful', 'tool')
('a', 'powerful', 'tool', 'for')
('powerful', 'tool', 'for', 'analyzing')
```

```
('tool', 'for', 'analyzing', 'text')
('for', 'analyzing', 'text', 'data.')
```

The above code shows the N-grams model, where the ngrams function is imported from the nltk package. The sentence is tokenized, and 4-grams is created using the **ngrams()** function that has the list of tokens and 4 as the input. For bigrams, 4 can be changed to 2. The output has a list of a set of 4 consecutive words. Each set has 4 consecutive words with a newly added word at the end and the first word from the previous set that is being removed.

Term Frequency-Inverse Document Frequency (TF-IDF)

While both the techniques of Bag-of-Words (BoW) and N-grams capture word frequency, they do not consider a word's importance within or across a document collection. TF-IDF (Term Frequency-Inverse Document Frequency) addresses this by assigning weights to words based on their frequency within a document (TF) and their rarity across the entire collection (IDF).

Term Frequency (TF)

Term Frequency is defined by how often a word appears in a document. A higher TF indicates the word might be more relevant to the document's content.

Inverse Document Frequency (IDF)

Inverse Document Frequency measures how rare a word is across the entire document collection. Words that appear frequently across all documents are less informative, and their IDF score will be lower in that case.

We need to put both parameters together to understand the importance of unique words and filter out common words.

```
TF*IDF
```

In NLP, there is a challenge of converting text data into numerical representations for machine learning models. But numbers cannot be directly understood by computers. So, TF-IDF comes into the picture by assigning numbers to the words based on their frequency and importance. Thus, algorithms can analyze the pattern within text data using TF-IDF. TF-IDF not only focuses on the word counts but also gives importance to the frequency of unique and less frequent words in the documents, thus helping in applications such as sentiment analysis, topic modeling, and information retrieval, to name a few.

To help sentiment analysis models identify sentiment-bearing words, **TF-IDF** converts text into weighted numerical vectors that emphasize phrases of high value in relation to the corpus. By lowering the noise in common words, this feature extraction method improves the efficiency of classification systems.

TF-IDF can be used in topic modeling to reduce the influence of ubiquitous phrases by highlighting and identifying essential terms that are distinctive of particular themes. The coherence and interpretability of themes produced by models such as **Latent Dirichlet Allocation (LDA)** might be enhanced by these weighted phrases, which act as informative characteristics.

We can also investigate some advantages and disadvantages of the TF-IDF model.

Advantages

- **Reduced Weight of Common Words:** TF-IDF reduces the influence of common words, thus helping focus on more specific words in the document. This way, the context can be understood well and analyzed.
- **Improved Text Representation:** TF-IDF considers both word frequency and document-specific importance.

Disadvantages

- **Rare Words:** Very rare words can have very high IDF scores that can lead to overfitting problems in machine learning models.
- **Absence of Semantic Meaning:** TF-IDF cannot help with semantic meaning. It weighs the words and considers them when determining their importance, but it cannot get the context of the phrase.
- **Sensitivity to Preprocessing:** TF-IDF can be sensitive to stemming or lemmatization since different word forms cannot be recognized as the same base words. This way, the TF-IDF numbers can vary, thus reducing accuracy.

To understand the TF-IDF concept mathematically, here is a very well-explained **blog.**

Now, let us explore Python code for TF-IDF.

```
from sklearn.feature_extraction.text import TfidfVectorizer
# Sample documents
documents = ["I am a good man.",
             "You are a good man too."]
# Create TF-IDF vectorizer
vectorizer = TfidfVectorizer()
# Fit the vectorizer on the documents
tfidf_matrix = vectorizer.fit_transform(documents)
# Print TF-IDF matrix (sparse matrix)
print(tfidf_matrix.toarray())
# Print feature names (vocabulary)
```

```
print(vectorizer.get_feature_names_out())


Output:
[[0.70490949 0.         0.50154891 0.50154891 0.         0.        ]
 [0.         0.49922133 0.35520009 0.35520009 0.49922133
0.49922133]]
['am' 'are' 'good' 'man' 'too' 'you']
```

In the aforementioned code example, we have demonstrated TF-IDF using **`TfidfVectorizer()`** function that is present in the scikit-learn library. We defined a list of documents. We then created the **`TfidfVectorizer()`** object. Then we called the **`fit_transform()`** method on the vectorizer with documents. This learns the vocabulary and calculates the TF-IDF weights for each term in each document. Then we get the TF-IDF matrix, and then we have the feature names (words in each document) learned by the vectorizer.

We can also calculate TF-IDF using tmtoolkit in spaCy (https://spacy.io/universe/project/tmtoolkit).

Unveiling Meaning with Word Embeddings

In this section, we will explore word embeddings and some techniques such as GloVe, FastText, and Word2vec. We will also explore Sentence embeddings along with some techniques such as SBERT, Sen2vec, Skip-thought vectors, and USE.

Word Embeddings

The techniques of BoW and TF-IDF represent text documents numerically, but they do not quite capture the semantic relationship between the words. Word embeddings make up this gap and transform words into numerical vectors, where similar words have similar vector representations.

Word embeddings are dense, low-dimensional vectors that capture semantic meaning and relationships between words. Words with similar meanings have similar vector representations. This way, applications such as word similarity comparisons, analogy reasoning, and sentiment analysis can be done by analyzing relationships between the vectors.

Now, to perform vectorization (word-to-number conversion), Euclidean distance and Cosine Similarity are used.

Semantic and grammatical information is captured by word embeddings, which turn words into dense numerical vectors. Metrics of similarity and distance are used to compare these vectors. The **Euclidean Distance** quantifies the numerical separation between two vectors in space by measuring their straight-line distance; a smaller distance indicates better similarity.

The angle between vectors is evaluated using **Cosine Similarity**, which is more useful in capturing semantic similarity because it concentrates on the directional alignment of the vectors rather than their magnitude.

Accordingly, a high cosine similarity suggests that two word vectors have comparable meanings even if their scales are different. This is important for tasks such as synonym recognition, grouping, and improving other NLP applications.

https://towardsdatascience.com/understanding-nlp-word-embeddings-text-vectorization-1a23744f7223

To demonstrate theoretically, if there are two sentences (like documents), we plot them in an N-dimensional vector space, and the angle between the two documents is the similarity. So, the smaller the angle between the documents, the higher the similarity.

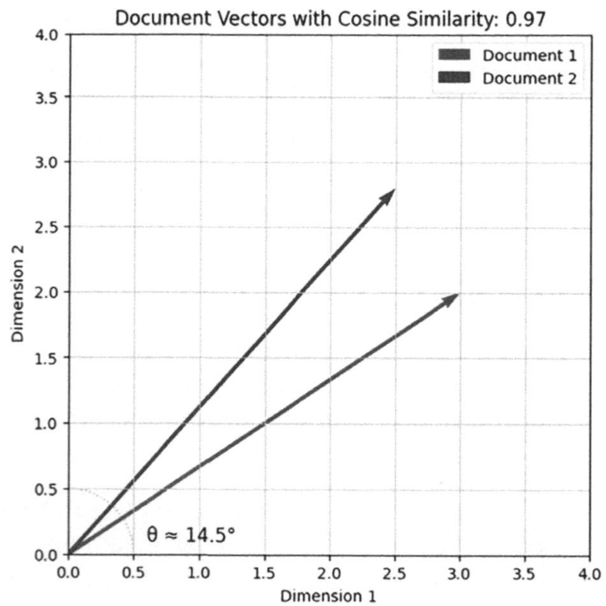

Figure 2.1: *Cosine similarity*

- **Vectors as Documents:** Each document is represented by a vector (here in 2D for simplicity). In practice, these vectors are derived from word embeddings or other vectorization techniques.
- **Cosine Similarity and Angle:** The cosine similarity is computed as the cosine of the angle between the two vectors. A smaller angle (closer to 0°) implies a higher similarity.

There are Word embeddings that come from primarily 3 pre-trained methods: Word2vec (by Google), Fasttext (by Facebook), and Glove (by Stanford).

https://spotintelligence.com/2022/11/30/word-embedding/

Word2Vec

Word2Vec is a powerful technique for learning word embeddings, which are dense, low-dimensional vectors that capture the semantic meaning and relationships between words. This approach goes beyond simply counting word occurrences, allowing NLP algorithms to understand the context and depths of a language.

Two main models are used to learn the word embedding using the word2vec method.

- **Continuous Bag-of-Words (CBOW):** CBOW is a neural network-based approach used in Word2Vec to predict a target word based on its surrounding words (context). It captures the semantic meaning of words by analyzing the patterns in which words appear together in a given window size.

  For example, given the sentence:
  "*The cat is sitting on the mat.*"

  If the context window size is 2, and we are predicting the missing word (`w_target`), a training example might look like:

Context words	**Target word**
(The, is)	cat
(cat, sitting)	is
(is, on)	Sitting

Table 2.1: *Context words and target word*

  CBOW helps understand the meaning of a word by leveraging its neighboring words, making it efficient for NLP tasks like text classification and word similarity detection.

Architecture of CBOW

CBOW consists of three layers:

- **Input Layer:** Takes multiple one-hot encoded words (context words).
- **Hidden Layer:** Converts one-hot vectors into a dense, low-dimensional representation (word embedding).
- **Output Layer:** Predicts the target word by applying a softmax function to generate probabilities for all words in the vocabulary.

Step-by-Step Working

1. **Input Representation:** Each context word is represented as a one-hot encoded vector.
2. **Embedding Lookup:** The input vectors are multiplied by the weight matrix to produce word embeddings.
3. **Averaging:** The embeddings of all context words are averaged.
4. **Prediction:** The averaged vector is passed through another weight matrix and a softmax activation to predict the target word.
5. **Training:** The model uses negative log likelihood loss (or cross-entropy loss).

Advantages of CBOW

- Faster training compared to Skip-gram.
- Works well with large datasets.
- Captures common words effectively.

Disadvantages of CBOW

- Does not perform well with rare words since it averages multiple word embeddings.
- Loses positional information as it treats all context words equally.
- **Skip-gram:** This architecture flips the concept and predicts the surrounding context words based on a given word.

For example, in the same sentence:

"The cat is sitting on the mat."

If "**cat**" is the target word and the window size is 2, Skip-gram generates training examples like:

Target word	**Context words**
cat	(The, is)
is	(cat, sitting)
Sitting	(is, on)

Table 2.2: *The target word and the context words*

Skip-gram assigns high probabilities to words that frequently appear together, making it more effective for learning rare word representations.

Architecture of Skip-gram

Skip-gram consists of the following key components:

- **Input Layer:** A single one-hot encoded word (target word).
- **Hidden Layer:** Maps the input to a dense vector representation (word embedding).
- **Output Layer:** Predicts multiple context words using softmax probability distribution.

Step-by-Step Working

1. **Input Representation:** The target word is converted into a one-hot encoded vector.
2. **Embedding Lookup:** The input vector is multiplied by the weight matrix to generate a word embedding.
3. **Prediction:** The model predicts multiple words surrounding the target word using another weight matrix and softmax activation.
4. **Training:** The model is trained using negative sampling or hierarchical softmax to improve efficiency.

Advantages of Skip-gram

- Works well for learning rare words since it generates more training data.
- Captures deeper semantic relationships between words.

Disadvantages of Skip-gram

- Slower to train compared to CBOW due to multiple predictions.
- Requires more computational resources.

Feature	CBOW	Skip-gram
Training speed	Faster	Slower but more accurate
Handles rare words	Does not do very well	Does well
Context use	Predicts a single word from multiple words	Predicts multiple words from a single word
Best use case	Large datasets, common words	Small datasets, rare words

Table 2.3: *CBOW vs Skip-gram*

https://www.geeksforgeeks.org/continuous-bag-of-words-cbow-in-nlp/

https://www.kdnuggets.com/2018/04/implementing-deep-learning-methods-feature-engineering-text-data-skip-gram.html

As far as training and capturing similarities are concerned, the explanation is as follows.

- **Training:** Word2Vec utilizes a neural network architecture to learn the word embeddings. The network is trained on a large corpus of text data, where each word is represented as a one-hot vector.
- **Similarity Capture:** By analyzing the relationships between words during training, Word2Vec embeds similar words close together in the vector space. Words with opposite meanings tend to be placed farther apart.

We will investigate some advantages and disadvantages of Word2Vec.

Advantages

- **Semantic Understanding:** It captures the semantic relationship between the words.
- **NLP Performance:** Continuing with the first advantage of Semantic Understanding, it enhances applications such as sentiment analysis, machine translation, and question-answering.

Disadvantages

- **Heavy data requirements:** Training Word2Vec requires a large text data corpus, which is computationally heavy.
- **Out of Vocabulary (OOV) Words:** Word2Vec only learns embeddings for words present in the training corpus. Thus, if a new word appears that was not present in the training data, the model cannot generate an embedding for it.
- **Computational cost:** From the first disadvantage, training Word2Vec can be computationally heavy due to a lot of text data.

GloVe (Global Vectors for Word Representation)

GloVe is another powerful technique for learning word embeddings. While Word2Vec utilizes neural networks, GloVe leverages co-occurrence information to capture semantic relationships between words.

GloVe constructs a large matrix where rows represent words and columns represent other words in the vocabulary. Each cell in the matrix contains a value indicating how often two words co-occur within a specific window size in the training corpus.

Example: How GloVe Builds a Co-occurrence Matrix

Let us consider a small corpus:
"*The cat sat on the mat. The dog sat on the rug.*"

Step 1: Define a Window Size

Assume a **window size of 2** (words on either side of the target word). This means that for each word, we count how often other words appear within this window.

Step 2: Construct the Co-occurrence Matrix

Below is a simplified **word-word co-occurrence matrix** for our corpus:

Words	The	cat	sat	on	mat	dog	rug
The	0	1	1	0	0	1	0
cat	1	0	1	0	0	0	0
sat	1	1	0	1	1	1	1
on	0	0	1	0	1	0	1
mat	0	0	1	1	0	0	0
dog	1	0	1	0	0	0	1
rug	0	0	1	1	0	1	0

Figure 2.2: *Co-occurrence matrix*

- The matrix stores co-occurrence counts.
- **Example:** The word **"sat"** appears with **"The" (1 time), "cat" (1 time), "on" (1 time), "mat" (1 time), "dog" (1 time), "rug" (1 time)** in the given window.

Step 3: Convert Co-occurrences into Probabilities

Each value in the matrix is transformed into probabilities:

$P(w_j|w_i)$ = (co-occurrence count of w_i and w_j)/total occurences of w_i

This helps determine how strongly words are related.

Step 4: Factorizing the Matrix

GloVe then applies **matrix factorization techniques** to reduce dimensionality. This creates dense vector representations where words with similar meaning have similar embeddings.

The code implementation for GloVe is as follows.

```
import numpy as np
import matplotlib.pyplot as plt
from sklearn.decomposition import PCA

# Sample word vectors obtained after matrix factorization
(simulated)
word_vectors = {
    "The": [0.8, 0.2],
    "cat": [0.6, 0.5],
```

```
    "sat": [0.5, 0.7],
    "on": [0.3, 0.9],
    "mat": [0.4, 0.6],
    "dog": [0.7, 0.3],
    "rug": [0.2, 0.8]
}

# Convert dictionary to array for PCA
words = list(word_vectors.keys())
vectors = np.array(list(word_vectors.values()))

# Apply PCA to reduce dimensions to 2D
pca = PCA(n_components=2)
reduced_vectors = pca.fit_transform(vectors)

# Plot the words in 2D space
plt.figure(figsize=(8,6))
plt.scatter(reduced_vectors[:,0], reduced_vectors[:,1],
color='blue')

# Annotate words
for i, word in enumerate(words):
    plt.annotate(word, (reduced_vectors[i,0]+0.02,
reduced_vectors[i,1]+0.02), fontsize=12)

plt.title("2D Representation of Word Embeddings (GloVe)")
plt.xlabel("PCA Component 1")
plt.ylabel("PCA Component 2")
plt.grid(True)
plt.show()
```

The code explanation is as follows.

The relevant libraries are imported, which are numpy, matplotlib, and sklearn. PCA from sklearn.decomposition is used to **reduce the dimensionality** of word vectors from a high-dimensional space to **2D**.

Then we define Sample Word Vectors

- The dictionary word_vectors contains **sample word embeddings** (each word is represented as a **2D vector**).
- Normally, **real GloVe vectors are high-dimensional (for example, 50D, 100D, 300D)**, but here we assume **2D embeddings** for simplicity.

Then we **convert Word Vectors into a Numpy Array**

- **words:** Stores the **word labels** (for example, `"The"`, `"cat"`, `"sat"`, etc.).

- **vectors:** Converts word embeddings from a dictionary format into a **NumPy array** for numerical processing.

Next, PCA is applied to reduce Dimensionality

`PCA(n_components=2)`: Creates a **PCA object** to reduce the vectors to **2D**.

`pca.fit_transform(vectors)`: Performs PCA transformation to **map high-dimensional vectors into a 2D plane** while preserving the relationships.

The scatter plot is used to visualize word embeddings.

Then, words are annotated on the graph.

- **Loops through each word** and places text labels **slightly offset** from the plotted points.
- Helps in **identifying** where each word is positioned in the 2D space.

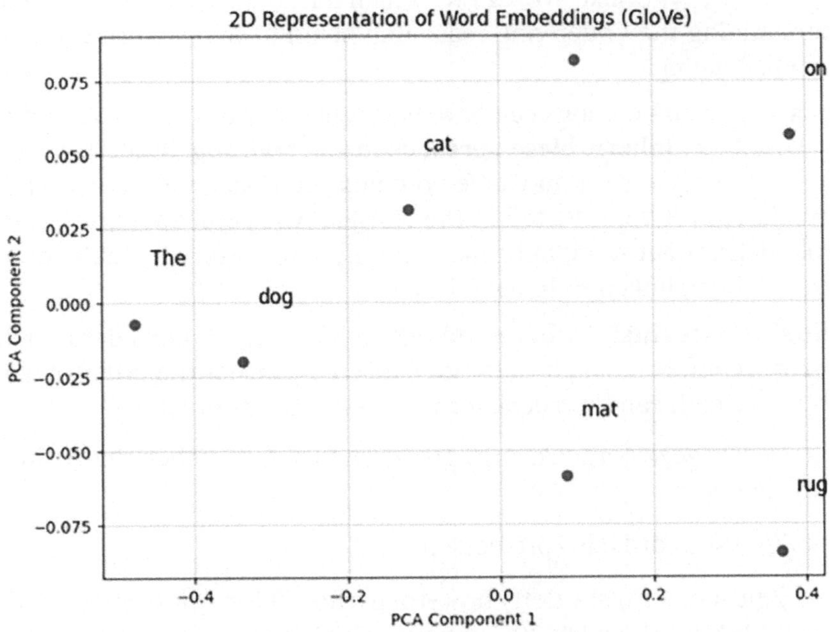

Figure 2.3: *GloVe representation using PCA*

- Each word is plotted in a **2D space** after applying **PCA** to reduce the dimensions from high-dimensional vectors.
- Words that **co-occur frequently** (for example, `sat`, `on`, `mat`) appear **closer** to each other.
- Words that are **semantically or contextually unrelated** (for example, `The`, `rug`) are positioned **farther apart**.

- This visualization demonstrates how GloVe captures relationships between words based on co-occurrence patterns.

GloVe explained in detail, now let us look into the advantages and disadvantages of GloVe.

Advantages

- **Efficient Training:** GloVe is more efficient to train in comparison to Word2Vec, specifically on large datasets, because of the presence of statistical techniques in GloVe.
- **Capturing Global Information:** GloVe considers the co-occurrence statistics, thus capturing global word relationships in comparison to Word2Vec, which captures local context.

Disadvantages

- **Interpretability:** Unlike Word2Vec, which has a neural network architecture, understanding the underlying reasoning behind GloVe's word vectors can be more challenging.
- **Biases:** GloVe embeddings can have biases like Word2Vec. GloVe embeddings, like Word2Vec, **inherit biases present in the training data**. This means that if the corpus used to train GloVe contains **societal, gender, or racial biases**, these biases will be reflected in the learned word embeddings. For example, words such as **doctor** might be more closely associated with **male** terms, while **nurse** might be linked to **female** terms.
- **Limited Contextual Understanding:** While GloVe considers global co-occurrence information, it does not explicitly process the order of words in a sentence, which can be crucial for understanding context.

  https://www.geeksforgeeks.org/pre-trained-word-embedding-using-glove-in-nlp-models/

  https://nlp.stanford.edu/projects/glove/

  https://github.com/shotleft/how-to-python/blob/master/How%20it%20works%20-%20Principal%20Component%20Analysis.ipynb

FastText

FastText, is an extension of Word2Vec that addresses a limitation in traditional word embedding approaches. Word2Vec excels at capturing semantic relationships between words, but it often struggles with out-of-vocabulary (OOV) words and words with rich morphology (for example, prefixes, suffixes). FastText tackles these issues by leveraging subword information.

FastText breaks down words into character n-grams (subwords of length n). These n-grams can be prefixes, suffixes, or even entire words. By learning representations for these n-grams, FastText can:

- **Handling OOV (Out of Vocabulary) Words:** Since many words share common subwords (for example, "`play`" and "`playing`" share "`play`"), FastText can create meaningful representations for unseen words by combining the embeddings of their constituent n-grams.
- **Embrace Morphology:** Languages with rich morphology often have many words derived from a smaller set of roots. By learning n-gram representations, FastText can capture the relationships between words that share common subword structures.

Advantages

- **Improved OOV Word Handling:** FastText can create meaningful representations for unseen words, enhancing its applicability for real-world scenarios.
- **Enhanced Performance for Morphologically Rich Languages:** FastText captures the relationships between words that share common subword structures, leading to better performance in languages such as Arabic, Turkish, and Finnish.
- **Lower Memory Footprint:** Compared to word-level embeddings, FastText often requires less memory due to the smaller vocabulary size (n-grams versus full words).

Disadvantages

- **Increased Training Time:** Breaking down words into n-grams and learning their embeddings can lead to longer training times compared to Word2Vec.
- **Hyperparameter Tuning:** Selecting the optimal n-gram size can be crucial for performance and requires experimentation.

Sentence Embeddings

The semantic meaning of individual words is captured in word embeddings, but in sentence embeddings, the whole sentences represent numerical vectors. These vectors encode the sentence's meaning and relationships between the words it contains. Sentence embeddings empower NLP algorithms to understand the overall sentiment, topic, or intent of a sentence.

Understanding Sentence Embeddings

- **From Words to Sentences:** Sentence embeddings build upon word embeddings. For each word in a sentence, there is a semantic meaning to the overall vector representation.

- **Capturing Sentence Meaning:** The resulting sentence embedding encapsulates the meaning and relationships conveyed by the entire sentence, not just individual words.
- **Applications:** Sentence embeddings are crucial for various NLP tasks, including:
    - Text classification (sentiment analysis, topic modeling)
    - Semantic similarity comparison (finding similar sentences)
    - Text summarization (capturing the main idea)
    - Machine translation (preserving meaning across languages)

Let us look at some advantages and disadvantages of Sentence embeddings.

Advantages

- **Improved NLP Performance:** Tasks such as sentiment analysis and text classification have enhanced performance by capturing the overall meaning of the sentence.
- **Versatility:** Sentence embeddings can be integrated into various NLP architectures for diverse applications.
- **Simplified Workflow:** Pre-trained models such as USE offer a convenient way to utilize sentence embeddings without extensive training.

Disadvantages

- **Bias:** Sentence embeddings can inherit biases present in the training data. Careful selection of pre-trained models and mitigation strategies is crucial. Consider an NLP model trained on biased data, where **names from different racial backgrounds** are associated with varying sentiment scores. If we use sentence embeddings for sentiment analysis, bias can manifest unfairly. It can lead to biased **hiring algorithms** that might rank resumes with certain names **lower**, thus reducing job opportunities. Bad **loan approval systems** can lead to biased sentence embeddings, therefore influencing creditworthiness predictions, which may lead to **unfair denials of loans**.
- **Computational Cost:** Encoding very large volumes of text can be computationally expensive.
- **Interpretability:** Understanding the meaning encoded in a sentence embedding vector can be challenging.

We can look into a few Sentence Embeddings tools.

Sent2Vec

- **Concept:** Sent2Vec is an **unsupervised learning model** that generates **sentence embeddings** by leveraging **pre-trained word embeddings**. It extends

Word2Vec principles to full sentences, allowing sentences to be represented as **dense vectors** in a high-dimensional space.

Important points:

- It **learns sentence representations** by reconstructing the sentence from its constituent **word embeddings**.
- It trains a **shallow neural network** (similar to Skip-gram in Word2Vec) to **predict surrounding sentences** given a target sentence.
- It captures **semantic meaning** better than simple averaging of word embeddings.

  Example: Let us consider two sentences:

  Sentence 1: "*The cat sat on the mat.*"

  Sentence 2: "*A dog rested on the rug.*"

- **How Sent2Vec Encodes These Sentences:**
  - It **splits words into n-grams** (for example, "*the cat*", "*sat on*", "*on the*").
  - It **generates sentence embeddings** by summing **word and n-gram embeddings**.
  - The output is a **dense numerical vector** for each sentence, which can be used for **text similarity, sentiment analysis, and retrieval tasks**.

Applications:

- **Text Similarity and Search Engines:** Sent2Vec does an efficient **semantic search** by representing sentences as numerical vectors.
- **Text Classification:** Can be used to classify emails, customer queries, or documents.
- **Chatbots & Question Answering:** Helps models understand the **context of user input** better.
- **Document Clustering & Retrieval:** Sent2Vec enables fast grouping of similar documents based on **semantic meaning** rather than just word overlap.

Skip-Thought Vectors

- **Concept:** Skip-Thought Vectors is an **unsupervised learning model** that learns **sentence embeddings** by leveraging a **sequence-to-sequence (seq2seq) framework**. It is inspired by the **Skip-gram model in Word2Vec**, but instead of predicting surrounding words, it **predicts surrounding sentences** in a given text.

Important points:

- Uses a **Recurrent Neural Network (RNN)-based encoder-decoder architecture** to generate sentence embeddings.
- Learns to **encode a sentence** into a dense vector that captures **semantic and syntactic features**.
- The encoded sentence representation is used to **predict the previous and next sentences** in a text corpus.
- This results in embeddings that capture **contextual and compositional meaning** better than traditional word-level embeddings.
- **Example:**
  - **Training data**: "*The weather is sunny today.*" -> "*I'm going to the beach!*" "*The movie was a disappointment.*" -> "*I will not recommend it to anyone.*"
  - Sentence embedding for "*The movie was a disappointment.*" captures the sentiment and context of the sentence.

Applications

- **Text Summarization:** By capturing **context and meaning**, Skip-Thought can help generate **better summaries** of documents.
- **Dialogue Systems and Chatbots:** Used in **context-aware** chatbot responses by encoding past conversations.
- **Semantic Search:** Enables **better ranking of search results** by comparing the context of sentences rather than just using keywords.
- **Paraphrase Detection:** Helps identify sentences that **mean the same thing** but are written differently.
- **Text Generation:** Used for **coherent** text generation in applications such as **story writing and automated reporting**.

SBERT (Sentence-BERT)

Concept: SBERT (Sentence-BERT) is a powerful technique for generating sentence embeddings. It builds upon pre-trained Transformer models such as BERT (Bidirectional Encoder Representations from Transformers) and fine-tunes them on a specific task involving semantic similarity. SBERT is specifically designed to produce **meaningful, fixed-size vector representations** for entire sentences.

Important points

- Fine-tunes **BERT** for generating **contextual sentence embeddings** that capture **semantic similarity** efficiently.

- Uses a **Siamese and Triplet Network** architecture to compare sentence embeddings.
- Performs better than the traditional sentence embedding methods such as **Word2Vec, GloVe, and Skip-Thought** in **semantic similarity and clustering** tasks.

How BERT works

- **Training:**
  - Siamese and Triplet Networks are used to train SBERT on sentence pairs rather than single sentences.
  - SBERT converts two phrases (S1 and S2) into vector embeddings.
  - The Cosine Similarity is used to measure the similarity.
    - The model is trained to **minimize the distance** between similar sentence pairs and **maximize the distance** between dissimilar ones.
- **Design:**
  - **Base Model:** BERT (or RoBERTa, DistilBERT, and so on) that has already been trained
  - **Pooling Layer:** Uses CLS token embedding, mean pooling, or max pooling to transform token embeddings into a fixed-size sentence vector.
  - **Similarity Computation:** Determines how close a text is by using the Dot Product or Cosine Similarity.
  - **Loss Function:** Triplet loss (for ranking tasks) or contrastive loss (for classification jobs).
  - **Example:** Imagine training SBERT on a dataset of movie reviews with labels (positive, negative). During fine-tuning, SBERT learns to differentiate between positive and negative sentences by capturing the overall sentiment conveyed. This allows SBERT to generate sentence embeddings that reflect the semantic similarity of reviews, even when they use different words to express similar sentiments.

Applications:

- **Semantic Search:** Improves **search engines** by ranking results based on **semantic meaning** rather than keyword matches.
- **Question-Answering Systems:** Help **retrieve the most relevant answers** by comparing the embeddings of questions and stored responses.
- **Paraphrase Detection:** Identifies **similar sentences** in NLP applications (for example, detecting duplicate Quora questions).
- **Text Clustering & Topic Modeling:** Groups sentences or documents into **thematic clusters** based on similarity.

- **Machine Translation Evaluation:** Measures similarity between **translated and reference sentences** for quality assessment.

Universal Sentence Encoder (USE)

- **Concept:** This is a pre-trained model by Google that uses a deep neural network architecture to generate sentence embeddings.
- **Example:** USE can capture the semantic similarity between sentences such as "*Climate change is a serious threat*" and "*Global warming is causing significant environmental damage.*"

Let's see the Python code for USE below.

```
import tensorflow as tf
import tensorflow_hub as hub
# Load the Universal Sentence Encoder model
model = hub.load('https://tfhub.dev/google/universal-sentence-
encoder/4')
# Sample sentences
sentence1 = "Natural Language Processing is a powerful tool for
text analysis."
sentence2 = "Machine learning algorithms are revolutionizing
NLP."
# Preprocess sentences (optional)
# ... (e.g., lowercase, remove punctuation)
# Convert sentences to tensors
sentences = tf.constant([sentence1, sentence2])
# Encode sentences
sentence_embeddings = model(sentences)
# Access the encoded vectors
embedding1 = sentence_embeddings[0].numpy()
embedding2 = sentence_embeddings[1].numpy()
# Calculate cosine similarity (optional)
# Utilize sentence embeddings for your NLP tasks
print("Sentence 1 Embedding:", embedding1)
print("Sentence 2 Embedding:", embedding2)
```

The steps of the code are as follows.

1. We import TensorFlow and TensorFlow Hub.
2. We load the pre-trained Universal Sentence Encoder model.
3. We define sample sentences.
4. Preprocess the sentences if needed.
5. We convert the sentences to TensorFlow tensors for model input.

6. We use the loaded model to encode the sentences, resulting in a tensor of sentence embeddings.
7. We access the individual sentence embedding vectors for further analysis.
8. We can calculate cosine similarity to compare the embeddings.
9. These embeddings can be used for various NLP tasks, depending on your application.

```
Sentence 1 Embedding: [-5.41178100e-02 -3.26636136e-02 -2.75272653e-02  6.40941784e-02
 -3.80900800e-02 -6.83193356e-02 -7.09311515e-02  3.02882437e-02
  8.62482861e-02  6.97460622e-02  1.38676949e-02 -7.05450028e-02
 -6.97766256e-04  1.41210463e-02 -4.87933904e-02  4.58583161e-02
  4.79612090e-02 -4.19744253e-02  5.75106069e-02 -3.65464464e-02
 -6.48946688e-02  3.44096720e-02 -7.16300011e-02 -8.51622410e-03
 -7.64904246e-02  1.76761262e-02  5.04398495e-02 -3.72950248e-02
 -2.41969246e-02 -2.94289235e-02  1.45016592e-02 -1.36453994e-02
 -3.37602869e-02  1.94099750e-02 -4.05665636e-02  3.96720059e-02
 -1.48004228e-02 -5.57609461e-02 -1.07883464e-03  4.32068104e-04
 -2.23424528e-02  1.06411625e-03 -4.06198502e-02  2.44681370e-02
  6.55382201e-02  2.96496437e-03 -2.23038718e-02 -9.93909407e-03
  3.97732817e-02 -5.36222272e-02 -2.64550559e-02 -6.61458215e-03
  5.84178306e-02  2.86148675e-02 -1.70262530e-02 -2.93206349e-02
  3.94201316e-02  5.86032830e-02  5.38289621e-02 -4.37597930e-02
  1.70678664e-02 -5.42656220e-02  4.71577607e-03  6.73855245e-02
 -1.43186385e-02  4.98260707e-02  5.83744831e-02  5.84481508e-02
 -2.42847707e-02 -1.86329372e-02 -2.87342705e-02  4.05627713e-02
  3.78088541e-02 -5.86119741e-02  2.61217710e-02  5.96112311e-02
 -8.44571739e-03  5.11747338e-02  2.57000104e-02 -1.26712751e-02
 -7.02122925e-03 -3.76966633e-02  6.99471608e-02 -4.60471362e-02
 -1.01853525e-02  8.95640696e-04 -4.51389551e-02 -1.19158970e-02
 -8.62106308e-02  7.66627789e-02 -2.27237660e-02 -3.77128720e-02
 -3.54560167e-02  1.70808043e-02  5.38427271e-02  7.26870373e-02
 -8.63700807e-02  9.48018488e-03  5.64857461e-02 -7.94683471e-02
...
 -2.96497587e-02  3.95804383e-02 -7.03143999e-02  1.03816185e-02
```

Figure 2.4: *Sentence embedding result*

https://www.analyticsvidhya.com/blog/2020/08/top-4-sentence-embedding-techniques-using-python/#:~:text=In%20NLP%2C%20sentence%20embedding%20refers,or%20similarity%20between%20these%20vectors.

https://cohere.com/blog/sentence-word-embeddings

https://spotintelligence.com/2022/12/17/sentence-embedding/

Word Sense Disambiguation

While models such as the **Universal Sentence Encoder** are designed to capture the overall semantic meaning of entire sentences, **Word Sense Disambiguation**

(WSD) addresses a more fine-grained challenge – determining the exact meaning of ambiguous words based on their context.

Unlike sentence embeddings that focus on sentence-level similarity, WSD ensures that each word is interpreted correctly, especially when it has multiple possible senses.

Concept

- **The Polysemy Challenge:** Words like "*bat*" can refer to a flying mammal or sporting equipment. WSD helps determine the intended meaning based on the right context.
- **Contextual Dependence:** The meaning of a word is often revealed by the surrounding words in a sentence. WSD algorithms leverage this context to decode the real meaning of the words.
- **Applications:** WSD has various applications in NLP, including:
  - Machine translation (ensuring accurate meaning transfer)
  - Information retrieval (improving search results)
  - Text summarization (capturing the intended meaning)
  - Sentiment analysis (understanding the sentiment expressed in a specific sense)

The Approaches to Word Sense Disambiguation

- **Knowledge-Based Methods:** These methods rely on external knowledge sources such as dictionaries and thesauri that define various word senses and their relationships.
- **Statistical Methods:** These methods utilize statistical information from large text corpora to analyze how words co-occur and determine the most likely sense in a given context.
- **Machine Learning Methods:** Supervised learning approaches can be trained on annotated text data where each word has its sense labeled. The trained model then predicts the sense for unseen words based on context.

Challenges and Future Directions

- **Data Ambiguity:** Sentences can be inherently ambiguous, making it difficult to determine the intended sense definitively.

- **Context Complexity:** Capturing intricate relationships and nuances of context remains an ongoing challenge.
- **Domain Specificity:** WSD algorithms often require domain-specific training data for optimal performance.

  https://web.stanford.edu/~jurafsky/slp3/slides/Chapter18.wsd.pdf

  https://www.geeksforgeeks.org/word-sense-disambiguation-in-natural-language-processing/

  https://www.mygreatlearning.com/natural-language-processing/tutorials/nlp-word-sense-disambiguation

  https://www.tutorialspoint.com/natural_language_processing/natural_language_processing_word_sense_disambiguation.htm

Part-of-Speech (PoS) Tagging

Part-of-Speech (POS) tagging is the fundamental NLP task that assigns grammatical labels (tags) to each word in a sentence. These tags categorize words based on their function within the sentence, such as nouns, verbs, adjectives, adverbs, prepositions, and so on.

To understand PoS tagging, we need to understand the concept below.

- **Grammatical Roles:** POS tags reveal a word's grammatical role in a sentence. A noun acts as a subject or object, while a verb describes an action or state of being.
- **Benefits:** POS tagging provides a fundamental layer of understanding for NLP algorithms.

PoS tagging can be used in the following applications.

- **Sentiment Analysis:** Identifying the sentiment expressed by adjectives and adverbs.
- **Named Entity Recognition (NER):** Recognizing entities such as people, places, and organizations based on their surrounding POS tags (for example, "New **York**" likely indicates a location).
- **Syntactic Analysis:** Unveiling the sentence structure by understanding the relationships between different POS tags.

Real-life Examples

Let us look into some real-life examples:

- Sentence: "*The quick brown fox jumps over the lazy dog.*"

    - **POS Tags**: (**The** - Determiner), (**quick** - Adjective), (**brown** - Adjective), (**fox** - Noun), (**jumps** - Verb), (**over** - Preposition), (**the** - Determiner), (**lazy** - Adjective), (**dog** - Noun).
- Sentence: "*Machine learning is revolutionizing the field of* NLP."
    - **POS Tags**: (**Machine** - Noun), (**learning** - Verb), (**is** - Verb), (**revolutionizing** - Verb), (**the** - Determiner), (**field** - Noun), (**of** - Preposition), (**NLP** - Proper Noun).

Approaches to POS Tagging

- **Rule-Based Tagging:** These methods rely on handcrafted rules that define patterns for assigning tags based on word morphology, presence of prefixes/suffixes, and surrounding words.
- **Statistical Tagging:** These techniques utilize statistical models such as Hidden Markov Models (HMMs) trained on large, annotated text corpora. The models learn the probability of a tag sequence given in a sentence.
- **Machine Learning Methods:** Supervised learning approaches such as Support Vector Machines (SVMs) can be trained on labeled data to predict POS tags for new sentences.

Let us look into the Python implementation of PoS tagging.

```
import spacy
# Load the English language model (replace "en_core_web_sm" with
a larger model for improved accuracy if needed)
nlp = spacy.load("en_core_web_sm")
# Sample sentence
sentence = "The Amityville Horror is one of the best horror
movies ever."
# Process the sentence using spaCy
doc = nlp(sentence)
# Access POS tags for each token
for token in doc:
  print(f"Word: {token.text}, POS Tag: {token.pos_}")
Output:
Word: The, POS Tag: DET
Word: Amityville, POS Tag: PROPN
Word: Horror, POS Tag: PROPN
Word: is, POS Tag: AUX
Word: one, POS Tag: NUM
Word: of, POS Tag: ADP
Word: the, POS Tag: DET
Word: best, POS Tag: ADJ
Word: horror, POS Tag: NOUN
Word: movies, POS Tag: NOUN
```

```
Word: ever, POS Tag: ADV
Word: ., POS Tag: PUNCT
```

In the above code, we tested the concept of PoS tagging using the .pos_ method. In the sentence, there are nouns, numbers, adjectives, auxiliaries, and so on. We have loaded the "**`en_core_web_sm`**" English model from spaCy. We have used spaCy to get the PoS results, but we can also use the nltk library to do the same.

Additional Considerations

- POS taggers may not always produce perfect results, especially for ambiguous cases.
- Different tag sets with varying levels of granularity might be used depending on the application.
- POS tagging accuracy can be improved by employing techniques such as rule-based corrections or ensemble methods combining multiple taggers.

  https://www.shiksha.com/online-courses/articles/pos-tagging-in-nlp/#:~:text=POS%20tagging%20is%20the%20process,natural%20language%20processing%20(NLP).

  https://www.analyticsvidhya.com/blog/2020/07/part-of-speechpos-tagging-dependency-parsing-and-constituency-parsing-in-nlp/

  https://www.nltk.org/book/ch05.html

  https://spacy.io/usage/linguistic-features

Named Entity Recognition (NER)

Named Entity Recognition (NER) is a crucial NLP task that identifies and classifies named entities within a text. These entities can be **people, organizations, locations, dates, monetary values**, and other predefined categories. NER enhances the algorithms to understand the real-world entities mentioned in the text, enabling various applications.

Core Components of NER:

- **Identifying Key Entities:** NER focuses on extracting specific named entities from text, providing a structured representation of the information.
- **Entity Types:** Common NER categories include:
  - People (names of individuals)
  - Organizations (companies, institutions)
  - Locations (countries, cities, landmarks)

- Dates (specific points or ranges in time)
- Monetary Values (amounts with currencies)
- Other custom-defined entities (for example, products, diseases)

Applications of NER:

- **Information extraction**: Populating knowledge graphs with entities and relationships.
- **Question answering**: Identifying relevant entities to answer factual questions.
- **Sentiment analysis:** Analyzing sentiment expressed towards specific entities (for example, companies).
- **Machine translation:** Preserving and translating named entities accurately across languages.

Approaches to Named Entity Recognition

- **Rule-Based NER:** These methods utilize hand-crafted rules based on patterns such as capitalization, gazetteers (lists of known entities), and Part-of-Speech (POS) tags.
- **Statistical NER:** This approach employs statistical models such as Hidden Markov Models (HMMs) trained on annotated text data, where entities are labeled with their types.
- **Machine Learning Methods:** Supervised learning models such as Conditional Random Fields (CRFs) or neural networks can be trained on labeled data to perform NER with increased accuracy.

We will look into the Python implementation of NER using spaCy.

```
import spacy
nlp = spacy.load('en_core_web_sm')

doc = nlp("I live in New York")
for word in doc.ents:
    print(word.text, word.label_)

spacy.explain('GPE'), spacy.explain('ORG'),spacy.explain('MONEY')

Output:
New York GPE
('Countries, cities, states',
 'Companies, agencies, institutions, etc.',
 'Monetary values, including unit')
```

In the aforementioned code, we have used the same "**`en_core_web_sm`**" as before and have used the **`.label_`** object to get the named entities. Here, we have **New York** as a

Geo-Political Entity (like a location). We also observe the **`spacy.explain()`** functions on **`GPE`**, **`ORG`**, **and `MONEY`** that give us responses such as **`'Countries, cities, states'`**, '**`Companies, agencies, institutions`**, etc.', and 'Monetary values, including unit' respectively.

In the next code, we check the dependencies between the words in the sentence.

```
from spacy import displacy
doc = nlp("I live in New York")
displacy.render(doc, style="dep")
```

Here, we see **`displacy.render()`** to check the dependencies between the words in the sentence. We will see the result below.

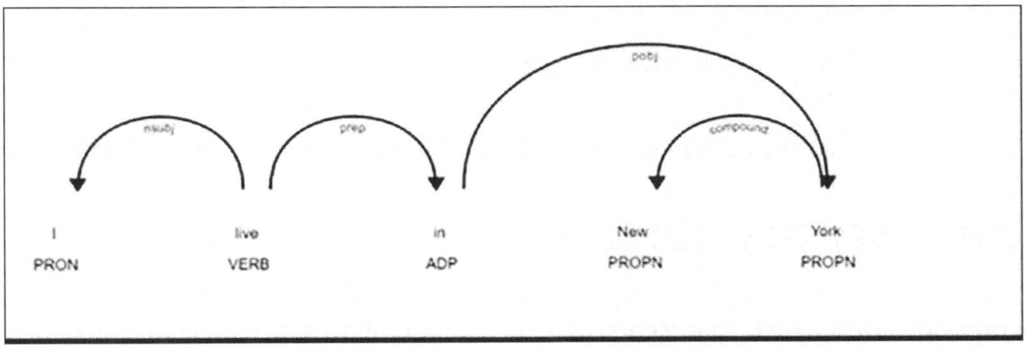

Figure 2.5: *Dependencies in the sentence*

We see the different Parts of Speech in the sentence (I live in New York) and see the root, subject, pronoun, preposition, and object. It is a dependency tree that shows how each word depends on others in the sentence to form a grammatically correct and meaningful statement.

In the next code, we will see the Named Entities in the form of tags.

```
doc = nlp("Bill Gates and Paul Allen founded Microsoft")
displacy.render(doc, style="ent")
```

The **`displacy.render (doc, style = "ent")`** is used to have the tags of different entities.

Figure 2.6: *Tags of the sentence*

The specific formatting and appearance of the highlighted entities are Person and Organization.

This output demonstrates spaCy's ability to identify and categorize named entities within the sentence, providing a structured representation of these entities relevant to real-world concepts.

Some extra situations of NER.

- NER models may struggle with ambiguous cases or entities not present in the training data.
- Customizing NER models can be done by defining specific entity types relevant to the application domain.
- Combining NER with other NLP techniques, such as co-reference resolution, can improve overall understanding of the textual information.

  https://www.kaggle.com/code/abhisarangan/ner-using-spacy

  https://www.analyticsvidhya.com/blog/2021/06/nlp-application-named-entity-recognition-ner-in-python-with-spacy/

  https://www.geeksforgeeks.org/python-named-entity-recognition-ner-using-spacy/

  https://spotintelligence.com/2022/12/06/named-entity-recognition-ner/

Coreference Resolution

Coreference resolution is a fundamental NLP task that identifies and links expressions in a text that refer to the same real-world entity or concept. It essentially deals with pronouns, noun phrases, or other referring expressions that do not explicitly repeat the entity's name. Let us see an example to understand Coreference Resolution.

Sentence:

John bought a new car. He loves driving it on weekends.

Coreference Resolution:

- "`John`" and "`He`" refer to the same person.
- "`a new car`" and "`it`" refer to the same object.

By resolving the coreferences, we can rewrite the sentence as: John bought a new car. John loves driving the car on weekends.

Understanding Coreference Resolution

Here, we will see the idea of Coreference Resolution and its different benefits.

- **Connecting the Dots:** Coreference resolution establishes relationships between mentions (different ways an entity is referred to) within a text.
- **Benefits:** Resolving coreference is crucial for various NLP applications, including:

- **Text Summarization:** By understanding coreference, summaries can accurately reflect the relationships between entities mentioned throughout the text.
- **Question Answering:** Coreference can help pinpoint relevant information by linking mentions of the same entity in a question and the answer passage.
- **Machine Translation:** Preserving coreference relationships improves the accuracy and coherence of translated text.
- **Information Extraction:** Coreference resolution empowers the system to build a more comprehensive understanding of the entities and their interactions within the text.

Approaches to Coreference Resolution

The various methods of Coreference Resolution are as follows.

- **Rule-Based Methods:** These strategies use manually created rules that take into account things such as discourse cues (such as "**first**," "**second**"), noun phrase similarity, and grammatical traits.
- **Statistical Models:** Labelled coreference connections in annotated datasets can be used to train statistical methods such as Conditional Random Fields (CRFs) or Hidden Markov Models (HMMs).
- **Machine Learning Techniques:** Neural networks and other deep learning models can be trained to recognize intricate patterns in vast volumes of data and enhance the accuracy of coreference resolution.

Challenges in Coreference Resolution

- **Disambiguation:** Pronouns can refer to multiple entities in complex sentences, requiring context analysis to identify the correct antecedent.
- **Anaphora:** Coreference resolution needs to handle anaphoric references, where the entity is mentioned later in the text compared to the pronoun referring to it.
- **Specificity:** Determining the intended meaning of vague expressions such as "*it*" or "*this*" poses a challenge.

  https://spotintelligence.com/2024/01/17/coreference-resolution-nlp/

  https://towardsdatascience.com/coreference-resolution-in-python-aca946541dec

  https://blog.devgenius.io/coreference-resolution-nlp-python-584c2ec50f5d

https://github.com/aleenaraj/Coreference_Resolution

https://stanfordnlp.github.io/CoreNLP/coref.html

NLP Evaluation Metrics

Evaluating the performance of NLP algorithms is important for understanding their strengths and weaknesses. NLP evaluation metrics provide quantitative measures to compare the performance of different models or assess a single model's accuracy on a particular task.

Importance of Evaluation: Evaluation helps us:

- Choose the best model for a specific NLP task.
- Identify areas for improvement in NLP algorithms.
- Track the progress of NLP research and development

Common Metrics: Different metrics are used depending on the type of NLP task. Here are some widely used ones:

- **Accuracy:** (Number of Correct Predictions/Total number of Predictions)
    - **Concept:** Measures the overall ratio of the correct predictions made by the model.
    - **Example:** In a spam classification task, accuracy represents the percentage of tags where the model correctly identified the sentences as spam or not spam tags.
- **Precision:** (True Positives/(True Positives + False Positives))
    - **Concept:** Measures the ratio of the correct positive predictions.
    - **Example:** In a sentiment analysis task, precision indicates the percentage of reviews flagged as positive that are truly positive messages.
- **Recall:** (True Positives / (True Positives + False Negatives))
    - **Concept:** Measures the ratio of actual positive cases that the model correctly identifies.
    - **Example:** In sentiment analysis, a high recall means the model identifies most actual positive (or negative) reviews, even if it also mistakenly classifies some neutral reviews as positive/negative.
- **F1 Score:** (2 * Precision * Recall) / (Precision + Recall)
    - **Concept:** Combines precision and recall into a single metric, balancing both aspects of model performance.

  - **Example:** In sentiment analysis, an F1 score of 0.85 indicates the model performs well at both correctly identifying positive and negative sentiment, balancing precision and recall.
- **BLEU (**BiLingual Evaluation Understudy) **Score** (Machine Translation):
  - **Concept:** Measures the similarity between machine-generated text and human-written references.

How BLEU Works:

- **N-gram Precision:** BLEU checks how many **n-grams** in the candidate translation appear in the reference translation. It calculates precision for different n-gram sizes (commonly 1- to 4-gram).
- **Clipping:** To avoid over-counting repeated n-grams, BLEU uses **clipped counts**–it only counts the number of n-grams up to the maximum number that appears in any reference.
- **Brevity Penalty (BP):** If the candidate translation is **shorter than the reference**, BLEU penalizes the score. This discourages the model from producing overly short translations that may have high precision but lack completeness.

  Example: A machine translation system that scores high on the BLEU score is likely to produce translations that are more similar in meaning and fluency to human-written references.

Reference: "*The cat is on the mat.*"

Candidate: "*The cat on mat.*"

BLEU will compare overlapping unigrams, bigrams, etc.

Unigrams match: The, cat, mat → 3/4

Bigrams match: The cat → 1/3

Candidate is shorter → Brevity penalty applied

Final BLEU score is a decimal between **0 (no match)** and **1 (perfect match)**, often shown as a percentage (for example, 0.45 → 45%).

BLEU is commonly used to benchmark **machine translation models** such as Google Translate, OpenNMT, and Transformer-based systems (for example, BERT2BERT, T5, and so on).

- **ROUGE (**Recall-Oriented Understudy for Gisting Evaluation**) Score**

  Definition: By comparing generated text with reference text (ground truth), a collection of measures known as ROUGE (Recall-Oriented Understudy for Gisting Evaluation) is used to assess the quality of text summarization, machine translation, and text generation algorithms. To evaluate how well a model-generated summary retains the essential components of a reference summary, it calculates n-gram overlap, recall, and precision.

Types of ROUGE Metrics

- **ROUGE-N (N-gram Overlap)**
  - Measures the **overlap of n-grams** between the generated and reference summaries.
  - ROUGE-1 uses **unigrams (single words)**, while ROUGE-2 considers **bigrams (two-word sequences)**.
- **ROUGE-L (Longest Common Subsequence - LCS)**
  - Measures the **longest shared sequence of words** between the reference and generated summaries.
  - Unlike n-grams, **LCS allows for gaps**, capturing sentence structure similarity.
  - ROUGE-L is useful when word order matters.
- **ROUGE-W (Weighted LCS)**
  - Similar to ROUGE-L but assigns **higher weights** to **longer consecutive matches** in LCS.
  - Prioritizes **longer contiguous overlapping phrases**, rather than sporadic words.
- **ROUGE-S (Skip-Bigram Based Co-Occurrence Statistics)**
  - Measures **skip-bigram** overlap, allowing for words to appear **out of order** but still count as a match.
  - A **skip-bigram** consists of **two words that appear in the same order** in both summaries, with gaps allowed.
- **ROUGE-WE (ROUGE with Word Embeddings)**
  - Uses **semantic similarity** instead of exact word matches.
  - Leverages **pre-trained word embeddings (Word2Vec, GloVe, BERT)** to detect similarity between **synonyms**.

  Example: In text summarization tasks, the ROUGE score measures how well a generated summary overlaps with human-written references, indicating how well it captures the key information and phrasing.

- **Perplexity**

  Definition: Measures how well a language model predicts the next word in a sequence. It measures a model's uncertainty when dealing with new data. It has lower values of perplexity, meaning the model is more confident with its predictions.

Importance of Perplexity:

- **Measures Predictive Performance:** Helps determine how well a model predicts unseen text.
- **Useful in Language Modeling:** Used in **N-gram models, RNNs, and Transformer-based models**.
- **Benchmark for Model Selection:** Lower perplexity suggests better generalization.
- **Helps in Hyperparameter Tuning:** Used to adjust model parameters for better results.

Perplexity in different language models

- **Recurrent Neural Networks (RNNs):**
  - RNNs compute next-word probabilities dynamically.
  - Lower perplexity means better long-term dependencies.
  - LSTMs and GRUs often outperform simple RNNs due to vanishing gradient issues.
- **Transformer Models (BERT, GPT)**
  - Transformer-based models such as GPT (Generative Pre-trained Transformer) optimize perplexity over large corpora.
  - GPT-3 has lower perplexity than GPT-2 due to better contextual understanding.
- **Word Error Rate (WER):**

  Definition: Ratio of the number of errors in a speech recognition output to the total number of words in the reference transcript.

  Example: In speech recognition, a WER of 15% indicates that the system makes 15 errors (substitutions, insertions, deletions) for every 100 words spoken.

Metrics Specific to Tasks:

- **Sentiment Analysis**: Accuracy, precision, recall, and F1-score for positive/negative sentiment.
- **Named Entity Recognition:** F1-score for different entity types.
- **Question Answering:** Accuracy, F1-score for answer selection, and answer generation.

  https://huggingface.co/spaces/evaluate-metric/bleu

https://www.cs.bu.edu/fac/snyder/cs505/PerplexityPosts.pdf

https://spotintelligence.com/2024/08/19/perplexity-in-nlp/

https://www.baeldung.com/cs/language-models-perplexity

Additional Considerations:

- Choosing the right evaluation metric depends on the specific NLP task, and its priorities.
- Metrics such as accuracy may not always be sufficient, and a combination of multiple metrics can provide a more comprehensive picture of performance.
- Human evaluation can be used alongside automated metrics to assess factors like relevance and natural language fluency.

https://medium.com/@sujathamudadla1213/nlp-model-metrics-b3fa32373269

https://www.geeksforgeeks.org/nlp-bleu-score-for-evaluating-neural-machine-translation-python/

https://medium.com/@mikeusru/common-metrics-for-evaluating-natural-language-processing-nlp-models-e84190063b5f

https://github.com/gcunhase/NLPMetrics/tree/master

https://datascience.fm/top-evaluation-metrics-for-nlp-models/

https://github.com/ChulinChen20/Predicting_Turnover_Types_on_Twitter/tree/main

Dependency Parsing

Dependency parsing is a fundamental NLP task that analyzes the grammatical relationships between words in a sentence. It goes beyond simply identifying parts-of-speech (POS) tags and aims to create a dependency tree that reveals how each word depends on others within the sentence structure.

At its core, dependency parsing represents a sentence as a **dependency tree**, where:

- Each word (except the root) is linked to a **head** (another word it depends on).
- The type of relationship between words is labeled with **dependency tags** (for example, **subject, object, modifier**).

For example, in the sentence:

"The cat sits on the mat."

A dependency tree might look like this:

- **sits** is the **root verb** (main action).
- **cat** is the **subject**, depending on **sits**.
- **on** is a **preposition**, linking **sits** to **mat**.
- **the** modifies **cat** and **mat**.

Understanding Dependency Parsing

- **Mapping Relationships:** Dependency parsing creates a dependency tree where words are nodes and edges represent grammatical relationships (for example, subject-verb, verb-object).
- **Benefits:** Dependency parsing provides a deeper understanding of a sentence's structure, impacting various NLP applications:
  - **Sentiment Analysis:** Identifying the subject and object of a verb helps determine who or what the sentiment is expressed towards.
  - **Question Answering:** Parsing the structure helps pinpoint the relevant information based on the question's grammatical form.
  - **Machine Translation:** Understanding the grammatical roles allows for more accurate word order and structure in the translated text.
  - **Text Summarization:** Dependency parsing can guide the summarization process by extracting the key elements and their relationships.

Approaches to Dependency Parsing:

- **Rule-Based Parsing:** These methods employ handcrafted rules based on syntax and POS tags to define dependency relationships between words.
- **Statistical Parsing:** Statistical models such as Transition-based Parsing or Graph-based Parsing utilize statistical learning from annotated data to predict dependencies.
- **Machine Learning Methods:** Neural networks, particularly Recurrent Neural Networks (RNNs) or transformers, can be trained to learn complex dependency patterns from large text corpora.

Additional Considerations:

- Dependency parsing models may encounter ambiguous cases where a word can have multiple possible dependencies, depending on the context.
- Projective versus Non-projective Dependencies: Projective parsing assumes all dependencies can be drawn as straight lines within the tree, while non-projective parsing handles cases where dependencies cross each, allowing the

parser to represent more complex linguistic phenomena such as word order variations and long-distance dependencies

https://www.analyticsvidhya.com/blog/2021/12/dependency-parsing-in-natural-language-processing-with-examples/

https://spotintelligence.com/2023/10/22/dependency-parsing/

https://towardsdatascience.com/natural-language-processing-dependency-parsing-cf094bbbe3f7

Coreference Resolution versus Dependency Parsing: Unveiling the Connections

Both coreference resolution and dependency parsing are crucial NLP tasks that analyze the relationships between words in a sentence. However, they focus on different aspects of this structure.

Similarities:

- Both tasks analyze the relationships between words within a sentence.
- They both contribute to a deeper understanding of sentence structure and meaning.
- Both can be implemented using rule-based, statistical, or machine learning approaches.

Differences:

- **Coreference resolution:** Deals with real-world entities, and how they are referred to within the text.
- **Dependency parsing:** Focuses on the grammatical roles of words within a sentence structure.
- **Coreference resolution:** Often involves reasoning about discourse structure and prior mentions.
- **Dependency parsing:** Primarily relies on the immediate syntactic context within the sentence.

In summary:

- Coreference resolution connects words that describe the same entity across a text.
- Dependency parsing analyzes the grammatical structure and relationships between words in a single sentence.

These tasks often complement each other. Dependency parsing can provide a foundation for coreference resolution by identifying potential coreference candidates (for example, pronouns as subjects). Similarly, coreference resolution can aid in dependency parsing when there are ambiguous cases involving pronouns or other referring expressions.

Conclusion

In this chapter, we explored various NLP techniques on the topic of representing data. We understood Bag of Words (BoW), N-grams, and TF-IDF, and explored some examples with relevant Python codes. We also went through the topics of word and sentence embeddings, where we saw Fasttext, GloVe, Word2vec, Sent2vec, USE, SBERT, and so on.

We also learned about the concepts of Word Disambiguation, Parts of Speech tagging, and Named Entity Recognition. Moreover, we also investigated various performance metrics for NLP models. Finally, we learned about the concepts of Coreference resolution and Dependency Parsing. In the upcoming chapter, we will investigate real-life use cases of the techniques used in this chapter and also look into interview questions on the concepts of TF-IDF, N-grams, BoW model, Word embeddings, and so on.

CHAPTER 3
Sentiment Analysis Using NLP

Introduction

The ever-growing field of Natural Language Processing (NLP) empowers machines to understand and manipulate human language. This chapter delves into a practical application of NLP, which is Sentiment Analysis. We will explore how to prepare text data for analysis and leverage methods such as bag-of-words, TF-IDF, and word embeddings to extract meaningful features. Furthermore, we will investigate techniques such as Part-of-Speech tagging and Named Entity Recognition (NER) to gain deeper insights into sentence structure and entities mentioned within the text. Moreover, we will also perform Sentiment Analysis using TextBlob, VADER Sentiment, and NLTK, and do a word cloud visualization to understand the usage frequency of various words in the reviews. This enables us to understand the themes, topics, and sentiments expressed in the reviews. Finally, we will do machine learning modeling using Multinomial Naïve Bayes, LinearSVC, and Logistic Regression to understand the classification of the positive, negative, and neutral reviews.

Structure

In this chapter, we will discuss the following topics:

- Sentiment Analysis of Amazon Reviews
- Data Acquisition
- Libraries and Tools Used
- Data Load and Exploration
- POS Tagging and NER
- Sentiment Analysis
- Word Cloud Visualization
- Machine Learning Modeling for Sentiment Analysis

Sentiment Analysis of Amazon Reviews

In today's data-driven world, understanding customer sentiment is imperative for businesses to thrive. One rich source of customer feedback is online product reviews. This topic of the chapter on Practical Applications of NLP Techniques delves into the application of sentiment analysis on Amazon mouse reviews, where we get a diverse and exhaustive resource of opinions and experiences. By extracting and analyzing the sentiment from these reviews, we aim to provide valuable insights into customer satisfaction, product strengths and weaknesses, and the areas for improvement.

Sentiment analysis, a subfield of natural language processing, involves the identification and quantification of subjective information in text. By applying sentiment analysis to Amazon product reviews, we can gain a deeper understanding of customer perceptions regarding product performance, features, and overall user experience. This knowledge can be very important in guiding product development, marketing strategies, and customer support initiatives.

This chapter will explore the end-to-end process of sentiment analysis, from data acquisition and preprocessing to feature engineering, model building, and evaluation. We will delve into the various NLP techniques, such as preprocessing, text cleaning, feature extraction, feature engineering, and some machine learning algorithms, to effectively classify reviews as positive, negative, or neutral. Ultimately, this analysis will provide valuable insights into customer sentiment toward various electronic products that Amazon has in its marketplace.

Data Acquisition

The dataset was taken from https://www.kaggle.com/datasets/danielihenacho/amazon-reviews-dataset/data where the dataset was created from the scraped reviews from products on Amazon for text classification. The data has columns that have sentiments (positive, negative, neutral), the **`cleaned_review`** column (where we have the reviews by the users), then we have the review length, and finally the review score of 1 to 5, with 5 being the most positive review and 1 being the most negative review.

Libraries and Tools Used

We will be using pandas for the data loading and exploration, and for the NLP applications, we will be using nltk and spaCy. The sklearn library is used to do machine learning modeling later in the chapter, as well as model evaluation. We will also be using libraries such as TextBlob, nltk, and **`VaderSentiment`** for sentiment analysis.

Data Load and Exploration

We will look into the following code for a better understanding of the data, and proceed with the data exploration.

```
import pandas as pd
import numpy as np
import seaborn as sns
import spacy
from spacy.lang.en.stop_words import STOP_WORDS
from sklearn.model_selection import train_test_split
from sklearn.feature_extraction.text import TfidfVectorizer
from sklearn.pipeline import Pipeline
from sklearn.metrics import accuracy_score, confusion_matrix,
classification_report,ConfusionMatrixDisplay
from sklearn import naive_bayes
from sklearn.linear_model import LogisticRegression
from sklearn.svm import LinearSVC
from nltk.corpus import stopwords

# Load the dataset (assuming it's in a CSV file)
# https://www.kaggle.com/datasets/danielihenacho/amazon-
reviews-dataset?resource=download
amazon_df = pd.read_csv("amazon_cleaned_reviews.csv")

# Load spaCy model
nlp = spacy.load("en_core_web_sm")

# Explore the dataset
print(amazon_df.shape)
amazon_df.head()
```

	sentiments	cleaned_review	cleaned_review_length	review_score
0	positive	i wish would have gotten one earlier love it a...	19	5
1	neutral	i ve learned this lesson again open the packag...	88	1
2	neutral	it is so slow and lags find better option	9	2
3	neutral	roller ball stopped working within months of m...	12	1
4	neutral	i like the color and size but it few days out ...	21	1

Figure 3.1: *Amazon review data*

In the preceding image, we see the first 5 rows of the dataset. The data set has **17340 rows and 4 columns**.

We can also see the distribution of the review scores.

```
sns.histplot(amazon_df['review_score'])
```

We are using **histplot** function, where we get the distribution of review scores from the seaborn library.

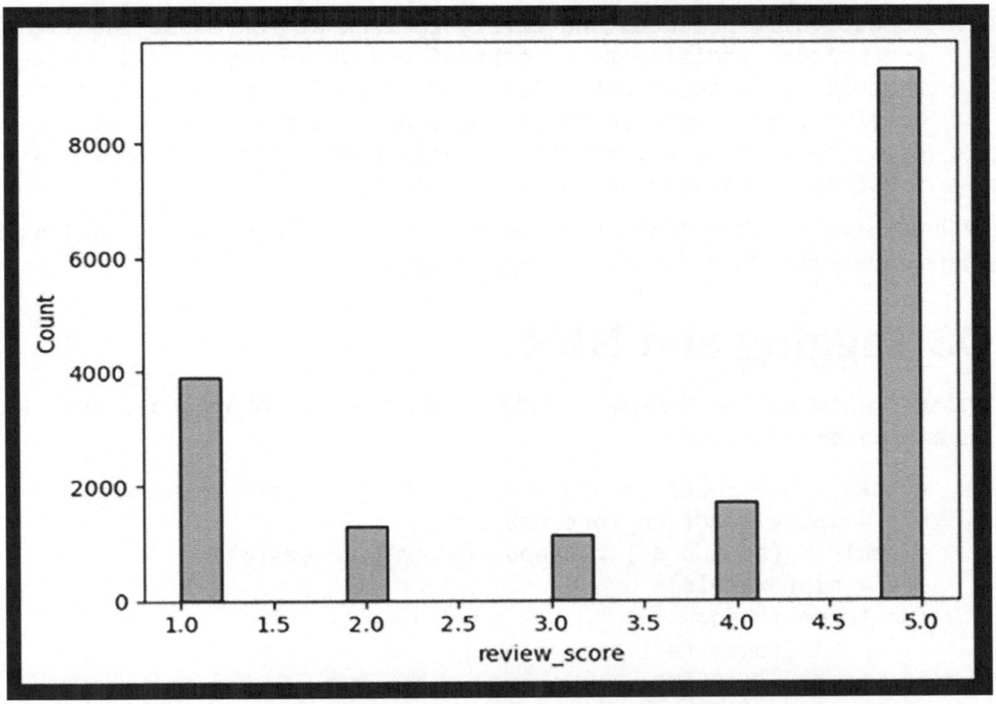

Figure 3.2: *Review scores distribution data*

The preceding picture shows that more than 8000 products have 5-star reviews, and almost 4000 products have 1-star reviews. We can check more details using **value_counts()** function.

```
amazon_df['review_score'].value_counts()
Output:
review_score
5    9316
1    3898
4    1714
2    1295
3    1117
Name: count, dtype: int64
```

We have the distribution of the review scores with numbers. Most of the users like the products, but a lot of users also dislike the products and give 1-star reviews. 1714 users gave 4-star reviews, which signifies that most users like the products.

Now, let us check out one of the reviews.

```
example = (amazon_df['cleaned_review'].values[10])
example
```

Output:

```
'beautifully produced and lovely to look at for mouse the lights
are welcome addition to an otherwise drab workspace did notice
that it tends to go into sleep mode quickly but takes longer wake
up time than expect on screen busy with windows the cursor freez-
es in position until the mouse fully comes back to life it is
frustrating for anyone who isn't patient '
```

We will use spaCy to understand a review's various parts of speech. We will check for a different example where the review length is smaller.

POS Tagging and NER

In this section, we will use the spaCy model and extract Parts of Speech from the texts in the **amazon_df** dataframe.

```
# Load spaCy model (replace with a larger model if needed)
nlp = spacy.load("en_core_web_sm")
example = (amazon_df['cleaned_review'].values[0])
doc = nlp(example)
for token in doc:
    print(token.text, token.pos_)

Output:
i PRON
wish VERB
would AUX
have AUX
gotten VERB
one NUM
earlier ADJ
love VERB
it PRON
and CCONJ
it PRON
makes VERB
working VERB
in ADP
my PRON
laptop NOUN
```

```
so ADV
much ADV
easier ADJ
```

In the preceding example review, we have various parts of speech such as verbs, adjectives, adverbs, pronouns, nouns, auxiliaries, and so on.

Next, will check the Named Entity Recognition (NER) using spaCy.

```
for ent in doc.ents:
    print(ent.text, ent.label_)
Output:
one CARDINAL
```

We are getting just one entity (one that is tagged as Cardinal in the review). However, if we consider news articles, blogs, and transcribed video texts, we can get various kinds of tags pertaining to geolocation, person, organization, and so on.

Next, we will understand the concept of dependency parsing with respect to sentiment analysis.

```
# Print dependency parse
for token in doc:
    print(token.text, token.dep_, token.head.text)
```

Output:

```
i nsubj wish
wish ROOT wish
would aux gotten
have aux gotten
gotten ccomp wish
one nummod love
earlier amod one
love dobj gotten
it dobj love
and cc wish
it nsubj makes
makes conj wish
working xcomp makes
in prep working
my poss laptop
laptop pobj in
so advmod much
much advmod easier
easier ccomp makes
```

In the preceding code, we get the various dependencies of the words adjacent to the other words. In sentiment analysis, there are some significances, while we do dependency parsing, such as subject identification, where dependency parsing can help identify the subject of a sentence, which is often crucial for understanding the target of sentiment.

Next, object identification helps identify the object of a verb that can reveal the entity or concept being evaluated. Then, we have adjectives and adverbs that can provide ideas on the intensity and direction of the sentiment. It also helps us understand the context of the sentiment from the sentence.

For example, the sentence has the word "**love**," which signifies that it is a positive sentiment, and the reviewer wishes that he/she had gotten the product earlier. Moreover, the reviewer also talks about the convenience of working on the laptop, which helps understand the overall positive sentiment of the review. We can also check the same for neutral and negative reviews.

We will now check the visualization of the dependency parser.

```
# Visualize dependency parse (optional)
from spacy.displacy import render
render(doc, style="dep")
```

Output:

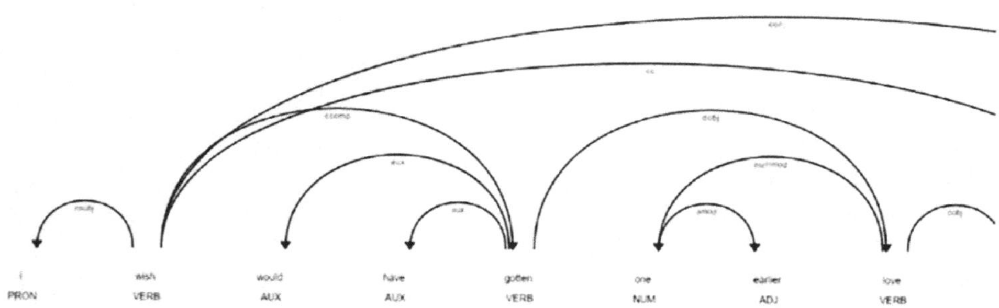

Figure 3.3: *Dependency parser visualized*

The preceding diagram shows the dependency parsing of the sentence. However, the whole diagram is not shown due to a lack of space, and we can check it while running the Python code. Dependency parsing provides a valuable tool for understanding the grammatical structure of a sentence, which can be directly related to sentiment analysis. Visualizing these dependencies can offer a more intuitive understanding of how different parts of the sentence contribute to the overall sentiment.

Key Insights from Dependency Parsing

Dependency Parsing helps in identifying relations between subjects, verbs, objects, and ultimately understanding the sentiment hidden inside the text. It also provides an understanding of the contexts that are essential for sentiment analysis.

- **Subject-Verb-Object Relationships:** Identifying the subject, verb, and object can help pinpoint the entity being evaluated and its sentiment.
- **Modifier Analysis:** Understanding how adjectives and adverbs modify nouns and verbs can provide clues about the intensity and direction of sentiment.
- **Negation Handling:** Dependency parsing can help identify negation words (for example, `"not"`, `"never"`) that can reverse the polarity of a sentiment.
- **Contextual Understanding:** Visualizing dependencies can reveal how words relate to each other within the sentence, providing a richer context for sentiment analysis.

In the next part, we will look into the TextBlob library to understand the usage of sentiment analysis. TextBlob is a Python library that provides a simple and intuitive interface for performing natural language processing tasks, including sentiment analysis. It simplifies the process of extracting sentiment polarity and subjectivity from text data.

Key Importance of TextBlob for Sentiment Analysis:

TextBlob is a library that does an array of tasks, from POS tagging, Noun extraction, Sentiment Analysis, Tokenization, Lemmatization, and so on. It uses NLTK to perform its tasks.

- **Ease of Use:** TextBlob offers a user-friendly API, making it accessible to both beginners and experienced NLP practitioners.
- **Sentiment Polarity and Subjectivity:** It provides functions to directly calculate the sentiment polarity (positive, negative, or neutral) and subjectivity (how opinionated the text is) of a given text.
- **Built-in Lexicon:** TextBlob comes with a pre-trained sentiment lexicon that helps in determining the sentiment of words and phrases.
- **Customization:** You can customize the sentiment lexicon or create your own to tailor the analysis to specific domains or contexts.
- **Additional NLP Tasks:** Beyond sentiment analysis, TextBlob can also be used for tasks such as part-of-speech tagging, noun phrase extraction, and translation.

Sentiment Analysis

We can see the succeeding code but before we need to install textblob.

```
from textblob import TextBlob
blob = TextBlob(example)
```

```
sentiment = blob.sentiment
print(sentiment.polarity)
print(sentiment.subjectivity)
Output:
0.23333333333333333
0.43333333333333335
```

In the preceding code, we see the polarity and subjectivity of the review. **Polarity** and **subjectivity** are two key metrics used in sentiment analysis to understand the emotional tone and opinionated nature of a text. **Polarity** refers to the sentiment orientation of a text, indicating whether it is positive, negative, or neutral, helps identify the overall sentiment, and provides a quantitative measure of the emotional intensity of the text. **Subjectivity** measures the degree to which a text expresses personal opinions or beliefs rather than objective facts. It can be useful to differentiate between biased or opinionated content, and it can also be combined with polarity to understand the overall emotional tone and objectivity of the text.

In the preceding review example, we have the polarity as 0.23 and subjectivity as 0.43. We can evaluate the numbers as follows:

- **Polarity:** 0.23 indicates a slightly positive sentiment. Values typically range from -1 (very negative) to 1 (very positive). A value of 0.23 suggests a mildly positive sentiment.
- **Subjectivity:** 0.43 indicates a moderately subjective text. Values range from 0 (objective) to 1 (highly subjective). A value of 0.43 suggests the text contains a mix of objective and subjective elements.
- **Combined Interpretation:** Given these values, the text can be interpreted as having a **mildly positive sentiment** with a **moderate degree of subjectivity**. This means the text is likely to express a positive opinion, but it also contains some factual or objective information.

In the next section, we will check sentiment analysis using nltk library (https://www.nltk.org/howto/sentiment.html). We will check the code as follows:

```
import nltk
from nltk.sentiment.vader import SentimentIntensityAnalyzer
nltk.download('vader_lexicon')
sid = SentimentIntensityAnalyzer()
def analyze_sentiment(text):
  sentiment_scores = sid.polarity_scores(text)
  compound_score = sentiment_scores["compound"]

  if compound_score >= 0.05:
    return "Positive"
  elif compound_score <= -0.05:
    return "Negative"
```

```
    else:
      return "Neutral"
# Example usage
sentiment = analyze_sentiment(example)
print(sentiment)
```

Output:

```
[nltk_data] Downloading package vader_lexicon to
[nltk_data] "Address where the data is downloaded"
Positive
```

To understand the code, we import the necessary modules from NLTK. We then download the VADER sentiment lexicon, which contains a list of words and their associated sentiment scores. Then we create a SentimentIntensityAnalyzer object.

The **analyze_sentiment()** function takes a text as input and returns the sentiment polarity based on the compound score. The compound score ranges from -1 (very negative) to 1 (very positive). We define thresholds to classify sentiment as positive, negative, or neutral.

The output sentiment is positive and matches that of the original label that we had in the data under the **sentiments** column in the data frame.

We will now look into **VADER (Valence Aware Dictionary and sEntiment Reasoner)** sentiment analyzer.

Key Features:

VADER is a rule-based sentiment analysis tool designed specifically for analyzing social media text. It combines a sentiment lexicon with a set of rules to accurately capture the emotional tone of the text. Here, there are Sentiment Lexicon, Rules, and Compound Score, which are detailed as follows:

- **Sentiment Lexicon:** Contains a list of words and their associated sentiment scores (positive, negative, or neutral).
- **Rules:** VADER incorporates rules to handle negation, intensifiers, and other linguistic constructions that can affect sentiment polarity.
- **Compound Score:** VADER calculates a "**compound**" score that represents the overall sentiment of a text, ranging from -1 (very negative) to 1 (very positive).

We will check the code where the VADER sentiment analyzer is used.

```
from vaderSentiment.vaderSentiment import SentimentIntensityAnalyzer
def sentiment_analysis_vader(text):
    sid = SentimentIntensityAnalyzer()
    score = sid.polarity_scores(text)
    return score
# Example usage:
sentiment_score = sentiment_analysis_vader(example)
```

```
print(sentiment_score)
Output:
{'neg': 0.0, 'neu': 0.616, 'pos': 0.384, 'compound': 0.8744}
```

This code defines a function **sentiment_analysis_vader** function that takes a text as input and returns the sentiment score using VADER. The **sentiment_score** will be a dictionary containing the following keys:

- **neg:** Negative sentiment score
- **neu:** Neutral sentiment score
- **pos:** Positive sentiment score
- **compound:** Overall compound score (ranges from -1 to 1)

In the preceding result, we have 0.616 for neu and 0.384 for pos, which suggests that the review is more in the neutral range than the positive range. This signifies that the text expresses a positive sentiment with some neutral elements. It suggests that the text is likely expressing a positive opinion or feeling.

In the context of the **e-commerce industry**, this sentiment analysis result—where the review has a **0.384 positive score** and a **0.616 neutral score**—can be interpreted as a **moderately satisfied customer**. For instance, a customer may have received their order on time and found the product acceptable, but the product was not exceptional.

This kind of feedback helps e-commerce businesses **pinpoint areas for value addition**—perhaps enhancing product quality, packaging, or the post-purchase experience. By segmenting such reviews, platforms can identify products that are meeting expectations but not exceeding them, allowing them to focus on **improving product listings, offering bundles, or initiating follow-up campaigns** to boost satisfaction, and turn neutral-positive customers into loyal advocates.

Word Cloud Visualization

We will now check the visualization of words using the word cloud. Word clouds are a visual representation of the frequency of words in a text corpus. By visualizing the most common words, we can quickly identify the key themes, topics, and sentiments expressed in the reviews.

The Python code is as follows:

```
from wordcloud import WordCloud
import matplotlib.pyplot as plt
# Combine all reviews into a single string
text = " ".join(amazon_df['cleaned_review'].astype(str))
wordcloud = WordCloud(width=800, height=400, background_
color='white').generate(text)
```

```
# Display the word cloud
plt.figure(figsize=(10, 7))
plt.imshow(wordcloud, interpolation='bilinear')
plt.axis('off')
plt.show()
```

In the preceding code, we import the WordCloud function and the matplotlib library. We concatenate all the reviews in the data frame and convert them into string data types. We then create the wordcloud variable with a white background and with a defined height and width of the visualization. Then we use the matplotlib library to display it as a visualization. The word cloud is as follows:

Figure 3.4: *Word cloud of the Amazon reviews*

In the preceding word cloud, we see **mouse** as the largest word. There are also big-sized words such as **love, work, use, great, one, light,** and so on. The largest word is the one that has been used frequently. The product mouse is being reviewed frequently. The words love and great signify positive sentiments, and there are indeed a lot of positive reviews. There are also words such as speaker, headphone, mic, laptop, and keyboard that are electronic accessories that are used with the mouse.

We can also remove the stopwords from the reviews and recreate the word cloud.

```
from nltk.corpus import stopwords
stopwords = set(stopwords.words('english'))
text = " ".join([word for word in text.split() if word not in
stopwords])
wordcloud = WordCloud(stopwords=stopwords, width=800, height=400,
background_color='white').generate(text)
# Display the word cloud
plt.figure(figsize=(10, 7))
```

```
    plt.imshow(wordcloud, interpolation='bilinear')
    plt.axis('off')
    plt.show()
```

In the preceding code, we made a minor change by removing the stop words from the reviews and then recreated the word cloud. Let us see how it looks now.

***Figure* 3.5:** *Word cloud of the Amazon reviews after stopwords removal*

We see that the most frequent words, such as **mouse, work, use, like, and love**, remain almost the same. The word **keyboard** has become more frequent in comparison to the earlier version.

Word cloud visualization can be used for **sentiment analysis** by providing an intuitive snapshot of the most frequently used words in a given text dataset–**filtered by sentiment**.

After running sentiment analysis, we can `segregate reviews/tweets/comments` into **positive, neutral, and negative categories**, and then generate a **separate word cloud** for each. This allows businesses to **visually understand** what words are most commonly associated with different types of sentiments.

Machine Learning Modeling for Sentiment Analysis

In the next parts of the project, we will explain the process of text cleaning, preprocessing, TF-IDF Vectorizer, and model training and evaluation for sentiment analysis.

- **Text Cleaning and Preprocessing:** Text cleaning and preprocessing are essential to preparing textual data for machine learning models. The raw text data usually contains noise such as punctuation, numbers, and stop words that do not contribute meaningfully to the model's understanding. Here is how to clean and preprocess text data:

1. **Tokenization:** Tokenization involves splitting a string of text into smaller pieces, usually words or phrases. This step converts sentences into individual words, which are called tokens. For example, the sentence "I *love Python programming*" would be tokenized into ["**I**", "**love**", "**Python**", "**programming**"].
2. **Lowercasing:** After tokenization, all tokens are converted to lowercase. This step ensures that the model treats words such as "*Python*" and "python" as the same token, reducing the complexity of the data.
3. **Stop Words Removal:** Stop words are common words that often do not add significant meaning to the text. Examples include "**is**," "**and**," "**the**," and so on. These words are removed from the text to reduce noise, and improve the model's efficiency.
4. **Lemmatization:** Lemmatization reduces words to their base or root form. For instance, "**running**" becomes "**run**," and "**better**" becomes "**good**." This process helps standardize words, and reduces the dimensionality of the text data.

The Python code is as follows:

```
import pandas as pd
import re
from sklearn.model_selection import train_test_split
from sklearn.feature_extraction.text import TfidfVectorizer
from sklearn.preprocessing import LabelEncoder
from nltk.corpus import stopwords
from nltk.stem import WordNetLemmatizer

# Simple text preprocessing
stop_words = set(stopwords.words('english'))
lemmatizer = WordNetLemmatizer()

def preprocess_text(text):
    if isinstance(text, str):  # Ensure the text is a string
        # Tokenization and converting to lowercase
        tokens = re.findall(r"\b\w+\b", text.lower())
        # Lemmatization and stop words removal
        tokens = [lemmatizer.lemmatize(word) for word in tokens
if word not in stop_words]
        return " ".join(tokens)
```

```
    else:
        return ""  # Return an empty string for invalid entries
# Apply preprocessing to the 'cleaned_review' column
amazon_df['processed_review'] = amazon_df['cleaned_review'].
apply(preprocess_text)

# Encode labels
le = LabelEncoder()
amazon_df['label'] = le.fit_transform(amazon_df['sentiments'])

# Train-test split
X_train, X_test, y_train, y_test = train_test_split(amazon_
df['processed_review'], amazon_df['label'], test_size=0.2,
random_state=42)
```

In the preceding code, we have utilized the nltk and scikit-learn libraries. For the preprocessing and cleaning of the data, we have tokenized the reviews and converted them to lowercase. Then we performed lemmatization using **`WordNetLemmatizer()`** object that we initialized to lemmatizer. Then we removed the stopwords specific to the English language and joined the final cleaned tokens. Then the above function is applied to prepare the final cleaned texts of the reviews. Then we use **`LabelEncoder()`** object to encode the sentiments variable. Next, we divide the dataset into train (80%) and test data (20%).

After that, we perform TF-IDF vectorization using the **`CountVectorizer()`** object that does the feature extraction process using the CountVectorizer class from scikit-learn.

1. **Instantiation:** A **`CountVectorizer`** object is created, which will be used to convert text data into numerical features.
2. **Fitting:** The **`fit_transform`** method is applied to the training data (**`X_train`**). This builds a vocabulary from the training data and converts the text into a numerical (document-term matrix) matrix.
3. **Transformation:** The transform method is applied to the testing data (**`X_test`**). This converts the testing data into numerical features using the vocabulary learned from the training data.
4. **Printing Shapes:** The shapes of the transformed training and testing data are printed, showing the number of samples and features in each dataset.

In essence, the code extracts numerical features from text data using the bag-of-words approach, where each column of the feature matrix represents a unique word from the vocabulary, and the values indicate the frequency of that word in the corresponding document.

```
from sklearn.feature_extraction.text import CountVectorizer
vect = CountVectorizer() # instantiate a vectorizer
X_train_dtm = vect.fit_transform(X_train)# use it to extract fea-
tures from training data
# transform testing data (using training data's features)
X_test_dtm = vect.transform(X_test)
print(X_train_dtm.shape, X_test_dtm.shape)
Output:
(13872, 7751) (3468, 7751)
```

In the preceding code, we get the results of the vectorized train and test data. **`X_train_dtm`** is the **document-term matrix** created from the training data using **`CountVectorizer`**.

We will do Machine Learning modeling and evaluation, and test three machine learning algorithms: **Multinomial Naïve Bayes**, **Logistic Regression**, and **Linear SVC**.

The code for Multinomial Naïve Bayes is as follows:

```
# import classifiers from sklearn
from sklearn.naive_bayes import MultinomialNB
from sklearn.linear_model import LogisticRegression
from sklearn.svm import LinearSVC
# import different metrics to evaluate the classifiers
from sklearn.metrics import accuracy_score

# from sklearn.model_selection import train_test_split
from sklearn.metrics import confusion_matrix
from sklearn import metrics
# import time function from time module to track the training
duration
from time import time
def plot_confusion_matrix(cm, classes,
                          normalize=False,
                          title="Confusion matrix",
                          cmap=plt.cm.Blues):
    """
    This function prints and plots the confusion matrix.
    Normalization can be applied by setting `normalize=True`.
    """
    if normalize:
        cm = cm.astype("float") / cm.sum(axis=1)[:, np.newaxis]

    plt.imshow(cm, interpolation="nearest", cmap=cmap)
    plt.title(title)
    plt.colorbar()
    tick_marks = np.arange(len(classes))
    plt.xticks(tick_marks, classes, rotation=45)
```

```
    plt.yticks(tick_marks, classes)

    fmt = ".2f" if normalize else "d"
    thresh = cm.max() / 2.
    for i, j in itertools.product(range(cm.shape[0]), range(cm.
shape[1])):
        plt.text(j, i, format(cm[i, j], fmt),
                 horizontalalignment="center",
                 color="white" if cm[i, j] > thresh else "black")

    plt.tight_layout()
    plt.ylabel("True label",fontsize=15)
    plt.xlabel("Predicted label",fontsize=15)
nb = MultinomialNB() # instantiate a Multinomial Naive Bayes model
%time nb.fit(X_train_dtm, y_train) # train the model(timing it
with an IPython "magic command")
y_pred_class = nb.predict(X_test_dtm) # make class predictions
for X_test_dtm
print("Accuracy: ", metrics.accuracy_score(y_test, y_pred_class))
# print the confusion matrix
cnf_matrix = confusion_matrix(y_test, y_pred_class)
plt.figure(figsize=(8,6))
plot_confusion_matrix(cnf_matrix, classes=['positive','neutral',
'negative'],normalize=True, title='Confusion matrix with max 5000
features')
Output:
CPU times: total: 0 ns
Wall time: 0 ns
Accuracy:  0.7084775086505191
```

In the preceding code, we have used the **MultinomialNB()** model that is specifically suited for multi-class classification tasks. This is appropriate for our scenario, having three sentiment categories (positive, neutral, and negative).

%time: This is an IPython magic command that executes the following code, while measuring its execution time.

Model Training

We are training the model using the **X_train_dtm** training data and **y_train** data.

- **.fit(X_train_dtm, y_train)**: This method trains the nb model using the training data.
- **X_train_dtm**: This is likely a document-term matrix created from the training documents using a vectorizer such as **CountVectorizer**. It represents the features extracted from the training text data.

- **`y_train`**: This is the corresponding target variable for the training data, containing the sentiment labels (positive, neutral, negative) for each document in the training set.

Predictions

The prediction is done on the test data.

- **`.predict(X_test_dtm)`**: This method uses the trained nb model to predict the sentiment category (positive, neutral, negative) for each document in the testing data (**`X_test_dtm`**).
- **`X_test_dtm`**: This is likely a document-term matrix created from the testing data using the same vectorizer as the training data. It represents the features extracted from the unseen text data.
- **`y_pred_class`**: This variable stores the predicted sentiment category for each document in the testing set.

Evaluating the Accuracy of the Model

The model is evaluated using the **`accuracy_score()`** function.

- **`metrics.accuracy_score(y_test`**, **`y_pred_class`**): This function from the sklearn.metrics module calculates the accuracy of the model's predictions.
- **`y_test`**: These are the true sentiment labels for the testing data, used as a reference for comparison.
- **`y_pred_class`**: These are the predicted sentiment labels for the testing data.

Confusion Matrix

The **`confusion_matrix()`** function uses the true labels (**`y_test`**) and the predicted labels (**`y_pred_class`**). The confusion matrix is a square matrix where rows represent true labels and columns represent predicted labels. The **`plot_confusion_matrix()`** was created to plot the confusion matrix.

- **`plt.figure(figsize=(8, 6))`**: Sets the figure size for the plot.
- **`plot_confusion_matrix`**: This custom function (likely defined elsewhere) plots the confusion matrix.
    - **`cnf_matrix`**: The calculated confusion matrix.
    - **`classes`**: A list of class labels (in this case, **`'positive'`**, **`'neutral'`**, **`'negative'`**).
    - **`normalize`**: Whether to normalize the confusion matrix (default is True).
    - **`title`**: The title for the plot.

We have 70.84% model accuracy. To elaborate more, we will understand the confusion matrix of the model.

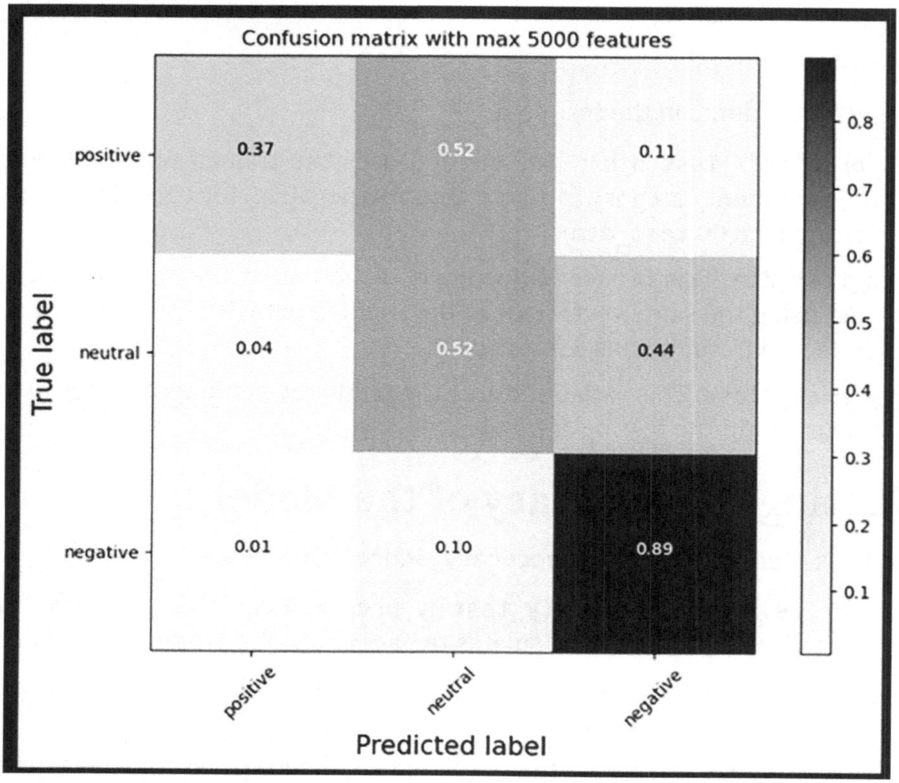

Figure 3.6: *Confusion matrix for Multinomial Naïve Bayes*

The preceding diagram is a confusion matrix for the **`MultinomialNB()`** model. From the confusion matrix, we can see that the '**`negative`**' sentiment is most accurately identified. Only 37% of positive sentiments are correctly identified. However, neutral sentiment is identified correctly in 52% of all cases. In 52% of cases, positive sentiments are identified as neutral sentiments, and 44% of neutral sentiments are identified as negative sentiments.

We will now test with the Logistic Regression model. The code is as follows:

```
from sklearn.linear_model import LogisticRegression # import the
function
logreg = LogisticRegression(class_weight="balanced") # instantiate
a logistic regression model
logreg.fit(X_train_dtm, y_train) # fit the model with training data

# Make predictions on test data
y_pred_class = logreg.predict(X_test_dtm)
```

```
# calculate evaluation measures:
print("Accuracy: ", accuracy_score(y_test, y_pred_class))
cnf_matrix = confusion_matrix(y_test, y_pred_class)
plt.figure(figsize=(8,6))
plot_confusion_matrix(cnf_matrix, classes=['positive','neutral',
'negative'],normalize=True,
                      title="Confusion matrix with normalization")
```

Output:

```
Accuracy:  0.8558246828143022
```

The code explanation is as follows:

`LogisticRegression`: This creates a Logistic Regression model object.

`class_weight="balanced"`: This argument specifies that class weights should be used to address potential imbalances in the training data. Setting it to "**`balanced`**" automatically calculates weights inversely proportional to class frequencies, giving more weight to underrepresented classes (for example, negative reviews if those are less frequent).

The training, prediction, and confusion matrix sections of the code remain the same as for the **`MultinomialNB()`**. The accuracy is 85.58%.

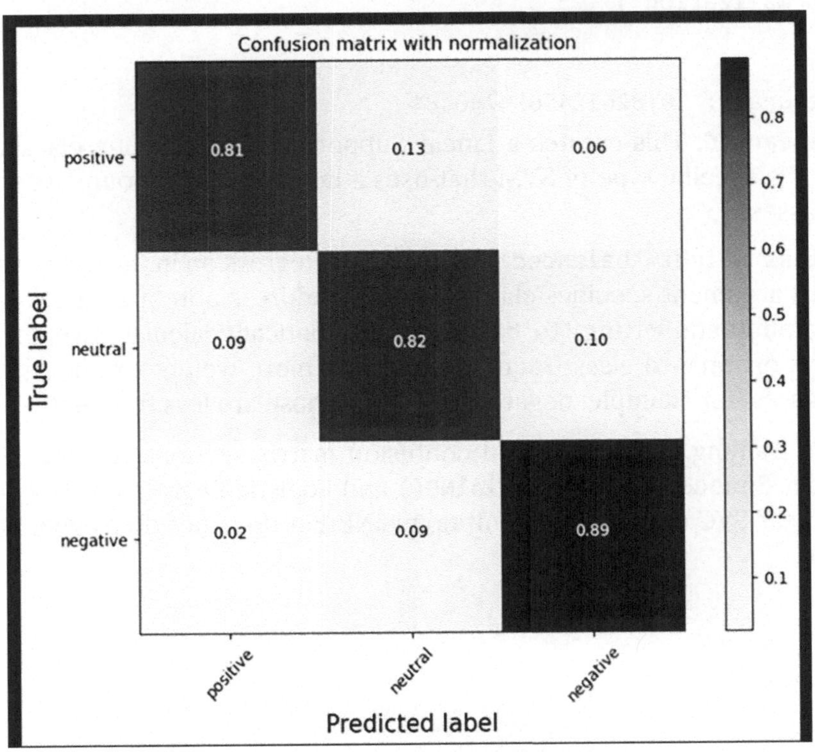

Figure 3.7: *Confusion matrix for Logistic Regression*

The confusion matrix for the negative sentiments remains the same at 89% like that of **MultinomialNB**. However, the positive and neutral sentiments are predicted correctly with 81% and 82% respectively. The Logistic Regression performs better than **MultinomialNB()** model.

Finally, we use the **LinearSVC()** model. The code is as follows:

```
classifier = LinearSVC(class_weight='balanced') # instantiate a
logistic regression model

classifier.fit(X_train_dtm, y_train) # fit the model with training
data
# Make predictions on test data
y_pred_class = classifier.predict(X_test_dtm)

# calculate evaluation measures:
print("Accuracy: ", accuracy_score(y_test, y_pred_class))
#print("AUC: ", roc_auc_score(y_test, y_pred_prob))
cnf_matrix = confusion_matrix(y_test, y_pred_class)
plt.figure(figsize=(8,6))
plot_confusion_matrix(cnf_matrix, classes=[ 'positive','neutral',
'negative'],normalize=True, title='Confusion matrix with
normalization')
```

Output:

```
Accuracy:  0.8261245674740484
```

- **LinearSVC**: This creates a Linear Support Vector Machine classifier object. It is a specific type of SVM that uses a linear decision boundary to separate classes.
- **class_weight='balanced'**: Like Logistic Regression in the previous example, this argument specifies class weights to address potential imbalances in the training data. Setting it to "**balanced**" automatically calculates weights inversely proportional to class frequencies, giving more weight to underrepresented classes (for example, negative reviews if those are less frequent).

The code's training, prediction, and confusion matrix sections remain the same as the previous 2 models of **MultinomialNB()** and Logistic Regression. The accuracy is 82.61%. Linear SVC outperforms MultinomialNB but does not do as good as Logistic Regression.

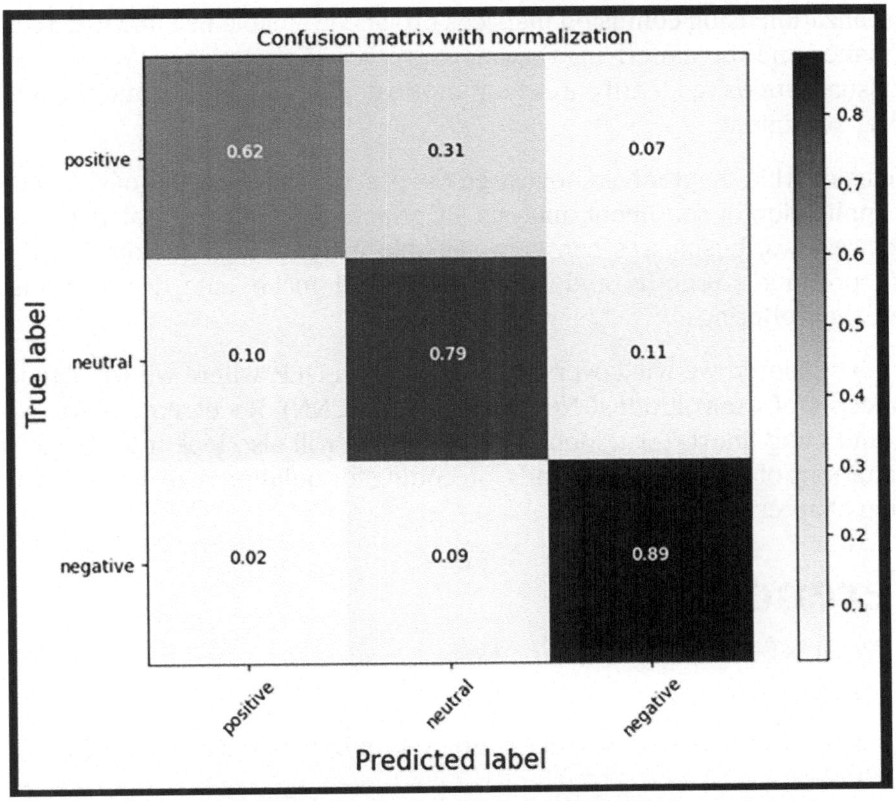

Figure 3.8: *Confusion matrix for Linear SVC*

The confusion matrix for the negative sentiments remains the same at 89% like that of MultinomialNB and Logistic Regression. For the neutral sentiment, 79% is predicted correctly, and 62% of positive sentiments are predicted correctly. However, the Linear Support Vector Machine Classifier does not perform as good as Logistic Regression. We can also experiment with other classification algorithms such as XGBoost, Decision Tree, Random Forest, and more complex Deep Learning models.

Conclusion

This chapter has demonstrated the power of NLP techniques in extracting valuable insights from Amazon reviews. By leveraging sentiment analysis, we have successfully classified reviews into positive, negative, and neutral categories, providing a deeper understanding of customer sentiment toward electronics products.

Through data preprocessing, feature engineering, and model selection, we achieved satisfactory results using various machine learning algorithms. The comparison of Multinomial Naive Bayes, LinearSVC, and Logistic Regression highlighted the strengths and weaknesses of each approach, allowing us to select the most suitable model for our task.

The visualization using confusion matrices provided valuable insights into the model's performance and the underlying themes expressed in the reviews. We also did Word Cloud visualizations to identify areas for improvement and understand the nuances of customer sentiment.

In conclusion, this chapter has showcased the practical applications of NLP techniques in the application of sentiment analysis. By effectively analyzing Amazon electronics product reviews, businesses can gain valuable insights into customer satisfaction, identify product strengths and weaknesses, and make data-driven decisions to improve their offerings.

In the next chapter, we will cover Deep Learning in NLP, where we will dig deep into the concepts of Convolutional Neural Networks (CNN), Recurrent Neural Networks (RNN), and Long Short-Term Memory (LSTM). We will also look into the advantages and limitations of these, and do hands-on coding for building real-life use cases in the following chapters.

References

- What is Sentiment Analysis? - AWS
- aws.amazon.com
- Expert Handbook on Sentiment Analysis in Digital Marketing [2024] | TimesPro Blog
- timespro.com
- https://medium.com/huawei-developers/unleashing-the-power-of-natural-language-processing-nlp-in-chatbot-development-2e7540356a00
- https://github.com/PranjalAyare/SENTIMENT_ANALYSIS
- https://www.geeksforgeeks.org/python-sentiment-analysis-using-vader/
- https://towardsdatascience.com/my-absolute-go-to-for-sentiment-analysis-textblob-3ac3a11d524
- https://github.com/cjhutto/vaderSentiment
- https://www.analyticsvidhya.com/blog/2021/06/text-preprocessing-in-nlp-with-python-codes/
- https://github.com/rehanraza24/Twitter-Text-Sentiment-Analysis-/tree/main
- https://iq.opengenus.org/text-preprocessing-in-spacy/
- https://www.kaggle.com/code/mesutssmn/sentiment-analysis-for-mental-health

- https://github.com/coderakib/Sentimental-analysis-of-amazon-customer-reviews
- https://www.mzes.uni-mannheim.de/socialsciencedatalab/article/bert-explainable-ai/
- https://github.com/MoinDalvs/Text_Mining_NLP/tree/main
- https://www.kaggle.com/code/faressayah/natural-language-processing-nlp-for-beginners#%F0%9F%A7%AE-Vectorization
- https://www.kaggle.com/learn-guide/natural-language-processing
- https://www.kaggle.com/discussions/getting-started/51445
- https://github.com/NirantK/awesome-project-ideas
- https://colab.research.google.com/github/practical-nlp/practical-nlp/blob/master/Ch4/01_OnePipeline_ManyClassifiers.ipynb
- https://notebooks.quantumstat.com/#/

CHAPTER 4
Deep Learning in NLP

Introduction

The field of Natural Language Processing (NLP) has witnessed marvelous advancements in recent years, mostly based on the research and development of various deep learning techniques. Deep learning is a subset of machine learning that leverages artificial neural networks with multiple layers to learn complex patterns and representations from data. For NLP, deep learning has revolutionized tasks such as sentiment analysis, machine translation, text summarization, and question-answering.

This chapter delves into the details of deep learning algorithms specifically tailored for NLP. We will explore Convolutional Neural Networks (CNNs), Recurrent Neural Networks (RNNs), and Long Short-Term Memory (LSTM) networks, each offering unique capabilities to address the challenges of language understanding.

By understanding the architecture, principles, and applications of these algorithms, we will gain a solid foundation in deep learning for NLP. This knowledge will empower us to develop sophisticated models that can extract meaningful insights from textual data, paving the way for innovative applications in various domains.

Structure

In this chapter, we will discuss the following topics:

- Deep Learning
- Deep Neural Networks
- Convolutional Neural Networks for NLP
    - Concept
    - Architecture
    - One-Dimensional Convolutions for Text Data
    - Mathematical Equations and Visualizations
    - Python Code Example

- Recurrent Neural Network for NLP
  - Concept
  - Architecture
  - Gated Recurrent Units (GRUs) and Long Short-Term Memory (LSTMs)
  - Mathematical Equations and Visualizations
  - Python Code Example
- Applications of CNNs and RNNs in NLP
  - Sentiment Analysis
  - Text Classification
  - Machine Translation
  - Question Answering

Deep Learning

In deep learning, multiple-layer neural networks are used for natural language processing (NLP) to process, comprehend, and produce human language. NLP tasks include language translation, content summarization, question answering, and understanding the semantics, grammar, and sentiment in text data. By allowing machines to comprehend and communicate with human language more effectively, Deep Learning models–especially those built on architectures such as RNNs, LSTMs, GRUs, CNNs, and Transformers–have made great strides in the field of NLP.

Applications of Deep Learning in NLP

- **Machine Translation:** Deep Learning models such as the Transformers fuel translation systems, such as Google Translate, by converting text from one language to another with high accuracy.
- **Sentiment Analysis:** Deep Learning models analyze text to determine its sentiment (for example, positive, negative, neutral). This is quite common today to monitor social media, analyze customer feedback to optimize products, and conduct market research.
- **Text Summarization:** Deep Learning techniques generate summaries of longer documents or articles that are useful in news aggregation, content creation, such as article and blog writing, and research paper summarization.
- **Chatbots and Virtual Assistants:** Models such as GPT are used in chatbots and virtual assistants such as Siri and Alexa, thus giving them the power to understand and respond to user queries like in a human conversation.

- **Named Entity Recognition (NER):** Deep Learning is also used to identify and classify important entities (for example, names, dates, locations) in text, thus helping in information extraction and document processing.
- **Speech Recognition:** Deep Learning models convert spoken language into text, which is crucial for voice-controlled applications and transcription services.
- **Question Answering Systems:** These systems use Deep Learning to find and provide accurate answers to questions posed in natural language, such as those used in search engines and virtual assistants.

Advantages of Deep Learning over Machine Learning in NLP

- **Ability to Capture Complex Patterns:** Traditional machine learning methods often rely on handcrafted features, which may not fully capture the complexities of human-level texts. Deep Learning models, on the other hand, learn hierarchical features directly from raw text, enabling them to understand the intricacies and extract language patterns.
- **Handling Large Datasets:** Deep Learning models perform better when it comes to processing and learning from large datasets, which is essential for NLP tasks given the vast, diverse, and complex nature of human language. This scalability allows them to outperform traditional machine-learning models on complex NLP tasks.
- **Contextual Understanding:** Deep Learning models, particularly those based on Transformers, can capture the context of words within sentences, allowing for more accurate language processing. Traditional machine learning models often struggle with context, especially in longer texts.
- **Transfer Learning:** Deep Learning enables the use of pre-trained models such as BERT and GPT, which can be fine-tuned for specific tasks with relatively small amounts of data. This approach has led to breakthroughs in NLP, where these models can be applied to various tasks with minimal additional training.

Here are some building blocks of Deep Learning

- **Neurons:** The fundamental units of a neural network, inspired by biological neurons, which process input data and pass on their output to other neurons.
- **Layers:**
    - **Input Layer**: The first layer, which receives the raw data.
    - **Hidden Layers**: Intermediate layers where the actual processing and feature extraction occur.
    - **Output Layer**: The final layer that produces the model's predictions.

- **Weights and Biases:** Weights are the parameters learned by the model, which determine the importance of inputs. Biases provide additional room for the model to better fit the data.
- **Activation Functions:** Functions such as **ReLU, Sigmoid, and Tanh** are the non-linear functions that help the network to identify complex relationships in the data.
- **Loss Function:** A function that is the difference between the predicted output and the actual target. This function helps to understand the amount of training needed to minimize this loss.
- **Optimization Algorithms:** Algorithms such as **Gradient Descent and Adam** are used to adjust the weights and biases during training to minimize the loss function.
- **Forward and Backward Propagation:**
    - **Forward Propagation**: The process by which input data passes through the network and produces an output.
    - **Backward Propagation**: The process by which the network's weights are updated based on the error calculated by the loss function.
- **Learning Rate:** A hyperparameter that controls how much the model's parameters are adjusted during training.

Core Concepts of Deep Learning

- **Deep Architectures:** Deep Learning models typically have multiple layers, allowing them to learn more complex data patterns at each layer. This depth enables the models to capture complex patterns that simpler models cannot.
- **Representation Learning:** Deep Learning models automatically discover representations needed for tasks such as classification or regression. This contrasts with traditional methods, where features are often manually created.
- **Generalization:** Despite the complexity of the models, Deep Learning aims to generalize well to unseen data, not just memorize the training set. Techniques such as regularization, dropout, and early stopping are used to improve generalization.
- **Transfer Learning:** A powerful concept where models trained on large datasets (such as BERT or GPT) are fine-tuned for specific tasks with smaller datasets. This reduces the need for large amounts of task-specific data.
- **Scalability:** Deep Learning models can be scaled to handle vast amounts of data and complex tasks. They benefit from advances in computational power, such as GPUs and TPUs, enabling them to process large-scale data efficiently.

- **End-to-end Learning:** In many cases, Deep Learning models can be trained in an end-to-end manner, meaning the model learns the entire process from raw input to the final output, without the need for intermediary steps or manual feature extraction.

Deep Neural Networks

Deep Neural Networks (DNNs) are a class of artificial neural networks (ANNs) that have multiple layers between the input and output layers. These layers allow DNNs to model complex patterns in data, making them very efficient for a wide range of tasks, including image recognition, natural language processing, and predictive analytics.

Types of Deep Neural Networks

- **Feedforward Neural Networks (FNNs):** The simplest type of DNN, where information flows in one direction from the input layer to the output layer through hidden layers. FNNs are used for tasks such as classification and regression.
- **Convolutional Neural Networks (CNNs):** They are primarily used for image and video processing, but they are also used for NLP tasks. CNNs apply convolutional filters to capture spatial features and patterns. They are also used in NLP for text classification and other tasks.
- **Recurrent Neural Networks (RNNs):** RNNs are designed for sequential data, such as time series or text, where the order of inputs matters. They have connections that form cycles, allowing them to have a memory of previous inputs. Variants such as Long Short-Term Memory (LSTM) and Gated Recurrent Unit (GRU) are popular for tasks such as language modeling and speech recognition.
- **Autoencoders:** Autoencoders are unsupervised DNNs used for tasks such as dimensionality reduction, data denoising, and anomaly detection. They consist of an encoder that compresses the input into a lower-dimensional representation and a decoder that reconstructs the original input from this representation.
- **Generative Adversarial Networks (GANs):** GANs consist of two networks, a generator and a discriminator, that compete with each other. The generator creates fake data, while the discriminator tries to distinguish between the real and the fake data. GANs are mainly used for generating realistic images, videos, and other types of synthetic data. **Deepfakes** are synthetic media, typically videos or audio, in which a person's likeness or voice is manipulated using deep learning techniques to make it appear as if they said or did something they never did. The term "*deepfake*" is a combination of "*deep*

learning" and "*fake.*" Deepfakes are created using Generative Adversarial Networks (GANs).

- **Transformers:** Transformers are a type of DNN architecture that has revolutionized NLP. They use self-attention mechanisms to process sequences of data in parallel, making them highly efficient for tasks such as machine translation, text summarization, and large language models (for example, GPT, BERT).

We will build a Deep Neural Network using the Breast Cancer dataset to predict whether a tumor is malignant or benign. The objective is to understand the steps needed to build a DNN. Thus, the kind of problem we are focusing on is not too complicated. However, in real life, there can be datasets that are extremely messy and complex to train models on.

To build a DNN, several Python libraries are commonly used for constructing and training neural networks. Below are some of the most relevant libraries and a step-by-step guide to building a simple DNN using them.

Relevant Libraries

- **TensorFlow:** A popular deep learning library developed by Google, TensorFlow provides a comprehensive ecosystem for building and training neural networks. It includes high-level APIs such as Keras.
- **Keras:** An easy-to-use, high-level API built on top of TensorFlow. Keras allows for quick prototyping and easy-to-understand code for building neural networks.
- **PyTorch:** Developed by Facebook, PyTorch is another widely used deep learning library. It is known for its flexibility and dynamic computation graph, making it popular among researchers.
- **NumPy:** A fundamental package for numerical computing in Python, used for handling arrays and performing mathematical operations.
- **Pandas:** The swiss-knife of data manipulation and analysis, useful for handling and preprocessing datasets.
- **Scikit-learn:** A machine learning library that provides tools for data preprocessing, feature engineering, creating models, model evaluation, and more.

We will build a basic DNN for a classification problem using TensorFlow and Keras. The steps are as follows.

Install the Required Libraries: We need to install the libraries.

```
! pip install tensorflow pandas numpy scikit-learn
```

Import the Libraries

```
import tensorflow as tf
from tensorflow.keras.models import Sequential
from tensorflow.keras.models import Dense
from sklearn.model_selection import train_test_split
from sklearn.preprocessing import StandardScaler
from sklearn.datasets import load_breast_cancer
import numpy as np
import pandas as pd
```

Data Preparation: We load the dataset, split it into training and test sets, and standardize the features.

- **`load_breast_cancer()`**: This function is from the sklearn.datasets module, which provides several built-in datasets for machine learning tasks. The Breast Cancer dataset is a well-known dataset for binary classification tasks. It contains features that describe characteristics of cell nuclei in breast cancer biopsies, and the goal is to predict whether a tumor is malignant or benign.
- **`data.data`**: This refers to the feature matrix X, which contains the input data. Each row corresponds to one sample (one tumor), and each column corresponds to a feature (for example, mean radius, mean texture).
- **`data.target`**: This refers to the target vector y, which contains the labels for the samples. The labels are binary: 0 for benign tumors and 1 for malignant tumors.
- **`train_test_split(X, y, test_size=0.2, random_state=42)`**: This function is from the sklearn.model_selection module. It splits the dataset into two parts: a training set and a test set. **X and y**: These are the input features and labels, respectively, that will be split. **`test_size=0.2`**: This indicates that 20% of the data should be allocated to the test set, and the remaining 80% will be used for training the model.
- **`random_state=42`**: This is a seed for the random number generator, ensuring that the split is reproducible. If we run this code multiple times, using the same **`random_state`** will yield the same split each time.
- **`X_train`**: The training set features, **`X_test`:** The test set features, **`y_train`:** The training set labels, **`y_test`:** The test set labels.
- **`StandardScaler()`**: This function is from the **`sklearn.preprocessing`** module, and is used to standardize features by removing the mean and scaling to unit variance. This is an important preprocessing step for many machine learning algorithms, especially those that rely on distance calculations (for example, SVM, KNN).

- **`scaler.fit_transform(X_train)`: `fit_transform()`**: This method first computes the mean and standard deviation from the training data (**`X_train`**) and then transforms the training data using these computed values.
- Why **`fit_transform`** on **`X_train`**? The model should learn the scaling parameters (mean and standard deviation) only from the training data to prevent information leakage from the test set.
- **`scaler.transform(X_test)`: `transform()`**: This method uses the mean and standard deviation computed from the training data to transform the test data (**`X_test`**).

Why only transform on **`X_test`**? The test data should be scaled using the same parameters (mean and standard deviation) learned from the training data to ensure a fair evaluation of the model's performance.

```
# Load dataset
data = load_breast_cancer()
X = data.data
y = data.target

# Split the data into training and test sets
X_train, X_test, y_train, y_test = train_test_split(X, y, test_
size=0.2, random_state=42)
# Standardize the features
scaler = StandardScaler()
X_train = scaler.fit_transform(X_train)
X_test = scaler.transform(X_test)
```

Model Building: We define a simple DNN with an input layer, two hidden layers, and an output layer. The activation function for the first and second hidden layers is relu, and the output layer is sigmoid. However, there are other activation functions too, such as **ELU, Leaky ReLU, Dying ReLU, Parametric ReLU, Tanh, Softmax, GELU** (Gaussian Error Linear Unit), and so on.

The '**`Sequential`**' model is a linear stack of layers. It helps us to build a model layer by layer in a sequential manner, where each layer has exactly one input tensor and one output tensor.

Dense: This is a layer type known as a fully connected or dense layer, where each neuron in the layer is connected to every neuron in the previous layer.

- **`units=16`**: This specifies the number of neurons in this layer. Here, the first hidden layer has 16 neurons.
- **`activation='relu'`**: The activation function used is ReLU (Rectified Linear Unit). ReLU introduces non-linearity to the model, enabling it to learn complex patterns. It outputs the input directly if it is positive; otherwise, it outputs zero.

- **input_shape=(X_train.shape[1],)**: This defines the shape of the input data. **X_train.shape[1]** represents the number of features in the input data. This is necessary for the first layer so that the model knows what shape of input data to expect. However, for subsequent layers, the input shape is automatically inferred.

In the **second hidden layer**, we have.

- **Dense(units=8, activation='relu')**: This is another fully connected layer with 8 neurons. The activation function is again ReLU, which helps in handling complex data by introducing non-linearity. No **input_shape** is specified here because the model automatically infers the input shape from the previous layer.

In the **Output layer**, we have:

- **Dense(units=1, activation='sigmoid')**: The output layer is a fully connected layer with just 1 neuron.
- **units=1**: Since this is a binary classification task, the output layer has 1 neuron, which outputs a single probability value between 0 and 1.
- **activation='sigmoid'**: The sigmoid activation function is used here because it is suitable for binary classification. It outputs a value between 0 and 1, which can be interpreted as the probability of the positive class. The model predicts the class with a threshold, typically 0.5 (for example, if the output is greater than 0.5, it predicts one class; otherwise, it predicts the other).

This model is simple yet effective for **binary classification** tasks, where the goal is to predict one of two possible outcomes (for example, "**yes**" or "**no**", "**positive**" or "**negative**"). The use of ReLU in the hidden layers helps the model learn complex patterns, while the Sigmoid function in the output layer converts the output to a probability that can be used for classification.

```
# Initialize the model
model = Sequential()

# Add the input layer and first hidden layer
model.add(Dense(units=16, activation='relu', input_shape=(X_
train.shape[1],)))

# Add the second hidden layer
model.add(Dense(units=8, activation='relu'))

# Add the output layer
model.add(Dense(units=1, activation='sigmoid'))  # Sigmoid
activation for binary classification
```

- **Model Compilation**: We compile the model using the Adam optimizer and binary cross-entropy loss.

```
model.compile(optimizer='adam', loss='binary_crossentropy',
metrics=['accuracy'])
```

- **Model Training:** We train the model using the training data.

```
# Train the model
history = model.fit(X_train, y_train, epochs=50, batch_size=32,
validation_split=0.2, verbose=1)
```

In deep learning training, epoch and batch size are key terms that describe how data is processed during model training:

- **Epoch:** An epoch refers to one complete pass through the entire training dataset. During each epoch, the model processes all the training data once, adjusting its parameters (weights and biases) based on the error from each batch.
- **Batch Size:** The batch size is the number of training samples processed before the model's internal parameters are updated. Instead of updating the model after each training sample, the model is updated after processing a batch of samples, making training more efficient and stable.

Model Evaluation: We evaluate the model's performance on the test set.

```
# Evaluate the model
test_loss, test_accuracy = model.evaluate(X_test, y_test,
verbose=0)
print(f"Test Accuracy: {test_accuracy:.4f}")
```

Output:

```
Accuracy: 0.9649
```

Prediction: We use the trained model to make predictions on new data.

```
# Make predictions
predictions = model.predict(X_test)
# Convert probabilities to binary predictions
predictions = (predictions > 0.5).astype(int)
```

Convolutional Neural Networks for NLP

CNNs, originally designed for image processing, have been successfully adapted for NLP tasks. By treating words as pixels in a 1D image, CNNs can effectively capture local patterns and dependencies within text sequences. This makes them well-suited for sentiment analysis, text classification, and named entity recognition tasks.

CNNs for NLP typically consist of embedding, convolutional, pooling, and fully connected layers. The embedding layer converts words into numerical representations, the convolutional layers extract features, the pooling layers downsize the feature maps, and the fully connected layers combine the extracted features to make predictions.

Concept

Convolutional Neural Networks (CNNs), originally designed for image processing, are also used effectively in Natural Language Processing (NLP). In NLP, CNNs are used to capture local patterns in text data, such as n-grams, by applying convolutional filters over word embeddings. These filters slide over the input text, detecting features such as phrases or sentences that are indicative of specific linguistic structures or sentiments.

The pooling layers in CNNs help in reducing the dimensionality while retaining the most significant features, making the model efficient. CNNs are especially useful for tasks such as sentence classification, sentiment analysis, and text categorization due to their ability to identify key phrases and important textual patterns. Despite their simplicity compared to more complex models such as RNNs or Transformers, CNNs are computationally efficient and provide strong baseline results for various NLP tasks.

Architecture

We will look into the architecture of CNNs.

- **Input Layer:** The input to a CNN for NLP tasks is a sequence of words or characters, represented as a matrix. Each word or character is mapped to a fixed-size vector through an embedding layer (for example, Word2Vec, GloVe), resulting in a 2D matrix where each row corresponds to the embedding of a word in the sentence.
- **Convolutional Layer:** This layer applies a set of convolutional filters (kernels) across the input matrix. Each filter slides over the input matrix, performing element-wise multiplication and summing up the results to produce a feature map. The filters are designed to detect specific patterns or features within the text, such as bigrams, trigrams, or semantic relationships between words.
- **Activation Function:** After the convolution operation, an activation function (usually ReLU) is applied to introduce non-linearity into the model. This helps CNN learn complex patterns and representations.
- **Pooling Layer:** The pooling layer reduces the dimensionality of the feature maps while retaining the most important information. The most common type

of pooling is max-pooling, where the maximum value from each patch of the feature map is selected, creating a smaller, more manageable representation of the data.

- **Fully Connected Layer (Dense Layer):** The output of the pooling layer is flattened into a 1D vector and passed through one or more fully connected layers. These layers combine the extracted features to make final predictions. For classification tasks, the final layer typically uses a SoftMax activation function to output a probability distribution over the possible classes.
- **Output Layer:** The output layer produces the final prediction, such as the class label for a classification task or the sentiment score for sentiment analysis.

One-Dimensional Convolutions for Text Data

One-Dimensional Convolutions (1D Convolutions) are a powerful tool in deep learning for processing sequential data, such as text. Unlike two-dimensional convolutions, which are commonly used in image processing, 1D convolutions operate along a single axis, making them particularly well-suited for handling time-series data or text, where the sequence of elements (for example, words or characters) is critical.

How 1D Convolutions Work with Text Data

- **Input Representation**: Text data is typically represented as a sequence of vectors. These vectors could be word embeddings (such as Word2Vec or GloVe) or character embeddings, where each word or character is mapped to a dense vector in a high-dimensional space.
- **Convolution Operation**: In a 1D convolution, a filter (or kernel) of a specific size slides over the input sequence, performing element-wise multiplication and summing the results to produce a feature map. The filter moves along the sequence (usually across words or characters) to capture local patterns, such as n-grams in the text.

  For example, a filter of size 3 might capture trigram patterns, detecting combinations of three consecutive words or characters that frequently appear together.
- **Multiple Filters**: Multiple filters can be applied in a convolutional layer, each detecting different types of patterns within the text. These filters help the model learn different n-gram features that are important for the task.

Benefits of 1D Convolutions for Text Data

- **Local Pattern Detection**: 1D convolutions are excellent at detecting local patterns in text, such as specific phrases, combinations of words, or even sentiment-bearing n-grams.
- **Parameter Efficiency**: Compared to fully connected layers, convolutional

layers use fewer parameters, which reduces the risk of overfitting, especially when the dataset is not very large.

- **Position-Invariant Feature Learning**: Convolutions can detect patterns regardless of their position in the text. For instance, a filter detecting the pattern "`not good`" would recognize it whether it appears at the beginning or end of a sentence.
- **Combining Local Features**: By stacking multiple convolutional layers, the model can combine local features learned from earlier layers to detect more complex patterns in the text.

We will see an example of how 1D convolutions work on text data, using mathematical representation. We will consider a simplified case where the input is a sequence of word embeddings, and we apply a single 1D convolutional filter.

Problem Setup

- **Input Sentence**: "*I love AI*"
- **Word Embeddings**: Let us assume each word in the sentence is represented by a three-dimensional word embedding vector.
    - I → [0.2,0.4,0.5]
    - love → [0.8,0.7,0.1]
    - AI → [0.6,0.9,0.3]

So, the input sequence X is:

X= 0.2 0.4 0.5 0.8 0.7 0.1 0.6 0.9 0.3

Here, X is a 3×3 matrix, where each row represents the embedding of a word, and each column represents a specific dimension of the embeddings.

1D Convolution

Filter Definition

- **Filter (Kernel)**: Let us define a filter WWW with size 2 (meaning it spans over 2 words) and 3 channels (matching the embedding size). The filter is represented as:

  0.1 0.2 0.3 0.4 0.5 0.6

So, W is a 2×3 matrix.

Convolution Operation

- **Stride**: Assume a stride of 1, meaning the filter moves one word at a time.

- **Output Calculation**: The filter slides over the input sentence, performing element-wise multiplication and summing the results.

Let us calculate the convolution manually for each step:

1. **First Position**:
    a. The filter covers the first two words: '**`I`**' and '**`love`**'.
    b. Perform element-wise multiplication and sum:
    $\text{Output1}= (0.2\times0.1)+ (0.4\times0.2)+(0.5\times0.3)+(0.8\times0.4)+(0.7\times0.5)+(0.1\times0.6) = 0.98$
2. **Second Position:**
    a. The filter moves one word to the right, and covers the words '**`love`**' and '**`AI`**'.
    b. Perform element-wise multiplication and sum:
    $\text{Output2} = (0.8\times0.1)+(0.7\times0.2)+(0.1\times0.3)+(0.6\times0.4)+(0.9\times0.5)+(0.3\times0.6)$
    $\text{Output2}=0.08+0.14+0.03+0.24+0.45+0.18=1.12$

Output Feature Map

- The convolution produces a feature map (output sequence):
  Feature Map=0.98 1.12

This feature map is a 2-dimensional vector representing the extracted features from the input sequence using the convolutional filter.

We will look into the 1D convolutional operation for text data by incorporating different filter sizes, padding options, and multiple filters.

Filter Sizes

- The size of the filter determines how many words (or characters) are considered together in a single operation. Larger filters capture more context but may blur finer details.
- **For example:**
    - **Filter Size = 2**: Captures bigrams (pairs of consecutive words).
    - **Filter Size = 3**: Captures trigrams (triplets of consecutive words).
    - **Filter Size = 4**: Captures four-grams (four consecutive words).

Padding Options

- **Valid Padding**: In this case, no padding is added to the input sequence, so the filter slides across only the available positions, resulting in a smaller output size.

  - **Example:** For an input sequence of length 5 and a filter size of 3, the output will have a length of 3 (that is, 5–3+1 = 3).
- **Same Padding**: For this scenario, the padding is added to the input sequence so that the output has the same length as the original sequence.
  - **Example**: For an input sequence of length 5 and a filter size of 3, the padding ensures that the output length remains 5.

Multiple Filters

- Using multiple filters allows the model to learn different feature types from the text. For example, one filter might focus on bigrams, while another might focus on trigrams.
- The output feature map will have a depth equal to the number of filters used. If we use 4 filters, each producing an output of size n, the final output will have the shape n×4.

Now, we will use the IMDB movie reviews dataset as a real use case containing sentiment-labeled text data. We will apply 1D convolutional layers with different filter sizes, padding options, and multiple filters to classify the sentiment of the reviews. The Python code is as follows.

```
import numpy as np
from tensorflow.keras.models import Sequential
from tensorflow.keras.layers import Dense, Conv1D, GlobalMax-
Pooling1D, Embedding
from tensorflow.keras.preprocessing import sequence
from tensorflow.keras.datasets import imdb

# Load the IMDB dataset
max_features = 5000  # number of words to consider as features
maxlen = 400  # cut texts after this number of words

(X_train, y_train), (X_test, y_test) = imdb.load_data(num_words=-
max_features)

# Padding sequences to ensure equal length
X_train = sequence.pad_sequences(X_train, maxlen=maxlen)
X_test = sequence.pad_sequences(X_test, maxlen=maxlen)

# Model architecture
model = Sequential()
model.add(Embedding(max_features, 128, input_length=maxlen))  #
Embedding layer

# First Conv1D layer with multiple filters and different filter sizes
```

```
model.add(Conv1D(filters=64, kernel_size=3, padding='same',
activation='relu'))
model.add(Conv1D(filters=64, kernel_size=4, padding='same',
activation='relu'))
model.add(Conv1D(filters=64, kernel_size=5, padding='same',
activation='relu'))

# Global max pooling to reduce the dimensionality
model.add(GlobalMaxPooling1D())

# Fully connected output layer
model.add(Dense(1, activation='sigmoid'))

# Compile the model
model.compile(optimizer='adam', loss='binary_crossentropy',
metrics=['accuracy'])

# Summary of the model
model.summary()

# Train the model
model.fit(X_train, y_train, epochs=5, batch_size=32, validation_
data=(X_test, y_test))

# Evaluate the model
score, acc = model.evaluate(X_test, y_test, batch_size=32)
print(f'Test accuracy: {acc:.3f}')
```

We load the IMDB dataset (from the TensorFlow library) that contains 50,000 movie reviews already labeled as positive or negative. The reviews are preprocessed into a sequence of word indices. We divide it into train and test datasets.

We then pad the sequences to ensure that all the input reviews have the same length (maxlen = 400).

Then the word indices are converted into dense vectors (word embeddings) of size 128.

We use 3 convolutional layers with different filter sizes (3,4,5) and **64 filters** each. The **`padding = 'same'`** means that the output has the same length as the input, even after convolution. The activation function is ReLU.

The **`GlobalMaxPooling1D`** Layer reduces the output from convolutional layers to a fixed size by taking the maximum value over the time dimension, which helps in summarizing the most important features detected by the filters.

A **fully connected layer** with a sigmoid activation function for binary classification.

Then the created model is trained for 5 epochs with a batch size of 32. Then the performance is evaluated on the test set.

```
Epoch 1/5
782/782 ━━━━━━━━━━━━━━━━━━━━ 76s 84ms/step - accuracy: 0.6796 - loss: 0.5504 - val_accuracy: 0.8610 - val_loss: 0.3165
Epoch 2/5
782/782 ━━━━━━━━━━━━━━━━━━━━ 52s 66ms/step - accuracy: 0.9090 - loss: 0.2264 - val_accuracy: 0.8908 - val_loss: 0.2612
Epoch 3/5
782/782 ━━━━━━━━━━━━━━━━━━━━ 51s 66ms/step - accuracy: 0.9526 - loss: 0.1274 - val_accuracy: 0.8872 - val_loss: 0.2842
Epoch 4/5
782/782 ━━━━━━━━━━━━━━━━━━━━ 101s 129ms/step - accuracy: 0.9768 - loss: 0.0727 - val_accuracy: 0.8755 - val_loss: 0.3997
Epoch 5/5
782/782 ━━━━━━━━━━━━━━━━━━━━ 54s 69ms/step - accuracy: 0.9890 - loss: 0.0376 - val_accuracy: 0.8813 - val_loss: 0.4468

<keras.src.callbacks.history.History at 0x21c46ad8430>
```

Figure 4.1: *Training the model with 5 epochs*

We see that the accuracy improves with each epoch, and the training accuracy is 0.9890 after the 5th epoch. Next, when we do the model evaluation, the test accuracy is 0.881. The model overfits, and there can be techniques such as regularization, cross-validation, and model simplification to avoid overfitting.

This demo dataset for CNN was used to showcase the padding sequence, Global Max Pooling, using multiple filters with different kernel sizes.

Recurrent Neural Network

Recurrent Neural Networks (RNNs) are specifically built to handle sequential data, such as text, where the sequence of words plays a crucial role. In contrast to standard feedforward networks, RNNs incorporate recurrent connections, allowing the output from one time step to be used as input in the next. This feature enables RNNs to preserve a hidden state that retains information over time, making it possible to capture and understand dependencies within a sequence.

Consider the sentence "*The cat sat on the mat.*" To fully understand the word "*mat*," it is essential to recognize that "*cat*" was mentioned earlier in the sentence. RNNs can remember information from previous words and utilize this information when processing subsequent words. This feature of capturing sequential dependencies is especially useful in tasks such as language modeling, where the meaning of previous words impacts the prediction of the next word.

Differences Between RNN and CNN

RNN	CNN
RNNs have recurrent connections, where outputs from one step are fed back into the network.	CNNs use convolutional layers to apply filters to input data, capturing local patterns.
Designed for processing sequential data and capturing temporal dependencies.	Primarily designed for spatial data, capturing local patterns (for example, images, text).

RNNs maintain a hidden state across time steps, allowing them to remember past information.	CNNs do not have a memory of past inputs; they process input data in parallel.
Natural Language Processing (NLP), time-series forecasting, and speech recognition.	Image processing, computer vision, and text classification (using 1D convolutions).
RNNs can struggle with very long sequences due to vanishing gradients. Variants like LSTM and GRU mitigate this.	CNNs are limited in capturing long-range dependencies but can be combined with pooling layers for hierarchical feature extraction.

Table 4.1: *Difference between* RNN *and* CNN

Where CNNs and RNNs are Applicable

- **CNNs**
  - **Image Processing**: CNNs are better for tasks such as image classification, object detection, and segmentation. They can efficiently capture spatial hierarchies in images by applying convolutional filters.
  - **Text Classification**: CNNs can be used in NLP tasks such as sentiment analysis or text classification, where they capture local patterns (for example, n-grams) using 1D convolutions.
  - **Audio Processing**: CNNs are also applied to spectrograms for tasks such as speech recognition and audio classification.
- **RNNs**
  - **Sequence Prediction**: RNNs are good for tasks where the order of input data matters, such as language modeling, machine translation, and time-series forecasting.
  - **Speech Recognition**: RNNs can process audio data as sequences, capturing temporal dependencies over time.
  - **Text Generation**: RNNs are used in generating text, such as in language models that predict the next word in a sequence based on previous words.

A simple Recurrent Neural Network (RNN) consists of the following key components:

- **Input Layer**: The input is typically a sequence of data (for example, a sequence of words in a sentence). Each element in the sequence is passed one at a time to the RNN.
- **Hidden Layer**: The hidden layer in an RNN is where the recurrence happens. At each time step t, the hidden layer receives the input x_t and the hidden state from the previous time step h_{t-1}. The hidden state is updated using the formula:

$$ht=\sigma(W_{xh}\cdot x_t+W_{hh}\cdot h_{t-1}+b_h)$$

Here, W_{xh} and W_{hh} are weight matrices, b_h is the bias, and σ is the activation function (often tanh or ReLU).

- **Output Layer**: The output at each time step is computed based on the hidden state. The output can be a prediction or classification based on the task. It is usually calculated as:

$$yt=softmax(W_{hy} \cdot h_t + b_y)$$

where W_{hy} is the weight matrix connecting the hidden state to the output, and b_y is the bias.

Recurrent Connections: The hidden state from each time step is passed to the next, allowing the RNN to retain the memory of previous inputs.

Challenges: Vanishing Gradient Problem and Exploding Gradient Problem

Vanishing Gradient Problem

- **Description**: The vanishing gradient problem occurs when the gradients used to update the weights in the network become very small during backpropagation. This happens particularly in deep networks or RNNs with long sequences, where the gradients diminish as they are propagated back through many layers or time steps.
- **Impact**: When gradients vanish, the network's weights receive very small updates, which can cause the learning process to become extremely slow or even stop. This issue is especially problematic for RNNs, as it limits their ability to learn long-range dependencies in sequences.

Solution

- **Long Short-Term Memory (LSTM) and Gated Recurrent Units (GRU)**: These architectures are designed to reduce the vanishing gradient problem by allowing the network to retain important information over longer periods.
- **ReLU Activation**: Using ReLU instead of tanh or sigmoid can help reduce the impact of vanishing gradients.

Exploding Gradient Problem

- **Description**: The exploding gradient problem is the opposite of the vanishing gradient problem. It occurs when the gradients become excessively large during backpropagation. This can happen when the weights in the network are initialized poorly or when the sequence length is long.
- **Impact**: Exploding gradients can cause the network's weights to update with excessively large values, leading to numerical instability, making the model's output unpredictable, or causing it to fail to converge during training.

Solution

- **Gradient Clipping**: This technique involves capping the gradients at a maximum value during backpropagation to prevent them from getting too large.
- **Proper Weight Initialization**: Initializing weights carefully can help prevent gradients from exploding.

Use Case: Sentiment Analysis Using RNN

Let us explore a real-life use case of RNNs in NLP by building a text classification model using the **IMDB movie reviews** dataset available in TensorFlow. This dataset is a common benchmark for sentiment analysis, where the goal is to classify movie reviews as positive or negative.

Objective: We will build an RNN-based model that classifies movie reviews as positive or negative.

Dataset: The IMDB dataset consists of 50,000 movie reviews, split into 25,000 training and 25,000 test reviews. Each review is labeled as either positive (1) or negative (0).

The Python code is as follows.

```
import tensorflow as tf
from tensorflow.keras.datasets import imdb
from tensorflow.keras.preprocessing.sequence import pad_sequences
from tensorflow.keras.models import Sequential
from tensorflow.keras.layers import Embedding, SimpleRNN, Dense

# Load the IMDB dataset
max_features = 10000  # Number of words to consider as features
max_len = 500  # Cut texts after this number of words (among top
max_features most common words)

(X_train, y_train), (X_test, y_test) = imdb.load_data(num_words
=max_features)
# Pad sequences to ensure uniform input size
X_train = pad_sequences(X_train, maxlen=max_len)
X_test = pad_sequences(X_test, maxlen=max_len)

# Build the RNN model
model = Sequential()
model.add(Embedding(max_features, 32, input_length=max_len))
model.add(SimpleRNN(32, activation='relu'))
model.add(Dense(1, activation='sigmoid'))

# Compile the model
```

```
model.compile(optimizer='adam', loss='binary_crossentropy',
metrics=['accuracy'])

# Train the model
history = model.fit(X_train, y_train, epochs=10, batch_size=64,
validation_split=0.2)

# Evaluate the model on the test set
test_loss, test_acc = model.evaluate(X_test, y_test)
print(f"Test Accuracy: {test_acc:.4f}")
Output:
Test Accuracy: 0.8434
```

To start with, the explanation of the code, the first part of importing the libraries, functions, and dataset, remains the same as CNN.

- **Preprocessing**: The reviews are padded to ensure they all have the same length (**max_len**). This is important because RNNs require input sequences to be of uniform length.
- **Model Architecture:**
  - **Embedding Layer**: Converts the integer-encoded words into dense vectors of fixed size (32 in this case). This helps the model learn word embeddings.
  - **SimpleRNN Layer**: This layer processes the sequences, learning to capture dependencies between words over time.
  - **Dense Layer**: A single neuron with a sigmoid activation function is used to produce a binary output (positive or negative sentiment).
- **Compilation**: The model is compiled with the Adam optimizer, binary cross-entropy loss (since it is a binary classification problem), and accuracy as the metric.
- **Training**: The model is trained for 10 epochs with a batch size of 64. We also reserve 20% of the training data for validation to monitor the model's performance.
- **Evaluation**: Finally, the model's accuracy is evaluated on the test set.

The final training accuracy is 0.9778, and the test accuracy is 0.8434. Here we have the data overfitting. These might be the situations on why overfitting has happened in the first place.

- **Complexity of Sequential Data**: RNNs are designed to capture dependencies in sequential data (such as text), which can lead them to over-learn these dependencies in the training data, especially if the training data is not sufficiently varied.
- **Long-Term Dependencies**: While RNNs are good at capturing sequences, they

might overfit by focusing too much on patterns in the training set without generalizing how those patterns might vary in unseen text.

- **High Capacity**: RNNs, particularly LSTMs and GRUs, have a large number of parameters, giving them the capacity to model complex functions. This also means they can easily overfit if regularization techniques are not applied.

We can use **Regularization** to reduce the overfitting:

- **Dropout**: Introduce dropout in the RNN layers. Dropout randomly drops units during training, which helps prevent the model from becoming too dependent on any single feature or pattern.
- **L2 Regularization**: Apply L2 regularization to penalize large weights, encouraging the model to find a more generalized solution.

```
from tensorflow.keras.layers import Dropout, LSTM
model = Sequential()
model.add(Embedding(max_features, 32, input_length=max_len))
model.add(LSTM(32, activation='tanh', recurrent_dropout=0.2))  #
Added recurrent_dropout
model.add(Dropout(0.5))  # Added dropout layer
model.add(Dense(1, activation='sigmoid'))
```

We can also use **Early Stopping** to mitigate the effect of overfitting:

- **Early Stopping**: Monitor the validation loss during training and stop training when the validation loss starts to increase, which indicates the onset of overfitting.

```
from tensorflow.keras.callbacks import EarlyStopping
early_stopping = EarlyStopping(monitor='val_loss', patience=3,
restore_best_weights=True)
# Compile the model
model.compile(optimizer='adam', loss='binary_crossentropy',
metrics=['accuracy'])
history = model.fit(X_train, y_train, epochs=10, batch_size=64,
validation_split=0.2, callbacks=[early_stopping])
```

After early stopping, the validation accuracy is 0.8266, training accuracy is 0.8915. So, we can elaborate on this as follows:

- **Monitoring Validation Loss:** Early stopping was likely monitoring the validation loss, which did not improve significantly after the second epoch. Instead, it fluctuated and showed signs of potential overfitting by the third epoch.
- **Overfitting Detection:** The model showed better performance on the training set, but this was not reflected in the validation set. The lack of improvement in validation loss and the slight instability suggested that further training would only lead to overfitting.

- **Optimal Stopping:** The training stopped at the 5th epoch, which was deemed optimal by the early stopping mechanism, as continuing beyond this point might have further degraded the model's generalization ability.

Gated Recurrent Units (GRUs) and Long Short-Term Memory (LSTMs)

Long Short-Term Memory (LSTM) and Gated Recurrent Unit (GRU) are types of Recurrent Neural Networks (RNNs) specifically designed to handle the vanishing gradient problem and to better capture long-term dependencies in sequential data, such as text or time series.

LSTM

LSTM networks are a special kind of RNN capable of learning long-term dependencies. LSTMs are explicitly designed to avoid the long-term dependency problem. They do this by maintaining a cell state that can carry relevant information throughout the sequence without the risk of it vanishing.

Key Components

- **Cell State**: The memory that carries information across many time steps.
- **Gates**: Structures that control the flow of information to the cell state, including:
  - **Forget Gate**: Decides what information to discard from the cell state.
  - **Input Gate**: Decides which new information to add to the cell state.
  - **Output Gate**: Decides what part of the cell state should be output.

GRU

GRU is a variation of LSTM. GRUs are similar to LSTMs but have a simpler architecture. They combine the forget and input gates into a single update gate, and they do not have a separate cell state. Instead, the hidden state is responsible for both short-term memory and long-term memory. This simplicity makes GRUs computationally more efficient and sometimes better performing than LSTMs, particularly on smaller datasets.

Key Components

- **Update Gate**: Combines the functionality of the forget and input gates.
- **Reset Gate**: Controls how much of the previous state needs to be passed to the next step.

Differences Between LSTM and GRU

- **Complexity**: LSTMs are more complex, with three gates (input, forget, output) and a cell state, whereas GRUs are simpler, with two gates (update, reset) and no separate cell state.
- **Training Speed**: GRUs are generally faster to train because they have fewer parameters.
- **Performance**: GRUs can perform better on smaller datasets due to their simplicity, while LSTMs might perform better on larger datasets with more complex sequences.

Real-World Applications

- **LSTM**: Often used in tasks where the context is crucial over long sequences, such as machine translation, text generation, or time series forecasting.
- **GRU**: Often used in tasks where training speed is a priority, or in cases with smaller datasets, such as speech recognition or simple sentiment analysis.

Applications of CNNs and RNNs in NLP

Various applications can be used to build text classifiers, document recognizers, speech recognition systems, sentiment analyzers, chatbots, machine translation systems, and voice assistants, to name a few, using CNNs and RNNs.

Sentiment Analysis

Convolutional Neural Networks (CNNs) are traditionally used in image processing, but they have also proven effective in NLP tasks such as sentiment analysis. CNNs are particularly good at capturing local patterns, such as n-grams in text data.

Analyzing Product Reviews: A company analyzes customer reviews on its e-commerce platform to understand the overall sentiment toward its products. These reviews (positive or negative) can be short (a few words) or long (multiple sentences).

Advantages of using CNN for Sentiment Analysis

- **Efficiency:** CNNs are computationally efficient, making them suitable for real-time sentiment analysis on large datasets.
- **Feature Extraction:** CNNs can automatically learn relevant features from the text without requiring extensive manual feature engineering.

Recurrent Neural Networks (RNNs) are designed to process sequential data by maintaining a hidden state that captures information from previous time steps, making them ideal for tasks where the order of words matters.

Analyzing Social Media Sentiment: A company wants to monitor the sentiment of tweets about their products to understand public opinion and respond to negative sentiment promptly. They can also do it in real-time, thus observing public sentiments and taking steps if negative reviews are affecting their normal marketing strategy.

Advantages of using RNN for Sentiment Analysis

- **Contextual Understanding:** RNNs can capture long-term dependencies in text, making them effective for understanding the sentiment of complex sentences where the meaning of a word depends on the preceding words.
- **Sequential Nature:** Sequential processing in RNNs allows them to consider the order of words, which is essential for tasks such as sentiment analysis, where context and word order are important.

In some cases, a hybrid approach combining CNNs and RNNs can be particularly effective for sentiment analysis. The CNN can capture local patterns in the text (such as specific phrases), while the RNN can consider the broader context provided by the sequence of words.

Comprehensive Sentiment Analysis: A news agency wants to analyze the sentiment of editorial content, where understanding both specific phrases and the overall narrative is important.

Text Classification

For Text Classification using CNNs, the input data is represented as a sequence of word embeddings (such as Word2Vec, GloVe, or fastText), which are learned representations of words in a high-dimensional space.

The convolutional layer in the CNN applies filters to the word embeddings, which allows the network to identify relevant n-grams regardless of their position in the sentence.

After the convolutional layer, the output is typically fed through a pooling layer to further reduce the dimensionality of the features, and retain the most important features.

The pooled features are then fed into one or more fully connected layers, which perform the classification.

Advantages

- **Local Feature Detection:** CNNs are excellent at identifying key phrases or specific combinations of words that are indicative of a particular class.
- **Efficiency:** CNNs are less computationally expensive compared to RNNs, making them faster to train.

- **Parallelism:** The architecture of CNNs allows for parallel processing, which speeds up computation.

For RNNs, it is similar to that of CNNs, where words are represented as word embeddings.

Then the RNN processes the sequence of word embeddings one at a time, updating its hidden state with each new word. This hidden state carries forward the context from the previous words, making RNNs sensitive to the order of words.

After processing the entire sequence, the hidden states are used to make a final classification.

- **Long Short-Term Memory (LSTM):** LSTM networks include mechanisms (gates) to regulate the flow of information, making them capable of learning long-term dependencies in the text.
- **Gated Recurrent Unit (GRU):** GRU is a simplified version of LSTM, with fewer gates and a more streamlined architecture.

Advantages

- **Sequential Dependency:** RNNs excel at capturing dependencies across different parts of the text, such as how earlier words in a sentence affect the meaning of later words.
- **Contextual Understanding:** RNNs are good at understanding context, making them effective for tasks that require understanding the nuance of language.

Machine Translation

CNNs can be used to build encoder-decoder models for translation. In such models, convolutions are applied to the input sequence to extract n-gram features. These features capture local dependencies in the text (for example, word pairs or triplets), which can be particularly useful in translation tasks where certain phrases or word combinations have specific meanings.

In translating "*How is work today*?" to "*Wie ist die Arbeit heute*?" a CNN-based model might focus on capturing the local context around words such as "*work*" and "*today*," ensuring that these phrases are correctly translated into the corresponding German words.

Recurrent Neural Networks (RNNs) are specifically relevant for sequence-to-sequence (Seq2Seq) tasks such as machine translation due to their ability to process and generate sequences of varying lengths.

Encoder-Decoder Architecture

- **Encoder**: The RNN-based encoder processes the input sentence (in English) word by word. As each word is processed, the RNN updates its hidden state, gradually building a vector representation (called the context vector) that captures the meaning of the entire sentence.

- **Decoder**: The decoder is another RNN that takes the context vector as its initial hidden state and generates the output sentence (in French), word by word. At each step, the decoder predicts the next word in the target language based on the current hidden state and the word generated in the previous step.

Challenges

- **Long Sentences**: Traditional RNNs struggle with very long sentences because of the vanishing gradient problem, making it difficult to retain information over many time steps.
- **Word Order**: Different languages may have different word orders, making it necessary for the model to learn not only translation but also the reordering of words.

Attention Mechanism

- To address the issue of long sentences, modern RNN-based translation models incorporate an attention mechanism. Attention allows the decoder to focus on specific parts of the input sentence (encoded by the encoder) when generating each word in the target language. This greatly improves the quality of translations, especially for longer sentences.

Machine translation models powered by CNNs and RNNs are used by Google Translate, Microsoft Translator, and Amazon Translate. These models are constantly being improved to handle more languages, dialects, and contextual nuances, making cross-language communication increasingly seamless.

- Google's early versions of Google Translate were heavily based on RNNs, specifically the Seq2Seq model with attention.
- More recent models, such as the Transformer, combine the best features of both CNNs and RNNs (along with attention mechanisms) to produce even more accurate translations.

Question Answering

Question Answering (QA) is a crucial application in Natural Language Processing (NLP) that involves automatically responding to questions posed in natural language. QA systems are essential in many domains, including customer support, information retrieval, and conversational AI.

QA systems leverage deep learning techniques such as CNNs and RNNs to understand the question and its context.

CNNs extract features from text data by capturing local patterns through convolutional filters. In the context of QA, CNNs can be used to:

- **Text Representation**: CNNs can generate vector representations of both questions and potential answers by extracting n-gram features (for example, sequences of words) from the text.
- **Matching Questions to Answers**: The CNN can compare the question vector with answer vectors to identify the most relevant answer. For example, in a passage-based QA system, CNNs can be used to scan the passage for patterns or phrases that align with the question.
- To explain a real-life use case for Customer Support, a company implements a QA system where customers can ask questions about products or services. The system must quickly match a customer's question with the relevant information in a large database of FAQs.
- The CNN extracts key features from both the customer's question and potential answers in the FAQ database. It then compares these features to identify the closest match, ensuring quick and accurate responses.

We can look into **RNNs** that are ideal for tasks that involve sequential data, making them right for understanding the context of a question and the answer. Now, to address some limitations of RNNs, there are **LSTMs (Long Short-Term Memory)** and **GRU (Gated Recurrent Unit)** that capture dependencies in text and maintain context over long sequences.

- **Contextual Understanding**: RNNs can model the sequential nature of text, so the system can understand the context of a question based on word sequences.
- **Answer Generation**: In generative QA systems, RNNs can be used to generate answers word by word, ensuring that the generated response is contextually relevant to the question.

If we look into a use case for RNNs, there is a healthcare provider that uses an RNN-based QA system to answer patient queries about symptoms, treatment options, and medication. Patients submit questions in natural language, and the system must provide accurate, context-aware answers.

The RNN processes the question word by word, capturing the dependencies between symptoms and treatments mentioned in the question. This understanding helps the system retrieve or generate the most contextually appropriate response.

Many modern QA systems combine CNNs and RNNs to have the best of both approaches. CNNs can be used for feature extraction, while RNNs handle the sequential dependencies and contextual understanding of the question.

For example, an educational platform offers an AI-powered tutor that answers student questions on various subjects. The system must understand both the content of the question and the context provided by the student's previous interactions. These days, we have dedicated AI assistants specific to the course, like on platforms such as Udacity and Khan Academy.

The CNN extracts key features from the student's question, while the RNN processes the sequence of words to understand the context. Together, they enable the system to provide accurate, context-aware answers that are tailored to the student's learning history.

Advantages

- **Accuracy**: Combining CNN and RNN models brings out the best of both models, thus improving the system's accuracy in understanding questions and answering them.
- **Flexibility**: These models can be adapted to different domains, making them versatile for various QA applications.
- **Efficiency**: CNNs speed up the processing by reducing the dimensionality of text data, while RNNs ensure that the sequential nature of language is preserved.

Disadvantages

- **Complexity**: Training these models requires significant computational resources and expertise.
- **Data Dependency**: High-quality, annotated datasets are necessary to train effective QA systems.
- **Real-Time Performance**: Ensuring that the system responds in real-time can be challenging, especially for complex queries.

These are some of the most important real use cases of CNNs and RNNs. There are also use cases such as text summarization, plagiarism detection, language modeling, named entity recognition, speech recognition, chatbot development, and so on.

Conclusion

To conclude, we covered the concepts of Deep Learning, its applications, and the advantages of Deep Learning over Machine Learning for NLP. We also discussed the building blocks of Deep Learning, such as neurons, weights and biases, optimization algorithms, activation functions, and loss functions, to name a few. We also covered the concepts of deep learning, such as deep architectures, representation learning, generalization, transfer learning, and scalability.

Then we covered Deep Neural Networks and various types such as CNN, RNN, GANs, and autoencoders. Then we covered the relevant libraries such as TensorFlow, Keras, PyTorch, scikit-learn, pandas, and numpy. We also covered a use case for binary classification of tumors using a breast cancer dataset available in the scikit-learn library.

We then covered the concepts and architectures of both CNNs and RNNs. We discussed the Disappearing Gradient and exploding gradient problems of RNNs and their solutions. We also discussed the variants of RNN, which are GRUs and LSTMs. We also covered a sentiment analysis use case using RNN.

Finally, we summarized various real-life use cases of CNNs and RNNs for NLP, such as sentiment analysis, text classification, machine translation, and question answering systems.

In the next chapter, we will dive deep into applying deep learning models for sentiment analysis using Convolutional Neural Networks (CNNs). Through hands-on projects, we will explore the intricacies of the model, and how to apply it effectively to real-world problems.

References

- https://www.datacamp.com/tutorial/introduction-to-deep-neural-networks
- https://www.datacamp.com/tutorial/tutorial-deep-learning-tutorial
- https://www.datacamp.com/tutorial/introduction-to-convolutional-neural-networks-cnns
- https://www.geeksforgeeks.org/convolutional-neural-network-cnn-in-machine-learning/
- https://medium.com/@draj0718/convolutional-neural-networks-cnn-architectures-explained-716fb197b243
- https://journalofbigdata.springeropen.com/articles/10.1186/s40537-021-00444-8
- https://www.v7labs.com/blog/neural-networks-activation-functions
- https://encord.com/blog/activation-functions-neural-networks/
- https://www.scaler.com/topics/deep-learning/optimizers-in-deep-learning/
- https://towardsdatascience.com/optimizers-for-training-neural-network-59450d71caf6
- https://mdrk.io/optimizers-in-deep-learning/
- https://towardsdatascience.com/nlp-with-cnns-a6aa743bdc1e

- https://www.kaggle.com/code/farjanakabirsamanta/imdb-movie-review-classification-using-cnn
- https://www.tensorflow.org/tutorials/keras/text_classification_with_hub
- https://medium.com/@praveenraj.gowd/understanding-recurrent-neural-networks-rnn-nlp-e2f4cae03a4f
- https://www.datacamp.com/tutorial/tutorial-for-recurrent-neural-network
- https://web.stanford.edu/class/archive/cs/cs224n/cs224n.1244/
- https://slds-lmu.github.io/seminar_nlp_ss20/
- https://slds-lmu.github.io/dl4nlp/chapters/
- https://paperswithcode.com/area/natural-language-processing
- https://github.com/Mahesh3394/Text-Classification-Using-CNN
- https://wandb.ai/wandb_fc/wb-tutorials/reports/Tutorial-Text-Classification-Using-CNNs--VmlldzoONTIxNDI5
- https://www.geeksforgeeks.org/text-classification-using-cnn/
- https://cnvrg.io/cnn-sentence-classification/
- https://medium.com/voice-tech-podcast/text-classification-using-cnn-9ade8155dfb9
- https://cs224d.stanford.edu/reports/LambAndrew.pdf
- https://medium.com/ai-society/why-convolutional-neural-networks-are-a-great-architecture-for-machine-translation-9258ca1263a8
- https://engineering.fb.com/2017/05/09/ml-applications/a-novel-approach-to-neural-machine-translation/
- https://towardsdatascience.com/implementing-question-answering-networks-with-cnns-5ae5f08e312b
- https://aclanthology.org/C16-1164.pdf
- https://journalofbigdata.springeropen.com/articles/10.1186/s40537-020-00341-6

CHAPTER 5
Working with CNN

Introduction

Sentiment analysis, a cornerstone of natural language processing, aims to extract the emotional tone of text. This chapter delves into the application of deep learning models, specifically **Convolutional Neural Networks (CNNs)**, for sentiment analysis. Through hands-on projects, we will explore the intricacies of these models, their strengths and weaknesses, and how to apply them effectively to real-world problems.

By understanding the architecture, principles, and applications of CNNs, we will gain a comprehensive grasp of deep learning for sentiment analysis. This knowledge will empower you to build sophisticated models capable of accurately classifying text as positive, negative, or neutral.

Structure

In this chapter, we will cover the following topics:

- Sentiment Analysis Using CNN
- Data Understanding and Exploration
- Data Preparation for the CNN Model
- CNN Model Preparation and Training
- Model Evaluation and Visualization

Sentiment Analysis Using CNN

Sentiment analysis aims to identify the emotional tone of text data, classifying it as positive, negative, or neutral. CNNs, originally designed for image processing, have proven effective for **text classification tasks** due to their ability to capture local patterns and dependencies within sequences. We are using the patient reviews dataset on specific drugs with related conditions and a 10-star patient rating reflecting overall patient satisfaction.

Data Understanding and Exploration

The data was obtained by crawling **online pharmaceutical review sites**. The intention was to study:

- sentiment analysis of drug experience over multiple facets, that is, sentiments learned on specific aspects such as effectiveness and side effects,
- the transferability of models among domains, that is, conditions, and
- the transferability of models among different data sources (see '`Drug Review Dataset (Druglib.com)`').

https://archive.ics.uci.edu/dataset/462/drug+review+dataset+drugs+com

The data is split into a train (75%) and a test (25%) partition and stored in two **`.tsv` (`tab-separated-values`) files**, respectively.

There are 7 variables in the 2 data sets. ID- Id of the drug, **`drugName`** that is the name of the drug, **`condition`** for which the drug is taken, **`review`** of the drug, **rating** with 10 stars being the highest rated drug, the **`date`** column, and the **`usefulCount`** column. The data is in tab-separated value format.

The train data has **161297 rows and 7 columns**, and the test data has **53766 rows and 7 columns**.

The datatype of each variable is as follows.

```
Unnamed: 0      int64
drugName       object
condition      object
review         object
rating          int64
date           object
usefulCount     int64
```

The **`drugName`**, **`condition`**, and **`review`** are strings. The **`date`** column is also a string, so we can convert it into a datetime datatype, but in this problem statement, we do not have the relevance of doing so. The **`usefulCount`** is an integer. The rating variable is an integer, but it is a categorical variable (like an ordinal categorical variable since it is a review, 1 being the lowest and 10 being the highest).

Data Preparation for the CNN Model

We will now do some preprocessing operations for the review (string) data, such as removing HTML tags (if any present), removing accented characters, converting to lowercase, removing punctuations and special characters, and removing stopwords. This way, we can prepare the data for further processing. The code is as follows.

```
import re
import nltk
from nltk.corpus import stopwords
from bs4 import BeautifulSoup
import unicodedata
import contractions
import string

def preprocess_corpus(text):
    """Preprocesses sports news text for CNN.

    Args:
        text (str): The input text.

    Returns:
        str: The preprocessed text.
    """

    # Remove HTML tags
    soup = BeautifulSoup(text, "html.parser")
    text = soup.get_text()

    # Remove accented characters
    text = unicodedata.normalize('NFKD', text).encode('ascii',
'ignore').decode('utf-8', 'ignore')

    # Convert to lowercase
    text = text.lower()

    # Remove punctuation and special characters
    text = text.translate(str.maketrans('', '', string.
punctuation))

    text = re.sub(r'\d+', '', text)  # Remove numbers

    # Remove stop words
    stop_words = set(stopwords.words('english'))
    words = [word for word in text.split() if word not in stop_
words]

    # Join words into a sentence
    preprocessed_text = ' '.join(words)

    return preprocessed_text
```

We imported regular expressions, the nltk library, beautiful soup, contractions, Unicode, and string in the above code. We first remove the HTML tags if any are present in the reviews, then we remove accented characters, and then we convert the texts into lowercase. We remove punctuations and special characters, and finally, we remove the English stopwords from the texts and join the texts.

We then load the train and test data using pandas and explore some basic information about the datasets.

```
drugs_df_train = pd.read_csv('drugsComTrain_raw.tsv', sep='\t')
drugs_df_test = pd.read_csv('drugsComTest_raw.tsv', sep='\t')

drugs_df_train.head()
```

We loaded the datasets using pandas and checked the top 5 rows of the train data.

	Unnamed: 0	drugName	condition	review	rating	date	usefulCount
0	206461	Valsartan	Left Ventricular Dysfunction	"It has no side effect, I take it in combinati	9	May 20, 2012	27
1	95260	Guanfacine	ADHD	"My son is halfway through his fourth week of	8	April 27, 2010	192
2	92703	Lybrel	Birth Control	"I used to take another oral contraceptive, wh	5	December 14, 2009	17
3	138000	Ortho Evra	Birth Control	"This is my first time using any form of birth	8	November 3, 2015	10
4	35696	Buprenorphine / naloxone	Opiate Dependence	"Suboxone has completely turned my life around	9	November 27, 2016	37

Figure 5.1: *The top 5 rows of the train data*

For each drug name, we see there is a condition that the drug treats. There are reviews for each drug and a rating for the drug. Next, we create a validation dataset from the train and test sets. The code is as follows.

```
from sklearn.model_selection import train_test_split
import pandas as pd

# Combine train and test data for splitting
combined_df = pd.concat([drugs_df_train, drugs_df_test], ignore_
index=True)

# Split combined data into new train and validation sets
train_df_new, val_df = train_test_split(combined_df, test_
size=0.2, random_state=42)
```

In the preceding code, we concatenated the train and test data frames and created a new combined data frame. The combined data frame is then split into a split of **80% (train)** and **20% (test)**. We finally have 3 datasets: a new train data frame (**train_df_new**), validation data **(val_df)**, and the test data (**drugs_df_test**).

In the next step, we will use the preprocess function on the **train**, **test**, and **validation** datasets.

```
# Preprocess text
train_df_new['review'] = train_df_new['review'].apply
(preprocess_corpus)
drugs_df_test['review'] = drugs_df_test['review'].apply
(preprocess_corpus)
val_df['review'] = val_df['review'].apply(preprocess_corpus)
```

We used the **preprocess_corpus** function on all the datasets before proceeding to the model training step. In the next step, we will split into **X_train, y_train, X_test, y_test, X_val, and y_val.**

```
X_train = train_df_new['review'].values
y_train = train_df_new['rating'].values

X_test = drugs_df_test['review'].values
y_test = drugs_df_test['rating'].values

X_val = val_df['review'].values
y_val = val_df['rating'].values
```

We extract the review and rating values from the train, test, and validation data. Then we will tokenize the train data.

```
# Tokenizing the Data (the Reviews)
t = Tokenizer(oov_token='<UNK>')
# fit the tokenizer on train documents
t.fit_on_texts(X_train)
t.word_index['<PAD>'] = 0
```

The **Tokenizer** class from Keras is used to convert text data into numerical representations that can be processed by machine learning models.

- The **oov_token** parameter specifies a token to be used for words that are not present in the vocabulary.
- The **fit_on_texts** method builds a vocabulary of unique words from the training data and assigns integer indices to them.
- The **word_index** attribute of the tokenizer contains a dictionary mapping words to their corresponding indices.
- Adding the padding token **'<PAD>'** ensures that all sequences have the same length, which is necessary for feeding data to neural network models.

  Then we transform the reviews into sequences.

```
# Transforming Reviews to Sequences
X_train = t.texts_to_sequences(X_train)
X_test = t.texts_to_sequences(X_test)
X_val = t.texts_to_sequences(X_val)
```

- **`t.texts_to_sequences()`**: This method from the Keras Tokenizer class is used to convert **text data into sequences of integers**. Each integer represents a unique word from the vocabulary created by the tokenizer. So, each text data from the train, test, and validation datasets is converted into numerical sequences.

We will visualize the sequence by matplotlib.

```
# Plotting the size of the sequences

import matplotlib.pyplot as plt
%matplotlib inline
train_lens = [len(s) for s in X_train]
test_lens = [len(s) for s in X_test]
fig, ax = plt.subplots(1,2, figsize=(12, 6))
h1 = ax[0].hist(train_lens)
h2 = ax[1].hist(test_lens)
```

- The code first calculates the length of each sequence in the training and testing sets.
- Then, it creates two subplots to visualize the distribution of sequence lengths for both sets.
- The histograms show the frequency of different sequence lengths in each set.

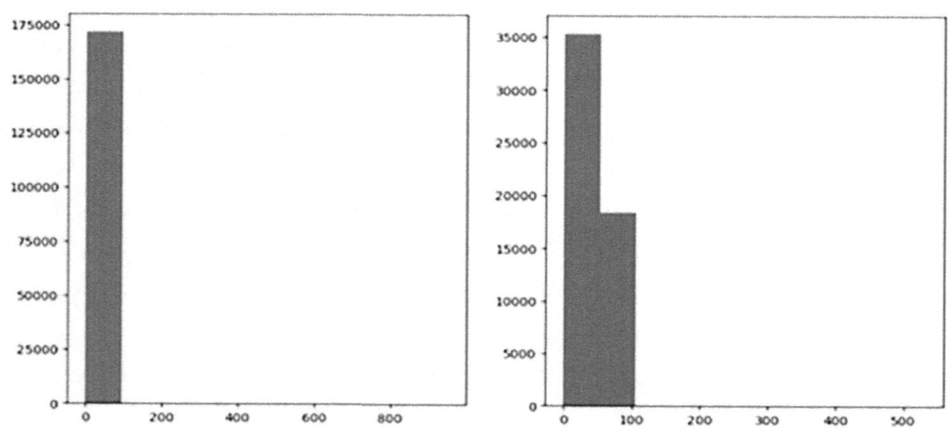

Figure 5.2: *Histogram of sequences of the train and test data*

The train data sequence is right-skewed, and the data is concentrated to the left; the test data sequence is almost the same, with a little bulge on the right. Next, we will do **sequence normalization** on the data train, test, and validation datasets. The purpose of sequence normalization is to:

- **Ensures Consistent Input:** Sequence normalization ensures that all input sequences have the same length. This is crucial for many machine learning models, including neural networks, as they require fixed-length inputs.
- **Prevents Errors:** If sequences have **varying lengths, padding** or **truncation** might be necessary. Incorrect padding or truncation can lead to errors in the model's predictions.

The code for sequence normalization is as follows.

```
# Padding the dataset to a maximum review length in words
MAX_SEQUENCE_LENGTH = 40
X_train = sequence.pad_sequences(X_train, maxlen=MAX_SEQUENCE_
LENGTH)
X_test = sequence.pad_sequences(X_test, maxlen=MAX_SEQUENCE_
LENGTH)
X_val = sequence.pad_sequences(X_val, maxlen=MAX_SEQUENCE_LENGTH)
```

We have added a maximum sequence length of 40, to which all sequences will be padded. For the training, test, and validation data, **`pad_sequences()`** pads the sequences to the specified maximum length. If a sequence is shorter than **`MAX_SEQUENCE_LENGTH`**, it will be padded with zeros at the end. If it is longer, it will be truncated.

Next, we will do label encoding. The purpose of label encoding is:

- **Machine Readability:** Most machine learning models require numerical labels. Encoding categorical labels (such as drug ratings) into numerical values makes them suitable for model training.
  - **Consistency:** It ensures that the model treats different categories consistently, preventing unintended biases.
  - **Evaluation Metrics:** Many evaluation metrics (for example, accuracy, precision, recall) require numerical labels for calculation.

The code for label encoding is as follows.

```
# Encoding Labels
le = LabelEncoder()
num_classes=10

y_train = le.fit_transform(y_train)
y_test = le.transform(y_test)
y_val = le.transform(y_val)
```

- The **`LabelEncoder`** class is used to encode categorical data into numerical representations.

- The `fit_transform()` method is used on the training labels to learn the unique categories and assign them integer indices.
- The `transform()` method is used on the testing and validation labels to encode them using the mapping learned from the training data.

There are **10 classes** in the **rating** column, starting from **1 to 10**, with 10 being the best rating and 1 being the worst.

CNN Model Preparation and Training

In this step, we will do CNN model preparation and training. In the first step, we define the vocabulary size, embedding size, and early stopping callback to prevent overfitting. The code is as follows.

```
# Setting Vocabulary size and Emmbedding size
VOCAB_SIZE = len(t.word_index)
EMBED_SIZE = 40

# Setting an Early_stopping callback to monitor accuracy with a
patience degree of 2

callback = tf.keras.callbacks.EarlyStopping(monitor='accuracy',
patience=2)
```

1. **Setting Vocabulary Size:**

   `VOCAB_SIZE = len(t.word_index)`: Calculates the vocabulary size based on the tokenizer (t) that was previously fitted on the training data. This defines the number of unique words in the vocabulary.

2. **Setting Embedding Size:**

   `EMBED_SIZE = 40`:

   Sets the embedding dimension, which determines the size of the word embeddings. A higher embedding dimension typically captures more complex semantic relationships between words.

3. **Creating Early Stopping Callback:**

   `callback = tf.keras.callbacks.EarlyStopping(monitor='accuracy', patience=2)`: Creates an early stopping callback object. This callback monitors the 'accuracy' metric during training and stops the training process if it does not improve for two consecutive epochs (patience=2). This helps prevent overfitting by stopping training when the model's performance on the validation set starts to deteriorate.

Significance:

- **Vocabulary Size:** A larger vocabulary size allows the model to capture more nuances in the text data. However, a very large vocabulary can also increase the model's complexity and computational requirements.
- **Embedding Size:** The embedding size determines the dimensionality of the word embeddings. A higher embedding size can capture more complex semantic relationships between words, but it also increases the model's parameter count.
- **Early Stopping:** This callback is crucial for preventing overfitting. By stopping training when the model's performance on the validation set stops improving it helps to find the optimal number of epochs and avoid overfitting the training data.

Now, we will create the CNN model.

```
# Creating the model
model = Sequential()
# The Embedding layer
model.add(Embedding(VOCAB_SIZE, EMBED_SIZE, input_length=MAX_
SEQUENCE_LENGTH))
# The first one dimensional convolutional layer (32,4,same,relu)
model.add(Conv1D(filters=32, kernel_size=4, padding='same',
activation='relu'))
model.add(Conv1D(filters=32, kernel_size=4, padding='same',
activation='relu'))
# The first Max pooling layer (2)
model.add(MaxPooling1D(pool_size=2))
# The first Dropout layer (10%)
model.add(Dropout(rate=0.10))
# The second one dimensional convolutional layer (32,4,same,relu)
model.add(Conv1D(filters=64, kernel_size=4, padding='same',
activation='relu'))
model.add(Conv1D(filters=64, kernel_size=4, padding='same',
activation='relu'))
# The second Max pooling layer (2)
model.add(MaxPooling1D(pool_size=2))
# The second Dropout layer (10%)
model.add(Dropout(rate=0.10))
# The third one dimensional convolutional layer (32,4,same,relu)
model.add(Conv1D(filters=64, kernel_size=4, padding='same',
activation='relu'))
model.add(Conv1D(filters=64, kernel_size=4, padding='same',
activation='relu'))
# The third Max pooling layer (2)
model.add(MaxPooling1D(pool_size=2))
```

```
# The third Dropout layer (10%)
model.add(Dropout(rate=0.10))
# The Flattening layer
model.add(Flatten())
# The First Dense Layer (256,relu)
model.add(Dense(256, activation='relu'))
# The Second Dense Layer or Prediction layer (1,sigmoid)
model.add(Dense(10, activation='softmax'))
# Compiling the Model using the Binary_Crossontropy as a loss
function and accuracy as a meseaure and Adam as an Optimizer
model.compile(loss='SparseCategoricalCrossentropy', optimizer=tf.
keras.optimizers.Adam(1e-4), metrics=['accuracy'])
# Displaying the Model Schema
model.summary()
```

This code defines a **Convolutional Neural Network (CNN)** model for text classification. The model is designed to process sequences of words and classify them into one of **10 categories**.

Create Sequential Model:

- **`model = Sequential()`**: Initializes a sequential model, which is a linear stack of layers.

Embedding Layer:

- **`model.add(Embedding(VOCAB_SIZE, EMBED_SIZE, input_length=MAX_SEQUENCE_LENGTH))`**: Adds an embedding layer to convert word indices into dense vectors.
    - **`VOCAB_SIZE`**: The size of the vocabulary.
    - **`EMBED_SIZE`**: The dimensionality of the word embeddings.
    - **`input_length`**: The maximum sequence length.

Convolutional Layers:

- **`model.add(Conv1D(filters=32, kernel_size=4, padding='same', activation='relu'))`**: Adds a 1D convolutional layer with 32 filters, a kernel size of 4, padding='same' to preserve input shape, and ReLU activation.
- Multiple convolutional layers are used to extract different features from the input sequence.

Pooling Layers:

- **`model.add(MaxPooling1D(pool_size=2))`**: Adds a max pooling layer to downsample the feature maps, reducing the dimensionality.

Dropout Layers:

- **`model.add(Dropout(rate=0.10))`**: Adds dropout layers to prevent overfitting by randomly dropping units during training.

Flatten Layer:

- **`model.add(Flatten())`**: Flattens the output of the convolutional layers into a 1D vector.

Dense Layers:

- **`model.add(Dense(256, activation='relu'))`**: Adds a fully connected layer with 256 units and ReLU activation.
- **`model.add(Dense(10, activation='softmax'))`**: Adds the final output layer with 10 units (for 10 classes) and softmax activation for probability distribution.

Compile Model:

- **`model.compile(loss='SparseCategoricalCrossentropy', optimizer=tf.keras.optimizers.Adam(1e-4), metrics=['accuracy'])`**: Compiles the model with the specified loss function (**`SparseCategoricalCrossentropy`** for multi-class classification), optimizer (Adam with a learning rate of 1e-4), and metrics (accuracy).

After the model is created, we will train the model using the code below.

```
# Training the Model with GPU
with tf.device('/GPU:0'):
    history1 = model.fit(X_train, y_train, validation_data=(X_
val,y_val),epochs=10, batch_size=64, verbose=1,
callbacks=[callback])
```

The code trains the model (model) on the **`training data (X_train, y_train)`** while validating on the **`validation data (X_val, y_val)`**. It leverages GPU acceleration (if available) to speed up the training process.

GPU Acceleration:

- **`with tf.device('/GPU:0')`**: This line ensures the computation happens on the first available GPU **`(/GPU:0)`**. TensorFlow automatically handles placing operations on the specified device.

Model Training:

- **`history1 = model.fit(...)`**: This part begins the model training using the fit method from the model object.
    - **`X_train`**: The training data for the model's input.
    - **`y_train`**: The training labels corresponding to the input data.
    - **`validation_data=(X_val, y_val)`**: The validation data used to monitor model performance during training.
    - **`epochs=10`**: The number of training epochs (iterations over the entire dataset).

  - **batch_size=64:** The number of samples processed in each training step.
  - **verbose=1:** Provides training progress information during each epoch.
  - **callbacks=[callback]:** List containing the early stopping callback (callback) defined earlier to monitor validation accuracy and stop training if it does not improve for two consecutive epochs.

Training History:

- **history1 = ...:** The fit method returns a History object containing the training history, including metrics such as loss and accuracy at each epoch for both training and validation data. The returned object is stored in the variable history1.

Model Evaluation and Visualization

In this step, we will evaluate the created model and visualize the accuracy and loss results for training and validation. The code snippet below evaluates the performance of the trained machine-learning model on the test set. It specifically calculates and prints the accuracy of the model's predictions.

```
# Final evaluation of the model
scores = model.evaluate(X_test, y_test, verbose=1)
print("Accuracy: %.2f%%" % (scores[1]*100))
Output:
Accuracy: 71.18%
```

model.evaluate(X_test, y_test, verbose=1):

- Evaluate the trained model (model) on the test data (**X_test**, **y_test**).
- **verbose=1** indicates that the evaluation process should print progress information.

scores = ...: The result of the evaluation is stored in the scores variable. This variable typically contains a list of metrics, such as loss and accuracy.

`print("Accuracy: %.2f%%" % (scores[1]*100)):`

- Extracts the accuracy score from the scores list (assuming accuracy is the second element).
- Prints the accuracy as a percentage with two decimal places.

In the next step, we will visualize the training and validation loss over epochs. The code is as follows.

```
import matplotlib.pyplot as plt
# Plot training and validation loss
plt.plot(history1.history['loss'], label='Training Loss')
plt.plot(history1.history['val_loss'], label='Validation Loss')
plt.title('Training and Validation Loss')
```

```
plt.xlabel('Epochs')
plt.ylabel('Loss')
plt.legend()
plt.show()
```

Plot Training and Validation Loss:

- **plt.plot(history1.history['loss'], label='Training Loss'):** Plots the training loss values from the **history1** object (returned by the model.fit method) in a line plot with the label **'Training Loss'**. The **history1** object from the model training step contains information about the training process, including loss values for both training and validation data at each epoch.
- **plt.plot(history1.history['val_loss'], label='Validation Loss'):** Similarly, plots the validation loss values with the label 'Validation Loss'.

Adding Titles and Labels:

- **plt.title('Training and Validation Loss'):** Sets the title of the plot.
- **plt.xlabel('Epochs'):** Labels the x-axis as 'Epochs'.
- **plt.ylabel('Loss'):** Labels the y-axis as 'Loss'.

Legend and Display:

- **plt.legend():** Adds a legend to the plot, identifying the different lines.
- **plt.show():** Displays the generated plot.

The resulting plot is as follows.

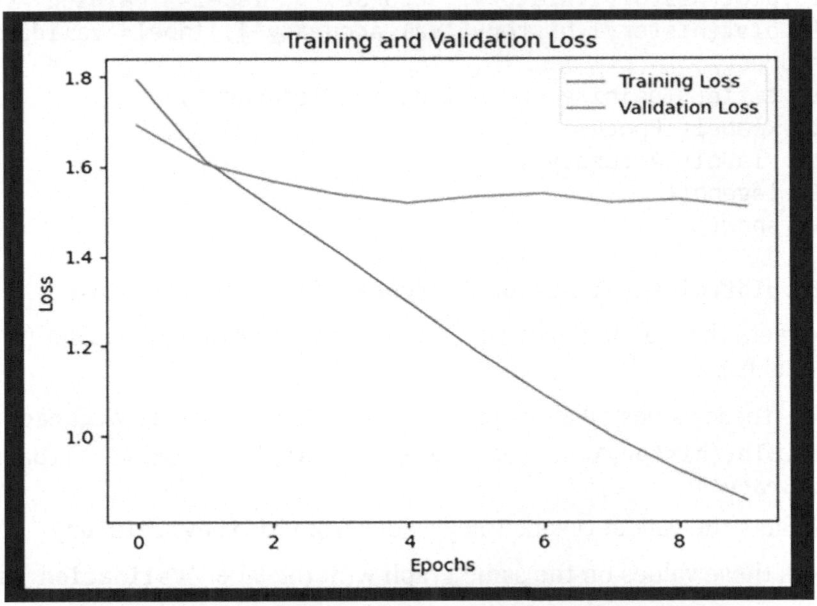

Figure 5.3: *Validation and training loss vs epochs*

From the graph above, the training loss decreases with each epoch, and the training and validation loss converges at some point where epoch ~ 1. The validation loss starts plateauing after that and reaches almost 1.55.

Interpretation of the Loss Graph:

The above description of the loss graph indicates a positive outcome for the model:

- **Decreasing Training Loss:** The training loss consistently decreases with each epoch, suggesting that the model is learning and improving its performance on the training data.
- **Converging Training and Validation Loss:** The fact that the training and validation loss curves converge around **epoch 1** suggests that the model is not overfitting significantly.
- **Plateauing Validation Loss:** The validation loss plateauing around 1.55 is a common occurrence. It indicates that the model has reached a point where further training is not significantly improving its performance on the validation data.

The graph suggests that your model has achieved a good balance between fitting the training data and generalizing it to unseen data.

Next, we will visualize the training and validation accuracy values over the training epochs. The code is as follows.

```
# Plot training and validation accuracy
plt.plot(history1.history['accuracy'], label='Training Accuracy')
plt.plot(history1.history['val_accuracy'], label='Validation
Accuracy')
plt.title('Training and Validation Accuracy')
plt.xlabel('Epochs')
plt.ylabel('Accuracy')
plt.legend()
plt.show()
```

`plt.plot(history1.history['accuracy'], label='Training Accuracy')`:

- Extracts the training accuracy values from the **`history1`** object (returned by model.fit).
- Plots these values on a line plot with the label **`'Training Accuracy'`**.

`plt.plot(history1.history['val_accuracy'], label='Validation Accuracy')`:

- Extracts the validation accuracy values from **`history1.history`**.
- Plots these values on the same graph with the label **`'Validation Accuracy'`**.

Adding Titles and Labels:

- `plt.title('Training and Validation Accuracy')`: Sets the title of the plot.
- `plt.xlabel('Epochs')`: Labels the x-axis as `'Epochs'`.
- `plt.ylabel('Accuracy')`: Labels the y-axis as `'Accuracy'`.

Legend and Display:

- `plt.legend()`: Adds a legend to the plot to distinguish the training and validation accuracy lines.
- `plt.show()`: Displays the generated plot.

The resulting plot is as follows.

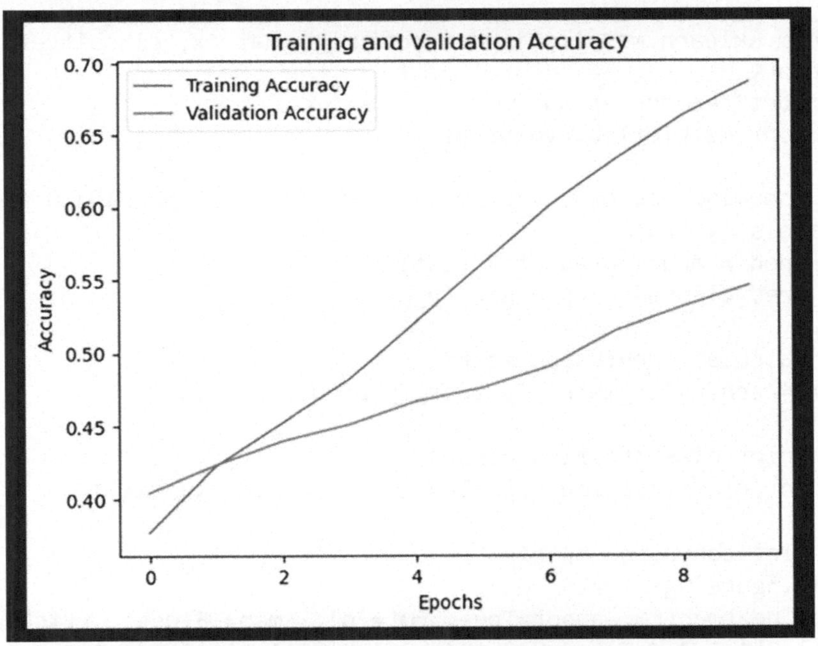

***Figure 5.4:** Validation and training accuracy vs epochs*

In the above graph, the training accuracy almost linearly increases and peaks at almost 70% at the 10th epoch. The training and validation accuracy values overlap at 41% and the validation accuracy slowly increases to almost 54%.

Interpretation of the Accuracy Graph:

Based on the description, the accuracy graph indicates the following:

- **Increasing Training Accuracy:** The training accuracy steadily increases, reaching around 70% by the 10th epoch. This suggests that the model is learning and improving its performance on the training data. We just trained with 10 epochs; we can do with more epochs.

- **Overlapping Training and Validation Accuracy:** The fact that the training and validation accuracy curves overlap at 41% initially suggests that the model might not be overfitting significantly at the beginning.
- **Increasing Validation Accuracy:** The gradual increase in validation accuracy up to 54% is a positive sign. It indicates that the model is generalizing well to unseen data.

Overall, the graph suggests that the model is learning effectively and improving its performance on both the **training and validation sets**.

In the next step, we will see the performance metrics in terms of the classification report and confusion metrics. We will observe the accuracy, precision, and recall for all 10 target classes. We will also visualize using a heat map. The code is as follows.

```
from sklearn.metrics import confusion_matrix, classification_
report
import seaborn as sns
import matplotlib.pyplot as plt

# Assuming you have your predicted labels (y_pred) and true
labels (y_true)
y_pred = model.predict(X_test)
y_pred_classes = np.argmax(y_pred, axis=1)

# Calculate confusion matrix
cm = confusion_matrix(y_test, y_pred_classes)

# Print classification report
print(classification_report(y_test, y_pred_classes))

# Plot confusion matrix
plt.figure(figsize=(8, 6))
sns.heatmap(cm, annot=True, fmt='d', cmap='Blues', xtickla-
bels=[1,2,3,4,5,6,7,8,9,10], yticklabels=[1,2,3,4,5,6,7,8,9,10])
plt.xlabel('Predicted')
plt.ylabel('Actual')
plt.title('Confusion Matrix')
plt.show()
```

Let's check the code step by step.

1. **Import Libraries:**

   `from sklearn.metrics import confusion_matrix, classification_report`: Imports functions for calculating the confusion matrix and classification report.

   `import seaborn as sns`: Imports the Seaborn library for creating heatmaps.

`import matplotlib.pyplot as plt`: Imports the Matplotlib library for plotting.

2. **Predict Labels:**

   `y_pred = model.predict(X_test)`: Uses the trained model (model) to predict labels for the test data (X_test).

3. **Get Predicted Classes:**

   `y_pred_classes = np.argmax(y_pred, axis=1)`: Converts the predicted probabilities (from y_pred) into class labels. The argmax function takes the index of the maximum value along the specified axis (axis=1 in this case).

4. **Calculate the Confusion Matrix:**

   `cm = confusion_matrix(y_test, y_pred_classes)`: Calculates the confusion matrix using confusion_matrix from sklearn.metrics. The confusion matrix shows how many instances of each true class were predicted as each class.

5. **Print Classification Report:**

   `print(classification_report(y_test, y_pred_classes))`: Prints a comprehensive classification report that includes metrics like precision, recall, F1-score, and support for each class.

6. **Plot Confusion Matrix:**

   `plt.figure(figsize=(8, 6))`: Creates a figure with a specific size (8 inches wide, 6 inches high).

   `sns.heatmap(cm, annot=True, fmt='d', cmap='Blues', xticklabels=[1,2,3,4,5,6,7,8,9,10], yticklabels=[1,2,3,4,5,6,7,8,9,10])`: Creates a heatmap visualization of the confusion matrix using **`sns.heatmap`**.

   - **`annot=True`**: Annotates each cell with the corresponding count.
   - **`fmt='d'`**: Formats the cell values as integers.
   - **`cmap='Blues'`**: Sets the colormap for the heatmap (blues in this case).
   - **`xticklabels`**: Sets the labels for the x-axis (predicted classes).
   - **`yticklabels`**: Sets the labels for the y-axis (actual classes).

   `plt.xlabel('Predicted')`: Labels the x-axis as **`'Predicted'`**.

   `plt.ylabel('Actual')`: Labels the y-axis as **`'Actual'`**.

   `plt.title('Confusion Matrix')`: Sets the title of the plot.

   `plt.show()`: Displays the generated heatmap.

Explanation:

- After training the model, we use it to **predict labels** for the test data.
- The confusion matrix provides a visual representation of how well the model performed on the test data. It shows the number of correct and incorrect predictions for each class.
- The classification report provides additional details about the model's performance, including **precision, recall, F1-score**, and support for each class. These metrics can help us understand the model's strengths and weaknesses for different classes.
- The heatmap visualization offers a clear way to interpret the confusion matrix, highlighting the **distribution of correct and incorrect predictions** across different classes.

By analyzing these evaluation results, we can gain valuable insights into how well the model generalizes to unseen data and identify areas for improvement.

We will see the precision, recall, and F1 scores for the 10 classes. We see that the classes here are 0 to 9, where 0 is class-1, 1 is class-2, and so on.

	precision	**recall**	**f1-score**	**support**
0	0.84	0.88	0.86	7299
1	0.53	0.54	0.53	2334
2	0.47	0.35	0.40	2205
3	0.45	0.19	0.27	1659
4	0.42	0.62	0.50	2710
5	0.49	0.31	0.38	2119
6	0.56	0.55	0.56	3091
7	0.63	0.69	0.66	6156
8	0.71	0.76	0.73	9177
9	0.89	0.86	0.87	17016
accuracy			0.72	53766
macro avg	0.60	0.57	0.58	53766
weighted avg	0.72	0.72	0.71	53766

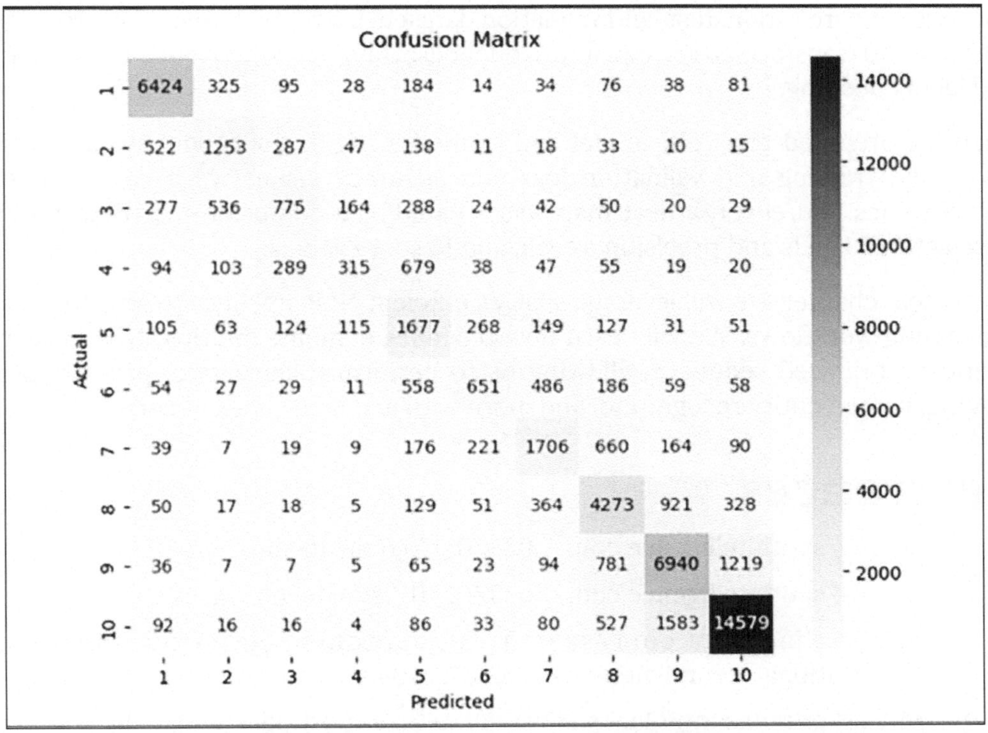

***Figure 5.5:** Confusion matrix of the 10 classes*

In the above heat map, we see a confusion matrix for the 10 classes, with the **x-axis as the predicted class and the y-axis as the actual class**. For **class 1**, **6424 reviews** are predicted to be correct. Of **class 1 reviews, 325** are predicted to be for **class 2,** and so on for the other classes. If we observe for each class, most of the reviews are classified correctly, and only a few reviews are misclassified, for example, **14579 reviews** are correctly classified for **class 10**. We can see one discrepancy for **class 4,** where **679 reviews** are **misclassified as class 5**. **558 reviews** for **class 6** are **misclassified as class 5**.

Conclusion

To conclude, we did sentiment analysis using CNN on a patient reviews dataset on specific drugs with related conditions and a 10-star patient rating for patient satisfaction. We explored the data in the preliminary stage. Then we prepared the data for the CNN model, we removed HTML tags, removed accented characters, converted to lower case, removed punctuation and special characters, removed stop words, and joined into sentences.

Then we prepared train, test, and validation datasets from the original data, tokenized the data, and transformed reviews into sequences. Then we did sequence normalization and label encoding.

Then we prepared the CNN model and trained it. Next, the model evaluation was done, and training and validation loss and accuracy values were visualized over epoch values. Moreover, a heat map was created as a confusion matrix to find the misclassified labels and precision, recall, and F1 score values.

In the next chapter, we will leverage spaCy's efficient NLP pipelines to streamline text processing workflows. We will learn how pipelines combine multiple NLP tasks into a single, optimized sequence, allowing us to perform tokenization, part-of-speech tagging, named entity recognition, and more with just a few lines of code.

References

- https://spotintelligence.com/2023/01/10/cnn-in-nlp/
- https://spotintelligence.com/2023/01/11/lstm-in-nlp-tasks/
- https://medium.com/saarthi-ai/sentence-classification-using-convolutional-neural-networks-ddad72c7048c
- https://github.com/Mahesh3394/Text-Classification-Using-CNN
- https://www.kaggle.com/code/aisuko/translation-nlp
- https://www.kaggle.com/code/rohitag13/bidirectional-gru-cnn
- https://www.kaggle.com/code/pushpakgote/natural-language-processing-with-rnn
- https://www.kaggle.com/code/oleksiiluppa/rnn-for-nlp
- https://www.kaggle.com/code/roblexnana/generating-text-for-nlp-using-simplernn-with
- https://www.kaggle.com/code/anetakovacheva/classifying-emotions-with-a-rnn
- https://www.kaggle.com/code/venkatkrishnan/rnn-lstm-nlp-topic-modeling
- https://www.kaggle.com/code/pushpakgote/natural-language-processing-with-rnn#Recurrent-Neural-Networks-(RNN's)
- https://www.kaggle.com/code/chanchal24/chatgpt-sentiment-analysis
- https://www.kaggle.com/code/atifaliak/chatgpt-review-classifier-lstm#-3.-Importing-Libraries-and-Checking-Data
- https://www.kaggle.com/code/cyrogai/sentiment-analysis-87-acc-lstm

CHAPTER 6
Building NLP Pipelines Using spaCy

Introduction

In Natural Language Processing (NLP), efficiency is paramount when dealing with large volumes of text data. spaCy, a popular Python library, offers a powerful toolset for streamlining NLP workflows through its pipeline architecture. Pipelines combine multiple NLP tasks into a single, optimized sequence, allowing us to perform **tokenization, part-of-speech tagging, named entity recognition**, and more with just a few lines of code.

This chapter will delve into spaCy pipelines, exploring their **capabilities, customization options, and practical applications**. By understanding how pipelines work and how to leverage them effectively, we will be able to build robust and efficient NLP applications that can handle a wide range of text-based tasks.

Structure

In this chapter, we will cover the following topics:

- Understanding spaCy Pipelines
- Creating and Customizing Pipelines
- Common NLP Tasks with Pipelines

Understanding spaCy Pipelines

spaCy pipelines are a powerful tool for efficient natural language processing. They combine multiple NLP tasks into a single sequence, allowing you to perform tokenization, part-of-speech tagging, named entity recognition, and more with just a few lines of code. This streamlined approach saves time and effort, making it easier to build complex NLP applications.

Concept of Pipelines

In spaCy, a pipeline is a sequence of components that are applied to text data in a specific order. Each component performs a particular NLP task, such as tokenization, part-of-speech tagging, or named entity recognition. By combining these components into a pipeline, you can efficiently process text data and extract valuable information.

Core Components of a Pipeline

- **Tokenizer:** Breaks text into individual words or tokens.
- **Tagger:** Assigns part-of-speech tags to each token (for example, noun, verb, adjective).
- **Parser:** Analyzes the syntactic structure of the text, identifying dependencies between words.
- **NER:** Identifies named entities in the text, such as persons, organizations, locations, dates, and times.
- **TextCategorizer:** Classifies text into predefined categories (for example, sentiment, topic).

Default Pipelines

spaCy provides several pre-trained pipelines for different languages and tasks. These pipelines include commonly used components and are optimized for performance.

Customizing Pipelines

We can customize spaCy pipelines to suit as per our specific needs by:

- **Adding or removing components:** Add or remove components to include or exclude certain NLP tasks.
- **Training custom models:** Train custom models for components such as taggers, parsers, or text categorizers.
- **Modifying component settings:** Adjust parameters or configurations of individual components.

Key Advantages of Pipelines:

- **Reusability:** Pre-trained pipelines can be reused for various tasks, saving development time.
- **Efficiency:** Pipelines combine multiple NLP tasks into a single sequence, optimizing processing time.
- **Flexibility:** We can customize pipelines to suit according to our specific needs and requirements.

- **Integration:** Pipelines can be easily integrated into other applications or workflows.

By understanding the concept of pipelines and their core components, we can effectively leverage spaCy to streamline your NLP tasks and extract valuable insights from text data.

Creating and Customizing Pipelines

spaCy pipelines offer flexibility in creating and customizing NLP workflows. We can start with pre-trained pipelines and add or remove components to suit the specific needs. For more tailored solutions, we can train custom models for components such as taggers, parsers, or text categorizers. Understanding these techniques helps create efficient and effective pipelines that align with your NLP tasks.

Creating a Basic Pipeline

To create a basic spaCy pipeline, we can use the **`nlp`** object, and add desired components:

```
import spacy
nlp = spacy.load('en_core_web_sm')  # Load a pre-trained English
pipeline
```

This will load the **`en_core_web_sm`** pipeline, including tokenization components, **part-of-speech tagging, dependency parsing**, and **named entity recognition**.

Adding or Removing Components

We can add or remove components from a pipeline using the **`nlp.pipe`** method:

```
# Check if 'ner' is already in the pipeline
if 'ner' not in nlp.pipe_names:
    # Add the ‹ner› component using its factory name
    nlp.add_pipe(‹ner›, last=True)
nlp.remove_pipe('ner')
```

We are checking existing components using **`nlp.pipe_names`** to get a list of component names currently in the pipeline. Then we do a conditional addition where we add the **`'ner'`** component if it is not already present. We can also remove the component.

Customizing a Text Processing Pipeline

We will create a simplified spaCy pipeline by excluding certain components. The goal is to reduce computational overhead and focus on specific NLP tasks while maintaining the core functionality of the pipeline.

```
# Create a simpler pipeline that doesn't use all components
simple_pipe = spacy.load(
 "en_core_web_sm",
 disable=["parser", "ner"])
simple_pipe.pipeline

Output:
[('tok2vec', <spacy.pipeline.tok2vec.Tok2Vec at 0x1cd8b2bb4c0>),
 ('tagger', <spacy.pipeline.tagger.Tagger at 0x1cd8b2bb520>),
 ('attribute_ruler',
  <spacy.pipeline.attributeruler.AttributeRuler at 0x1cd8c-
de2780>),
 ('lemmatizer', <spacy.lang.en.lemmatizer.EnglishLemmatizer at
0x1cd8cf3f2c0>)]
```

In the code above, we use **`disable=["parser", "ner"]`** when loading the pipeline; we are instructing spaCy to exclude the **parser and named entity recognizer components**. This means that the pipeline will only perform **tokenization and part-of-speech tagging**.

The **`simple_pipe.pipeline`** attribute returns a list of the components included in the pipeline. This can help debug or understand the pipeline's configuration.

From the output, we see the pipeline. The pipeline can **create embeddings using tok2vec, can perform part-of-speech tagging using tagger, and can perform lemmatization**.

We have the following advantages of customized pipelines:

- **Reduced Computational Overhead:** Removing unnecessary components can significantly improve processing speed, especially for large datasets.
- **Focused Functionality:** By focusing on specific tasks, we can optimize the pipeline for your particular use case.
- **Customizable:** We can still add or remove components as needed to create a pipeline that perfectly suits our requirements.

Common NLP Tasks with Pipelines

spaCy pipelines offer a streamlined approach to performing various NLP tasks. By combining multiple components, we can efficiently extract valuable information from text data. Common tasks include:

- **Tokenization and Lemmatization:** Breaking text into individual words (tokens), and reducing words to their base form.
- **Part-of-Speech Tagging:** Assigning grammatical categories to words.

- **Named Entity Recognition:** Identifying named entities such as persons, organizations, and locations.
- **Dependency Parsing:** Analyzing the syntactic structure of sentences.
- **Text Classification:** Categorizing text into predefined categories (for example, sentiment, topic).
- **Sentiment Analysis:** Identifying the emotional tone of text.

spaCy provides pre-trained pipelines for many languages and tasks, making it easy to get started. You can also customize pipelines to suit your specific needs by adding or removing components, training custom models, or modifying component settings.

Tokenization and Lemmatization

- **Tokenization:** Breaking text into individual words or tokens.
- **Lemmatization:** Reducing words to their **base forms (lemmas)** that have grammatical meaning.

The code is as follows.

```
import spacy
nlp = spacy.load('en_core_web_sm')
text = "The cats are running around the house."
doc = nlp(text)
# Tokenization
for token in doc:
    print(token.text)

# Lemmatization
for token in doc:
    print(token.lemma_)
Output:
The
cats
are
running
around
the
house
.
the
cat
be
run
around
the
house
.
```

In the preceding code, we are performing tokenization and lemmatization. For **tokenization**, we are using **token.text** to generate the individual tokens; for **lemmatization**, we are using **token.lemma_** to generate the base forms of the tokens.

Part-of-Speech Tagging

Assigning grammatical categories to words (for example, noun, verb, adjective).

The code is as follows.

```
for token in doc:
    print(token.text, token.pos_)
```

Output:

```
The DET
cats NOUN
are AUX
running VERB
around ADP
the DET
house NOUN
. PUNCT
```

The output gives us each token along with its parts of speech, such as nouns, verbs, determiners, auxiliary verbs, and so on.

Named Entity Recognition (NER)

Identifying named entities in text (for example, persons, organizations, locations).

The code is as follows.

```
import spacy
nlp = spacy.load('en_core_web_sm')

text = "Although last month's measures were mainly targeted at
making it easier for middle-class Chinese families to buy homes,
analysts still believe the country's 5% growth target is too
optimistic. Beijing's central bank has cut interest rates on
mortgages and lowered the amount of money lenders must keep on
hand. However, experts have warned more substantial reforms are
needed if China wants to boost its property sector following the
downfall of development firms like Evergrande."
doc = nlp(text)
for ent in doc.ents:
    print(ent.text, ent.label_)
```

Output:

```
last month's DATE
Chinese NORP
5% PERCENT
Beijing GPE
China GPE
Evergrande PRODUCT
```

In the preceding code, we find the tokens tagged as entities in a paragraph. The entities are **Date, NORP (National Origin or Nationality, percent, GPE (Geopolitical entity), and Product (Evergrande)**. We have used a larger paragraph from a newspaper to have various kinds of entities such as GPE, Product, percent, NORP, and Date.

Dependency Parsing

Analyzing the syntactic structure of sentences and identifying dependencies between words.

The code is as follows:

```
text = "The cats are running around the house."
doc = nlp(text)
for token in doc:
    print(token.text, token.dep_)
```

Output:

```
The det
cats nsubj
are aux
running ROOT
around prep
the det
house pobj
. punct
```

In the above result, we have preposition, object, auxiliary, determiner, punctuation, and so on.

Sentiment Analysis Using Spacy

For sentiment analysis following is a simple Python library for sentiment analysis of English sentences. We can install the package using the following.

The code is as follows.

```
import eng_spacysentiment
nlp = eng_spacysentiment.load()
text = "The movie was incredible! I loved every minute of it."
doc = nlp(text)
print(doc.cats)
```

Output:

```
{'positive': 0.5999119281768799, 'negative': 0.10723476856946945,
'neutral': 0.29285332560539246}
```

The output indicates the sentiment analysis results for the given text using the **eng_spacysentiment** library.

Interpretation:

- **Positive:** 0.5999
- **Negative:** 0.1072
- **Neutral:** 0.2929

The model has assigned probabilities to each sentiment category. In this case, the model is most confident that the text expresses a **positive** sentiment, as it has the highest probability. We can also test out various sentences of positive, negative, and neutral tones.

Conclusion

To conclude, we understood the concepts of spaCy pipelines and the core components of pipelines, as well as created and customized pipelines with some explanation. We also customized a text processing pipeline using pos tagging, token to vectorization, and lemmatization. We also explored various NLP applications in the pipelines such as tokenization, pos tagging, ner, dependency parsing, text classification, and sentiment analysis.

In the next chapter, we will use spaCy to build efficient pipelines for extracting structured information from unstructured text. We will learn how to combine spaCy's pre-trained models and custom components to create powerful information extraction tools. We will cover tasks such as tokenization, named entity recognition, dependency parsing, and rule-based matching to identify and extract key information such as names, dates, events, and relationships from documents or websites.

References

- https://spacy.io/usage/training
- https://www.edlitera.com/blog/posts/text-processing-pipelines-spacy
- https://www.ibm.com/topics/named-entity-recognition#:~:text=These%20categories%20can%20include%2C%20but,%2C%20quantities%2C%20medical%20codes%2C%20monetary
- https://www.datacamp.com/blog/what-is-tokenization
- https://spacy.io/usage/processing-pipelines
- https://spacy.io/usage/spacy-101
- https://www.getyourguide.careers/posts/building-custom-ner-models-with-spacy-to-enhance-travel-product-inventory
- https://www.dataquest.io/blog/tutorial-text-classification-in-python-using-spacy/
- https://www.kaggle.com/code/satishgunjal/tutorial-text-classification-using-spacy
- https://www.youtube.com/watch?v=ibi5hvw6f3g
- https://www.w3computing.com/articles/advanced-text-analytics-using-nltk-spacy/
- https://spacy.io/universe/project/eng_spacysentiment
- https://pypi.org/project/eng-spacysentiment/
- https://spacy.pythonhumanities.com/intro.html
- https://importsem.com/evaluate-sentiment-analysis-in-bulk-with-spacy-and-python/

CHAPTER 7
Building a spaCy Pipeline for Extracting Information

Introduction

In the previous chapter, we built and customized pipelines using spaCy that involved identifying and extracting meaningful entities, relationships, and patterns from unstructured text. In this chapter, we will build real-life applications that involve analyzing news articles, emails, or legal documents to help automate tedious tasks, saving time and effort, while uncovering valuable insights.

By integrating techniques such as Named Entity Recognition (NER), dependency parsing, and rule-based matching, we will learn to build end-to-end solutions for real-world problems. These projects will not only reinforce our understanding of NLP concepts but also prepare us to tackle diverse text-processing challenges in professional environments.

Structure

In this chapter, the following topics will be covered:

- Objectives of the Chapter
- Pre-Requisites
- Extracting Events and Dates from News Articles
    - Problem Statement and Dataset
    - Implementation: Combining NER, Rule-Based Matching, and Dependency Parsing
    - Visualization and Key Insights

- Extracting Customer and Transaction Information from Business Emails
    - Problem Statement and Dataset
    - Implementation: Parsing Emails and Extracting Patterns with NER and Matching
- Legal Document Analysis for Entity and Relationship Extraction
    - Problem Statement and Dataset
    - Implementation: Customizing spaCy Pipelines for Legal Texts
- Common Challenges in Information Extraction Projects
    - Data Quality Issues
    - Domain-Specific Adaptations
    - Optimizing for Scale

Objectives of the Chapter

The goal of this chapter is to provide readers with practical experience in utilizing spaCy to construct effective information extraction solutions. The emphasis is on using spaCy's sophisticated natural language processing skills to address practical issues. By the chapter's conclusion, readers will:

- **Recognize how information is extracted in real-world situations**
    - Learn how to identify and extract meaningful data, such as **events, dates, customer details, and relationships**, from unstructured text.
    - Develop an understanding of how NLP techniques can be applied to automate tasks and streamline workflows across different domains.
    - Integrate Multiple spaCy Techniques into End-to-End Solutions
    - Combine **Named Entity Recognition (NER), rule-based matching, and dependency parsing** to extract complex insights from text.
    - Use spaCy pipelines effectively for diverse use cases, such as event tracking, data extraction from emails, and legal document analysis.
- **Work with Realistic Datasets and Understand Data Challenges**
    - Get hands-on experience with real-world data sources, including news articles, email communications, and legal contracts.
    - Learn how to handle data challenges, such as noise, ambiguity, and domain-specific language, through preprocessing and pipeline customization.
- **Visualize and Interpret Extracted Information**
    - Explore methods to present extracted data in a meaningful and visually appealing way using Python visualization libraries.

- Understand how to convert raw text insights into actionable results, such as timelines, dashboards, and knowledge graphs.

- **Enhance Problem-Solving Skills for Real-World Applications**
  - Tackle real-world projects that require integrating multiple NLP techniques to address complex information extraction problems.
  - Gain insights into debugging, improving pipeline performance, and handling edge cases in text processing.
- **Build Readiness for Advanced NLP Projects**
  - Strengthen the foundation for pursuing advanced NLP topics, such as domain-specific model training or integrating spaCy with deep learning frameworks.
  - Encourage readers to apply the learned techniques to their own datasets and projects, fostering innovation and practical skill-building.
  - By focusing on practical, project-driven learning, this chapter prepares readers to tackle real-world information extraction challenges with confidence.

Pre-Requisites

Readers should have a solid understanding of the fundamental concepts of natural language processing and information extraction techniques before beginning the projects in this chapter.

The following requirements guarantee that you are prepared to follow successfully the following techniques:

- **Basics of NLP knowledge**
  - **Tokenization:** Knowing how text is divided into smaller units, such as words or phrases, and how this affects subsequent natural language processing tasks. The ability to recognize people, dates, organizations, and locations in the text is known as Named Entity Recognition, or NER.
  - **Rule-Based Matching:** This is the fundamental understanding of employing patterns to look for particular word sequences in text. Understanding the syntactic relationships between words in a phrase, and how to use them to extract meaningful structures is known as dependency parsing.
- **Hands-On Experience with spaCy**
  - Understanding how to set up and use spaCy pipelines.
  - Experience with loading pre-trained spaCy models and using their components (for example, `nlp.pipe`, `doc.ents`).

  - Ability to customize spaCy pipelines for specific tasks such as NER or rule-based matching.
- **Basic Knowledge of Text Preprocessing**
  - Techniques for cleaning and normalizing text such as removing special characters, stop words, and whitespace.
  - Familiarity with token normalization techniques such as lemmatization and lowercasing.
- **Understanding of Data Handling with Python Libraries**
  - **pandas**: For handling tabular data (for example, loading, filtering, and saving data to/from CSV or JSON).
  - **numpy**: For numerical operations and efficient array handling.
  - **json and csv modules**: For working with structured data formats.
- **Basic Visualization Skills**
  - Knowledge of Python visualization libraries such as **matplotlib, seaborn**, or plotly to create charts, timelines, or graphs.
- **Understanding of Real-World Data Challenges**
  - Awareness of common issues such as incomplete data, noisy or irrelevant content, and domain-specific terminology.
  - Ability to design preprocessing steps to handle such challenges before applying NLP techniques.

These prerequisites ensure you are ready to focus on the practical, project-based approach of this chapter. If you are missing any of these skills, it is recommended to revisit the relevant sections in earlier chapters or consult supplementary resources before proceeding.

Extracting Events and Dates from News Articles

In this section, we will analyze news articles and extract key events and the relevant dates.

- **Problem Definition:** Here, we need to build an NLP pipeline to extract key events and associated dates from news articles automatically. We will focus on meetings, announcements, incidents, or other time-sensitive events. The output will be a structured dataset (for example, CSV) containing the extracted events, dates, and context sentences.

- **Collect and Preprocess Data:** The dataset we will be using is the publicly available Kaggle dataset, BBC News Dataset. However, we need to ensure the dataset includes a variety of articles with clear events and dates ready to be extracted.

For the preprocessing, we will clean the text to remove irrelevant characters (HTML tags, special symbols). Moreover, we will also normalize text by converting it to lowercase and applying lemmatization. Then we need to segment the articles into sentences using spaCy's sentence tokenizer.

Next, we will look into the relevant code of the BBC news dataset. Firstly, we load the relevant libraries of Spacy and pandas. We also load the NLP Spacy pipeline.

```
import spacy
import pandas as pd
nlp = spacy.load('en_core_web_sm')  # Load a pre-trained English
pipeline
nlp.pipeline
Output:
[('tok2vec', <spacy.pipeline.tok2vec.Tok2Vec at 0x25b18f09060>),
 ('tagger', <spacy.pipeline.tagger.Tagger at 0x25b18f08ee0>),
 ('parser', <spacy.pipeline.dep_parser.DependencyParser at
0x25b18d5d150>),
 ('attribute_ruler',
  <spacy.pipeline.attributeruler.AttributeRuler at
0x25b15083400>),
 ('lemmatizer', <spacy.lang.en.lemmatizer.EnglishLemmatizer at
0x25b18f7fc00>),
 ('ner', <spacy.pipeline.ner.EntityRecognizer at 0x25b18d5d070>)]
```

As mentioned in the previous chapter, we have the components as

- **`tok2vec`**: generates token embeddings.
- **`tagger`**: assigns POS tags.
- **`parser`**: identifies dependencies.
- **`lemmatizer`**: finds the base forms of words.
- **`ner`**: identifies any named entities.

In the next step, we load the BBC news data set, find the shape of the data, and observe the first few rows of the data.

```
#Loading BBC News Data
df_bbc_data = pd.read_csv("bbc_news.csv")
print(f'Shape of data: {df_bbc_data.shape}')
# Show top 5 records
df_bbc_data.head()
```

The above code gives the shape of the data and the first 5 rows of the dataset.

Shape of data: (42115, 5)

	title	pubDate	guid	link	description
0	Ukraine: Angry Zelensky vows to punish Russian ...	Mon, 07 Mar 2022 08:01:56 GMT	https://www.bbc.co.uk/news/world-europe-60638042	https://www.bbc.co.uk/news/world-europe-606380...	The Ukranian president says the country will ...
1	War in Ukraine: Taking cover in a town under a...	Sun, 06 Mar 2022 22:49:58 GMT	https://www.bbc.co.uk/news/world-europe-60641873	https://www.bbc.co.uk/news/world-europe-606418...	Jeremy Bowen was on the frontline in Irpin, as...
2	Ukraine war 'catastrophic for global food'	Mon, 07 Mar 2022 00:14:42 GMT	https://www.bbc.co.uk/news/business-60623941	https://www.bbc.co.uk/news/business-60623941?a...	One of the world's biggest fertiliser firms sa...
3	Manchester Arena bombing: Saffie Roussos's par...	Mon, 07 Mar 2022 00:05:40 GMT	https://www.bbc.co.uk/news/uk-60579079	https://www.bbc.co.uk/news/uk-60579079?at_medi...	The parents of the Manchester Arena bombing's ...
4	Ukraine conflict: Oil price soars to highest l...	Mon, 07 Mar 2022 08:15:53 GMT	https://www.bbc.co.uk/news/business-60642786	https://www.bbc.co.uk/news/business-60642786?a...	Consumers are feeling the impact of higher ene...

Figure 7.1: *The top 5 rows of the BBC news data*

The above dataset has **42115 rows and 5 columns**. We have the title, publication date, link, guide, and description of the news.

Next, we find the data frame information and see that there are no missing rows.

```
#Data Information
df_bbc_data.info()
Output:
<class 'pandas.core.frame.DataFrame'>
RangeIndex: 42115 entries, 0 to 42114
Data columns (total 5 columns):
 #   Column       Non-Null Count  Dtype
---  ------       --------------  -----
 0   title        42115 non-null  object
 1   pubDate      42115 non-null  object
 2   guid         42115 non-null  object
 3   link         42115 non-null  object
 4   description  42115 non-null  object
dtypes: object(5)
memory usage: 1.6+ MB
```

In the next step, we convert the pubDate column into the right datatype and drop the pubDate column.

```
df_bbc_data['pubDate'] = pd.to_datetime(df_bbc_data['pubDate'])
df_bbc_data['date'] = df_bbc_data['pubDate'].dt.date
df_bbc_data = df_bbc_data.drop('pubDate', axis=1)
```

We have used the **`to_datetime()`** function on the **`pubDate`** column, and then converted using dt.date into the **YYYY-MM-DD** format for the new column **date**. Then we drop the old column **`pubDate`**.

Next, we take a sample of 1000 rows from the **`df_bbc_data`** data frame to process on a few rows. This reduces the time and load on the system to process **42115 rows** altogether.

```
df = df_bbc_data.sample(n=1000).copy()
```

In the next step, we find the first and last dates of the news publication and the frequency of news publications per month in the form of a bar graph. The code is as follows.

```
import matplotlib.pyplot as plt
import numpy as np
# Convert the date column to datetime format
df["date"] = pd.to_datetime(df["date"], format="%d-%m-%Y")
# Function to analyze dates
def analyze_dates(df, date_col):
    # Find oldest and newest dates
    oldest_date = df[date_col].min()
    newest_date = df[date_col].max()
    print(f"Oldest Date: {oldest_date.date()}")
    print(f"Newest Date: {newest_date.date()}")

    # Create a new column for Year-Month
    df["year_month"] = df[date_col].dt.to_period("M")

    # Group by Year-Month to count articles per month
    density = df.groupby("year_month").size()
    # Plot the density as a bar graph
    density.plot(kind="bar", figsize=(10, 6), color="skyblue")
    plt.title("Number of Articles Published per Month")
    plt.xlabel("Year-Month")
    plt.ylabel("Number of Articles")
    plt.xticks(rotation=45)
    plt.grid(axis="y", linestyle="--", alpha=0.7)
    plt.tight_layout()
    plt.show()
# Calling the function
analyze_dates(df, "date")
```

The code explanation is as follows.

- **Date Conversion**: The **`pd.to_datetime()`** function converts the date column from the format DD-MM-YYYY to a pandas datetime object, for easy manipulation.
- **Oldest and Newest Dates**: The **`.min()`** and **`.max()`** on the date column to find the oldest and newest publication dates.
- **Monthly Grouping**: The **`dt.to_period("M")`** method creates a new column for grouping dates by year and month (for example, 2022-07).
- **Density Calculation**: The **`.groupby("year_month").size()`** method counts the number of articles published in each month.
- **Bar Graph**: The density data is plotted as a bar graph using Matplotlib, with labels, titles, and grid lines for clarity.

Output:

```
Oldest Date: 2021-10-20
Newest Date: 2024-12-03
```

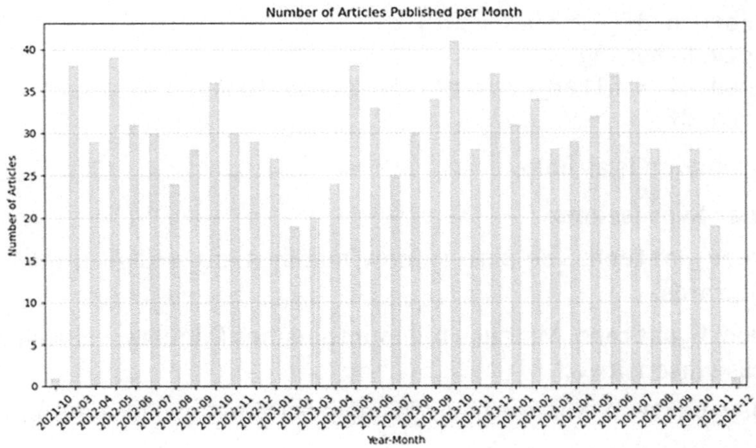

Figure 7.2: *The frequency of articles published by each month*

The oldest date in the dataset is 20th October 2021, and the newest date is 3rd December 2024.

From the above bar graph, we can observe that October 2023 has the maximum number of article posts, followed by May 2022. There are 8 months with more than 35 article posts per month.

In the following step, we will identify events based on day, month, and year. The code is as follows.

```
# Conditions
year_pattern = r'\b([1-9][0-9]{3})\b'  # Matches any 4-digit year
from 1000 onward
month_pattern = r'\b(January|February|March|April|May|June|July
|August|September|October|November|December)\b'
day_pattern = r'\b(Monday|Tuesday|Wednesday|Thursday|Friday|
Saturday|Sunday)\b'
currency_pattern = r'[\$\€\₹]\d+|\d+[\$\€\₹]'  # Matches numbers
with currency symbols

# Function to filter rows
def filter_rows(df, column):
    filtered_rows = df[column].apply(
        lambda x: (
            bool(re.search(year_pattern, x)) or  # Matches years
            bool(re.search(month_pattern, x, re.IGNORECASE)) or
# Matches months
            bool(re.search(day_pattern, x, re.IGNORECASE))  #
```

```
Matches days
        ) and not bool(re.search(currency_pattern, x))  #
Excludes currency-related rows
    )
    return df[filtered_rows]
# Apply filtering
filtered_df = filter_rows(df, "description")
filtered_df
```

The code explanation is as follows.

- **Regular Expressions:**
    - **`year_pattern`**: The pattern now matches any 4-digit number from 1000 onwards.
    - **`month_pattern`**: Matches full month names (January, February, and so on), case insensitive.
    - **`day_pattern`**: Matches full-day names (Monday, Tuesday, and so on), case insensitive.
    - **`currency_pattern`**: Matches numbers prefixed or suffixed by $, ₹, or €.
- **Filtering Logic:**
    - **`bool(re.search(...))`**: Ensures the condition matches (for example, year, month, or day).
    - **`not bool(re.search(currency_pattern, x))`**: Ensures rows with currency-related numbers are excluded.
- **Apply Function:**
    - The **`.apply()`** function is used to check each row of the description column against the filtering logic.

Output:

title	guid	link	description	year_month
Three men held after girl, 13, goes missing fr...	https://www.bbc.co.uk/news/uk-england-66049512	https://www.bbc.co.uk/news/uk-england-66049512...	Carmelle Heps, from Barnsley, travelled to Lon...	2023-06
Banning pro-Palestinian march would be last re...	https://www.bbc.co.uk/news/uk-67349474	https://www.bbc.co.uk/news/uk-67349474?at_medi...	Thousands are due to attend a London march, pl...	2023-11
Patrick Lyoya: Video shows fatal US police sho...	https://www.bbc.co.uk/news/world-us-canada-611...	https://www.bbc.co.uk/news/world-us-canada-611...	The shooting of an apparently unarmed black ma...	2022-04
Local elections 2023: When are they and who ca...	https://www.bbc.co.uk/news/uk-politics-65013652	https://www.bbc.co.uk/news/uk-politics-6501365...	Local elections in some parts of England and N...	2023-04
Emma Raducanu: Briton pulls out of charity mat...	https://www.bbc.co.uk/sport/tennis/67920598	https://www.bbc.co.uk/sport/tennis/67920598?at...	Britain's Emma Raducanu pulls out of a charity...	2024-01
Euro 2022: Have France gone from ticking time...	https://www.bbc.co.uk/sport/football/62169629	https://www.bbc.co.uk/sport/football/62169629?...	France are through to the Euro 2022 knockouts...	2022-07
Anthony Joshua: Eddie Hearn set to announce Di...	https://www.bbc.co.uk/sport/boxing/66434189	https://www.bbc.co.uk/sport/boxing/66434189?at...	Anthony Joshua will fight on Saturday night, w...	2023-08

Figure 7.3: *The filtered articles that have events*

We have the output that has 135 records, which have events recorded by day, month, or year.

For example, for this article description,

> "*AC Milan reach the Champions League semi-finals for the first time since winning the competition in 2007 as they see off Serie A rivals Napoli in an incident-packed game*," which was published in April 2023. 2023-04

Or this article's description

"*The Prince and Princess of Wales hear from the first person born after the* NHS *was founded, in* 1948," which was published in July 2023.

This way, we can identify dates using regular expressions.

In the next step, we will identify labels in the article descriptions such as **GPE (Geopolitical entity), ORG (Organization), DATE (date event), PERSON, and EVENT.** The code is as follows.

```
def extract_named_entities(text):
    doc = nlp(text)
    entities = [{"entity": ent.text, "label": ent.label_} for ent
in doc.ents]
    return entities
  # Apply the function to the dataframe
df['named_entities'] = df['description'].apply(extract_named_
entities)
df
```

The code is explained as follows.

- **NER Function:**
    - o The **`extract_named_entities`** function processes each row of text using spaCy's nlp model.
    - o It iterates through the **`ents` (named entities)** in the doc object, creating a list of dictionaries containing **`entity` (the text) and `label` (its entity type)**.
- **Apply the Function:**
    - o Use pandas' **`.apply()`** method to apply the **`extract_named_entities`** function to every row of the news column.
    - o A new column **`named_entities`** is created, storing the extracted entities.

Result: The resulting dataframe includes the original news column and a new **`named_entities`** column containing lists of extracted entities.

Output:

title	guid	link	description	year_month	named_entities
Copa 71: The Lost Lionesses - Storyville	https://www.bbc.co.uk/iplayer/episode/m0020541	https://www.bbc.co.uk/iplayer/episode/m0020541	Story of an extraordinary tournament, told thr...	2024-06	[]
Ros Atkins on... How the Ukraine war has stagnated	https://www.bbc.co.uk/news/world-europe-68255879	https://www.bbc.co.uk/news/world-europe-682558...	Almost two years on from Russia's invasion, th...	2024-02	[{'entity': 'Almost two years', 'label': 'DATE...
Plan for taxi drivers to carry stab wound band	https://www.bbc.com/news/articles/cgk7xdxklp2o#9	https://www.bbc.com/news/articles/cgk7xdxklp2o	About 50 taxis will carry bandage kits that co...	2024-09	[{'entity': 'About 50', 'label': 'CARDINAL'}]
Arab and Muslim leaders	https://www.bbc.co.uk/news/world-middle-east-6...	https://www.bbc.co.uk/news/world-middle-east-6...	Leaders accuse the US and	2023-11	[{'entity': 'US', 'label': 'GPE'

Figure 7.4: *The various labels that have been extracted using spaCy*

In the above output, we have various labels, such as **`CARDINAL`, `EVENT`, `DATE`, `ORG`, `PERSON`, `GPE`**, and so on, that have been extracted from the articles using the spaCy pipeline. For example, we have this article:

"*Carmelle Hepi, from Barnsley, travelled to London on Saturday for a party and has not been seen since.*" The entities are

```
[{'entity': 'Carmelle Hepi', 'label': 'ORG'}, {'entity':
'Barnsley', 'label': 'ORG'}, {'entity': 'London', 'label':
'GPE'}, {'entity': 'Saturday', 'label': 'DATE'}]
```

We have various labels for the above article. The words Barnsley and Carmelle Hepi are not rightly labeled since Carmelle is a PERSON and Barnsley is a GPE. However, London and Saturday are rightly labeled.

We can check this article:

"*Manchester United scrape into the FA Cup final on penalties despite throwing away a three-goal lead against Championship side Coventry in an epic semi-final at Wembley.*"

It is a football-related news from April 2024.

The entity labels are as follows.

```
[{'entity': 'Manchester United', 'label': 'GPE'}, {'entity': 'the
FA Cup', 'label': 'EVENT'}, {'entity': 'three', 'label':
'CARDINAL'}, {'entity': 'Championship side Coventry', 'label':
'ORG'}, {'entity': 'Wembley', 'label': 'ORG'}]
```

Manchester United and Coventry are football clubs. Manchester is a place, so it is tagged as a GPE, but it should be an Organization. FA Cup is an event. Three is a cardinal number. Wembley is a stadium that is tagged as an Organization. Coventry is rightly tagged as an Organization.

We can see in some cases that the words are not rightly tagged with the appropriate entities.

The result that we got from the spaCy and regular expressions can be extracted into .csv files.

Extracting Customer and Transaction Information from Business Emails

Problem Statement: Business emails often contain customer and transaction information, such as **customer names, dates, organization names, events, and other relevant details**. Manually extracting this information is time-consuming. Automating the process using NLP (spaCy) and regular expressions can save time, and uncover valuable insights.

We will be using the **Enron Email dataset.** The Enron email dataset contains approximately **500,000 emails** generated by employees of the Enron Corporation. It was obtained by the Federal Energy Regulatory Commission during its investigation of Enron's collapse.

Dataset Load and Sample Use:

In this step, we will load the dataset in the form of a data frame, and take a sample of the data as we did previously for the event and date extraction. The code is as follows:

```
data = pd.read_csv('emails.csv')
data.shape
```

There are **517401 rows and 2 columns**.

```
#Take a sample of the data for ease of analysis
data = data.sample(n=1000).copy()
```

We are using 1000 rows of data as the sample.

In the next step, we will retrieve the sender email, recipient email, dates, events, and email subject using regular expressions. We will also extract PERSON, GPE, EVENT, DATE, and ORG using the NER spaCy pipeline. The code is as follows:

```
# Load spaCy model
nlp = spacy.load("en_core_web_sm")

# Function to extract relevant details
def extract_email_details(email_text):
    details = {}

    # Extract sender email
```

```
    sender_match = re.search(r"From: ([\w\.-]+@[\w\.-]+)", email_
text)
    details["Sender Email"] = sender_match.group(1) if sender_
match else None

    # Extract recipient email
    recipient_match = re.search(r"To: ([\w\.-]+@[\w\.-]+)",
email_text)
    details["Recipient Email"] = recipient_match.group(1) if
recipient_match else None

    # Extract subject
    subject_match = re.search(r"Subject: (.+)", email_text)
    details["Subject"] = subject_match.group(1).strip() if
subject_match else None

    # Extract date
    date_match = re.search(r"Date: (.+)", email_text)
    details["Date"] = date_match.group(1).strip() if date_match
else None

    # Parse text for additional details
    doc = nlp(email_text)

    # Extract names from the text
    names = [ent.text for ent in doc.ents if ent.label_
== "PERSON"]
    details["Names in Text"] = ", ".join(names)

    # Extract dates from the text
    dates = [ent.text for ent in doc.ents if ent.label_
== "DATE"]
    details["Dates in Text"] = ", ".join(dates)

    # Extract names from the text
    geopolitical_entity = [ent.text for ent in doc.ents if ent.
label_ == "GPE"]
    details["GPEs in Text"] = ", ".join(geopolitical_entity)

    # Extract names from the text
    Organization = [ent.text for ent in doc.ents if ent.label_
== "ORG"]
    details["ORGs in Text"] = ", ".join(Organization)

    # Extract names from the text
    Events = [ent.text for ent in doc.ents if ent.label_
== "EVENT"]
```

```
        details["Events in Text"] = ", ".join(Events)

        return details
    # Apply extraction function
    data_extracted = data["message"].apply(extract_email_details)
    # Convert to DataFrame
    data_extracted = pd.DataFrame(data_extracted.tolist())
```

In the above function, we have extracted the **sender email, recipient email, date of the email, and subject** using regular expressions. Next, the spaCy pipeline extracted **person, dates, geopolitical entities, organizations, and events** present in the email body. The function is applied to the **message** variable in the data frame to retrieve the above records.

Sender Email	Recipient Email	Subject	Date	Names in Text	Dates in Text	GPEs in Text	ORGs in Text	Events in Text
40enron@enron.com	None	Outage for Applications Residing on R Drive	Thu, 21 Jun 2001 15:08:53 -0700 (PDT)	Chris Jeska, Sitara	21 Jun 2001, 6:26:02 PST, Friday, June 22, 200		Mime Version, ALL Enron Corp, X Origin, SALUS8	
stanley.k.horton@dynegy.com	joe.parks@enron.com	Raymond James Energy Daily Update (Wednesday 0	Wed, 23 Jan 2002 06:46:33 -0800 (PST)	Parks, Joe, joe parks, Alexandra Fasoli, Mcf...	23 Jan 2002, Wednesday, Wednesday, Wednesday,	U.S., U.S., Canada, U.S	PST, Raymond James Energy Daily Update, Mime V	
v.weldon@enron.com	philip.polsky@enron.com	Basis History	Tue, 24 Apr 2001 20:36:00 -0700 (PDT)	V Charles Weldon, Philip Polsky, Philip Polsky			V Charles pst, Enron North America Corp	

Figure 7.5: *Extracted emails and other details by spaCy*

In the above figure, we have extracted sender emails, recipient emails, subject of the email, and date of the email. We have extracted names, emails, geopolitical entities such as locations, organization names, and events from the email bodies using spaCy. This way, we can create a customized pipeline for performing operations step by step using spaCy.

The final data frame can be converted into a .csv file for a comprehensive understanding of the output.

Legal Document Analysis for Entity and Relationship Extraction

We aim to analyze legal documents to extract entities (for example, people, organizations, laws, dates, case references) and relationships (for example, plaintiff-defendant, agreement clauses, legal obligations). Using spaCy, we will process the text, identify entities and relationships, and visualize them as a **knowledge graph**.

Dataset: We will be using the train_data from the legal contracts dataset present on the Hugging Face website.

The data is loaded, and it has **26539 rows and 1 column**.

```
legal_data = pd.read_csv('train_data.csv')
legal_data.shape
Output:
(26539, 1)
```

Like the previous exercises, we take a random sample of 1000 rows for ease of processing and saving time.

```
#Take a sample of the data for ease of analysis
legal_data = legal_data.sample(n=1000).copy()
```

Next, we will preprocess the data.

```
# Preprocess text
legal_data['cleaned_text'] = legal_data['text'].str.replace(r'\
s+', ' ', regex=True).str.strip()
legal_data['cleaned_text'].head()
```

In the preceding code, we do the following things for preprocessing:

Removed special characters, multiple spaces, or irrelevant metadata.

Split text into paragraphs or clauses for easier processing.

Next, we will customize the spaCy pipeline.

Custom NER for Legal Entities: We will identify:

Parties: For example, "*Party* A," "*Company* XYZ."

Dates: For example, "*January* 1, 2023."

Legal References: For example, "*Section* 3.1," "*Article* 5."

Rule-Based Matching for Clauses: Use patterns to extract structured sections (for example, "*This Agreement is governed by...*").

Dependency Parsing for Relationships: Extract syntactic relationships such as subject-action-object patterns.

```
# Add rule-based matching for legal sections
matcher = Matcher(nlp.vocab)
patterns = [{"label": "SECTION", "pattern": [{"LOWER":
"section"}, {"IS_DIGIT": True}]}]
for pattern in patterns:
    matcher.add(pattern["label"], [pattern["pattern"]])
```

```
def extract_entities(doc):
    entities = {"PARTIES": [], "DATES": [], "SECTIONS": [],
"REFERENCES": []}
    for ent in doc.ents:
        if ent.label_ == "PERSON":
            entities["PARTIES"].append(ent.text)
        elif ent.label_ == "DATE":
            entities["DATES"].append(ent.text)
        elif ent.label_ in ["ORG", "LAW"]:
            entities["REFERENCES"].append(ent.text)
    matches = matcher(doc)
    for match_id, start, end in matches:
        entities["SECTIONS"].append(doc[start:end].text)
    return entities
```

The code is explained as follows.

Rule-Based Matching for Legal Sections: The Matcher class in spaCy is used to implement rule-based matching patterns. The aim here is to identify text patterns that correspond to legal sections (for example, "*Section* 23"):

```
matcher = Matcher(nlp.vocab)
```

Matcher is initialized with the **`nlp.vocab`** object, which is the vocabulary of the current spaCy language model.

This allows matching patterns to work seamlessly with the tokens in a processed Doc object.

Defining patterns:

```
patterns = [{"label": "SECTION", "pattern": [{"LOWER":
"section"}, {"IS_DIGIT": True}]}]
```

`"label": "SECTION"`: Specifies the label for this pattern. It indicates we are looking for sections in the text.

`"pattern": [{"LOWER": "section"}, {"IS_DIGIT": True}]:`

`{"LOWER": "section"}` matches the word "section" regardless of case.

`{"IS_DIGIT": True}` matches a token that is a number (for example, "23").

Together, this pattern identifies phrases such as "*section* 23".

Adding Patterns to Matcher:

for pattern in patterns:

```
    matcher.add(pattern["label"], [pattern["pattern"]])
```

For each pattern in the patterns list, the matcher is configured to recognize the specified pattern under the given label.

Extracting Entities

The function **extract_entities** processes a given Doc object to extract various types of entities.

```
def extract_entities(doc):
        entities = {"PARTIES": [], "DATES": [], "SECTIONS": [],
    "REFERENCES": []}
```

entities dictionary: Stores extracted entities in categories:

"**PARTIES**": Names of people or entities involved.

"**DATES**": Dates mentioned in the document.

"**SECTIONS**": Legal sections identified by the matcher.

"**REFERENCES**": References to laws, organizations, and so on.

Processing named entities:

```
    for ent in doc.ents:
            if ent.label_ == "PERSON":
                entities["PARTIES"].append(ent.text)
            elif ent.label_ == "DATE":
                entities["DATES"].append(ent.text)
            elif ent.label_ in ["ORG", "LAW"]:
                entities["REFERENCES"].append(ent.text)
```

- **doc.ents**: This is the list of entities recognized by the spaCy model.

For each entity:

If the entity label (**ent.label_**) is "PERSON", it is added to "PARTIES".

If the entity label is "DATE", it is added to "DATES".

If the entity label is "**ORG**" (organization) or "**LAW**" (legal reference), it is added to "**REFERENCES**".

Applying the Rule-Based Matcher:

```
    matches = matcher(doc)
```

matcher(doc): Applies the predefined patterns to the document.

Returns a list of matches, where each match includes:

- **match_id**: ID of the matched pattern.
- **start**: Start index of the matched span in the document.
- **end**: End index of the matched span.

Extracting Sections:

for **match_id**, **start**, **end** in matches:

```
entities["SECTIONS"].append(doc[start:end].text)
```

For each match:

- The span of text between start and end is extracted using **doc[start:end].text**.
- This text, corresponding to a legal section, is added to "**SECTIONS**".

Finally, we use the **extract_entities** function to extract the relevant entities from the cleaned text.

```
legal_data['entities'] = legal_data['cleaned_text'].apply(lambda
x: extract_entities(nlp(x)))
legal_data[['cleaned_text', 'entities']]
```

The final dataframe is as follows.

	cleaned_text	entities
13036	(a)the declaration ~~and payment of dividends ...	{'PARTIES': [], 'DATES': [], 'SECTIONS': [], '...
9042	(b) Authorization of Transaction. Seller has f...	{'PARTIES': ['Seller', 'Seller', 'Seller', 'Se...
9192	4.7 Restrictions on Transferability. Buyer und...	{'PARTIES': ['Buyer', 'Buyer', 'Buyer'], 'DATE...
13396	(b) To request a Swingline Borrowing, ~~a~~ th...	{'PARTIES': ['~~a~~', 'Borrower', 'Local Time'...
9527	(c) Form of Payment. Unless otherwise agreed t...	{'PARTIES': [], 'DATES': [], 'SECTIONS': [], '...
...	...	...
25065	4.1 Term. The term of this Agreement shall beg...	{'PARTIES': [], 'DATES': ['March 6, 2018', 'on...
17541	(b)Borrowing Procedures. Each Swing Line Borro...	{'PARTIES': ['Borrower', 'Borrower', 'Borrower...
14390	THIS FIRST AMENDMENT TO SECOND AMENDED AND RES...	{'PARTIES': ['P.H. GLATFELTER COMPANY', 'Lende...
4201	(i) Except as otherwise expressly set forth in...	{'PARTIES': [], 'DATES': [], 'SECTIONS': [], '...
9068	(a) Except as specifically disclosed on Schedu...	{'PARTIES': [], 'DATES': ['the Most Recent Fis...

1000 rows × 2 columns

***Figure 7.6**: Extracted entities using spaCy*

In *Figure* 7.6, we see the extracted entities for the labels **SECTIONS**, **PARTIES**, **DATES**, and **REFERENCES**.

The extracted entities labeled as **SECTIONS** represent specific legal provisions, clauses, or statutory references, such as **"Section 8" and "Section 280,"** which are critical in understanding the scope and applicability of legal documents. These provide the technical backbone of legal arguments, often outlining **rights, obligations, or violations.**

Entities under **PARTIES** capture the individuals or organizations (**Borrower, Lien, Transactions, Arrangers,** and so on) involved in the document, such as signatories or contracting entities. These names are vital for identifying the stakeholders bound by the terms or those participating in legal proceedings.

The **DATES** label extracts temporal information, such as dates of agreement, deadlines, or historical references, providing context and timelines essential for interpreting the events or obligations within the legal framework.

Entities labeled **REFERENCES** include citations of laws, acts, or organizations such as (**'the Age Discrimination', 'the Civil Rights Act', 'the Civil Rights Act', 'the Employee Retirement Income Security Act', 'the Family and Medical Leave Act', 'the Americans With Disabilities Act')** establishing the legal basis or authority that makes the document valid. These references help link the content to established legal doctrines or regulatory frameworks.

Together, these extracted entities form a comprehensive understanding of the legal document, connecting the who **(PARTIES), when (DATES), what (SECTIONS), and by what authority (REFERENCES)**, facilitating structured analysis and enabling insights such as compliance checks or contractual validations.

However, it was a straightforward spaCy pipeline without any complicated customizations for the legal document analysis. There are packages such as legal-NER that are already built on spaCy. We also have a text retrieval library based on spaCy and other Python libraries, which focuses on legal documents. We also have a spaCy language model on the Romanian legal domain trained with floret 4-gram to 5-gram embeddings and LEGAL entity recognition.

Common Challenges in Information Extraction Projects

When working on information extraction (IE) projects using spaCy, various challenges arise that can affect the accuracy, scalability, and adaptability of the models. The following is a detailed discussion of the key challenges:

Data Quality Issues

Data quality significantly impacts the performance of information extraction systems. Common data-related challenges include:

- **Noisy Data:** Text from scanned documents or poorly formatted sources often includes OCR errors, inconsistent formatting, or missing information.
- **Ambiguity in Language:** Many terms can have multiple meanings based on context, requiring careful preprocessing and linguistic analysis.

- **Incomplete Data:** Missing entities or references in the text can lead to partial or inaccurate extractions, especially in datasets without proper annotations.
- **Unstructured Text:** Many legal or business documents are written in free-flowing text, making it difficult to detect entities without additional pre-processing.
- **Lack of Annotation:** Creating labeled datasets for training custom models is time-consuming and labor-intensive, especially for domain-specific projects.

Mitigation Strategies

- Apply text cleaning techniques to preprocess data (for example, removing unnecessary characters, handling encoding issues).
- Use pre-trained models, and adapt them to specific domains through fine-tuning.
- Employ active learning to iteratively improve labeled datasets for more reliable results.

Domain-Specific Adaptations

spaCy's out-of-the-box models are trained on general-purpose datasets, which may not capture the nuances of specialized domains such as legal, medical, or financial texts. This creates challenges in accurately identifying and extracting entities.

- **Domain-Specific Language:** Technical jargon, abbreviations, and domain-specific syntax may not be recognized by general models.
- **Custom Entities:** Standard Named Entity Recognition (NER) models might not include domain-specific entities such as legal clauses, contractual obligations, or technical terminologies.
- **Complex Relationships:** Extracting hierarchical or nested relationships between entities often requires custom pipeline components or additional parsing.

Mitigation Strategies

- Train custom NER models using spaCy on annotated domain-specific datasets.
- Extend spaCy pipelines with rule-based matchers for specific patterns (for example, legal sections such as "*Section* 8" and "*Section* 280").
- Incorporate external knowledge bases or ontologies for enhanced context understanding.

Optimizing for Scale

When scaling up to handle large datasets or high-throughput applications, several challenges can emerge:

- **Performance Bottlenecks:** Processing large volumes of text in real time may lead to performance degradation or excessive resource consumption.
- **Parallel Processing:** spaCy's single-threaded pipelines can slow down when applied to large datasets unless optimized for multi-threading.
- **Model Size and Complexity:** Larger models, such as transformer-based pipelines (for example, **`en_core_web_trf`**), offer better accuracy but are computationally expensive.
- **Integration Challenges:** Deploying information extraction solutions in production requires seamless integration with the existing data pipelines or software systems.

Mitigation Strategies:

- Use batch processing with spaCy's **`nlp.pipe()`** for efficient handling of large datasets.
- Optimize hardware resources by leveraging GPU-based processing for transformer models.
- Profile and monitor pipeline performance to identify and address bottlenecks.
- Deploy scalable APIs or serverless solutions for production use cases.

Conclusion

This chapter is primarily a project-based chapter, where we briefly discussed the objectives of the chapter and the relevant prerequisites. For the projects, we extracted **events and dates** from the **BBC news dataset** (updated till December 2024). Moreover, we extracted sender and recipient email IDs, and the relevant information from the email body, such as **Person name, Organization name, location, dates, and events** from the whole email conversation from the **Enron email dataset**. Finally, we extracted information from a legal dataset such as **Parties, References, Sections, and Dates**. The dataset was utilized from the Hugging Face website. In the next chapter, we will understand the transformer architecture in detail, with BERT and GPT, and train as well as fine-tune the models using Hugging Face.

References

- https://www.kaggle.com/code/ekaterinabrepina/bbc-news-extract-locations-with-without-spacy#Solution-1:-using-SpaCy-for-entity-recognition
- https://www.qualicen.de/natural-language-processing-timeline-extraction-with-regexes-and-spacy/
- https://www.shiksha.com/online-courses/articles/extracting-information-from-text-data-using-spacy-in-nlp/
- https://towardsdatascience.com/extract-knowledge-from-text-end-to-end-information-extraction-pipeline-with-spacy-and-neo4j-502b2b1e0754
- https://medium.com/analytics-vidhya/introduction-to-information-extraction-using-python-and-spacy-858f5d6416ca
- https://www.kaggle.com/code/jamestollefson/enron-network-analysis
- https://www.kaggle.com/datasets/wcukierski/enron-email-dataset/data
- https://www.kaggle.com/code/pavansanagapati/knowledge-graph-nlp-tutorial-bert-spacy-nltk
- https://domino.ai/blog/natural-language-in-python-using-spacy
- https://programminghistorian.org/en/lessons/corpus-analysis-with-spacy
- https://thesai.org/Downloads/Volume14No3/Paper_89-Legal_Entity_Extraction_An_Experimental_Study.pdf
- https://thegrenze.com/pages/servej.php?fn=531_1.pdf&name=Legal%20Document%20Summarizer%20using%20Spacy%20and%20BART&id=2646&association=GRENZE&journal=GIJET&year=2024&volume=10&issue=2
- https://github.com/ahamadshaik/Information-Extraction-from-legal-documents-using-Spacy
- https://spacy.io/universe/project/rolegal
- https://github.com/Legal-NLP-EkStep/legal_NER
- https://huggingface.co/datasets/hugsid/legal-contracts/blob/main/train_data.csv

CHAPTER 8
Building a Transformer Using Hugging Face

Introduction

Transformer architectures have revolutionized the field of Natural Language Processing (NLP), enabling groundbreaking inventions such as language translation, text summarization, and conversational AI. Transformers that can process and understand language contextually have set new standards in terms of performance and versatility. Unlike traditional models that struggled with long-range dependencies, transformers leverage attention mechanisms to focus dynamically on relevant parts of the input, making them highly efficient and adaptable.

This chapter delves into the detailed architecture of transformers, moving beyond using pre-trained models to understanding the core principles that make them powerful. By exploring components such as self-attention and positional encoding, we aim to uncover how transformers process language effectively. Readers will gain insight into the architectures of popular models such as BERT and GPT, each tailored to specific NLP challenges.

Through hands-on examples using the Hugging Face library, this chapter provides a practical guide to training and fine-tuning transformer models for real-world applications across industries such as healthcare, e-commerce, IT, and fintech. We will also learn how to build custom transformer models from scratch, offering the flexibility to address niche tasks and domains. By the end, readers will be equipped with theoretical knowledge and practical skills to harness the full potential of transformers for diverse NLP applications.

Structure

In this chapter, the following topics will be covered:

- Introduction to Transformers
- Understanding Transformer Architecture
- Hugging Face Overview
- Working with Pre-Trained Models
- Training a Custom Transformer
- Case Studies

Introduction to Transformers

Transformers have revolutionized how robots interpret human language and have become the mainstay of contemporary NLP. Transformers provide a paradigm shift in the way that sequential data is handled. They were first presented in the 2017 publication **"Attention Is All You Need"** by Vaswani et al. With its fully parallelizable architecture, transformers are far more efficient and scalable than conventional models such as Recurrent Neural Networks (RNNs) and Long Short-Term Memory (LSTM) networks, which process sequences step-by-step.

The **self-attention** mechanism, a novel idea at the core of transformers, enables the model to assess the relative value of several words in a sequence. No matter how widely apart words are in a phrase, this approach allows transformers to capture intricate linguistic connections. The model can readily correlate "dog" with "barked" and "cat" with "scared," for example, in the sentence "The dog that barked loudly scared the cat," irrespective of their geographic distance.

The transformer architecture is built around a stack of **encoder and decoder layers**, each comprising **self-attention and feed-forward networks**. The encoder processes the input sequence and generates context-rich embeddings, while the decoder uses these embeddings to produce output sequences, making transformers highly versatile for understanding and generating language. **Positional encoding** is another key innovation, enabling transformers to retain information about the order of words in a sequence, a challenge for traditional feed-forward networks.

Transformers have proven their versatility across a wide range of NLP tasks, from machine translation and text summarization to question answering and sentiment analysis. Popular models such as BERT (Bidirectional Encoder Representations from Transformers) and GPT (Generative Pre-trained Transformer) have built upon the original transformer design to achieve state-of-the-art performance in numerous benchmarks. BERT excels at understanding the context in both directions (bidirectional), while GPT shines in generative tasks such as text completion and creative writing.

Beyond NLP, transformers have found applications in other domains such as vision (Vision Transformers or ViT) and reinforcement learning. Their ability to process large datasets and generalize effectively has made them the backbone of many AI systems in healthcare, e-commerce, IT, and fintech. For example, transformers can analyze patient records for predictive diagnosis, optimize product recommendations, or enhance fraud detection systems.

We will delve deeply into the foundations of transformer design in this chapter, breaking down elements such as feed-forward networks, positional encodings, multi-head attention, and self-attention. By expanding on these fundamental ideas, we hope to provide readers with the skills necessary to use transformer models that have already been trained, and even develop unique solutions that are suited to particular industry requirements.

With the tools provided by Hugging Face, one of the most comprehensive libraries for working with transformers, we will explore hands-on examples that translate theoretical understanding into practical implementation.

Understanding Transformer Architecture

Transformers rely on several foundational components—**word embeddings**, **positional encodings**, **self-attention**, and **residual connections**—to achieve state-of-the-art performance in Natural Language Processing. Let us delve into each of these concepts to understand their role and importance.

Word Embeddings: Dense vector representations of words or tokens in a high-dimensional space are called **word embeddings**. They help models comprehend linguistic context by capturing the syntactic and semantic links between words.

Role in Transformers: In transformers, raw text cannot be directly fed into the model. Instead, tokens (subwords, words, or characters) are mapped to embeddings through a learned embedding matrix during training.

- **Why embeddings?** Embeddings transform discrete tokens into continuous representations that are easier for neural networks to process. For example, the words "king" and "queen" will have embeddings that are semantically close in the vector space.

Implementation in Transformers

The embedding layer assigns each token a fixed-length vector. For instance, if a vocabulary size is 50,000 and the embedding dimension is 768, the embedding matrix will be of size 50,000×768.

- **Subword Tokenization**: Models such as BERT and GPT use subword tokenization (for example, WordPiece or Byte-Pair Encoding) to handle out-of-vocabulary words and improve efficiency.

Example

For the input sentence: "*Transformers are powerful models*," the embedding layer will map each token into a dense vector like this:

"Transformers"→ `[0.25, -0.15,...,0.78]`

Positional Encodings

Transformers lack an inherent sense of sequential order because they process tokens in parallel. Positional encodings inject information about the position of tokens in a sequence.

Transformers cannot see words sequentially since they process the tokens in parallel. Positional encodings help with the information about token positions in a sequence.

Mathematical Formulation

Positional encodings are added to word embeddings, using sinusoidal functions to represent positions in a sequence.

$$PE_{(pos,2i)}=\sin(pos/10000^{(2i/d)})$$

$$PE_{(pos,2i+1)}=\sin(pos/10000^{(2i/d)})$$

Here, pos is the position, i is the dimension index, and d is the embedding dimension.

Why Sinusoidal Functions?

- These functions allow the model to generalize to longer sequences, as the encodings can extrapolate positions beyond the training data.
- The combination of sine and cosine ensures that each position has a unique representation.

Visualization

Positional encodings create patterns, such as waves, that differ for each position. For example:

Example with Embedding Dimension = 4

Let us say our model uses an embedding dimension of 4 (**`d_model`** = 4).

We will calculate the positional encodings for two positions: pos=0 and pos=1

Step 1: Compute Positional Encoding for pos = 0

```
PE(0,0)=sin(0)=0(even index)
PE(0,1)=cos(0)=1(odd index)

PE(0,2)=sin(0)=0
PE(0,3)=cos(0)=1
```

So, **positional encoding for pos=0** = [0, 1, 0, 1]

Step 2: Compute Positional Encoding for pos = 1

We use the same formula but with pos = 1.

```
For i = 0:

PE(1,0) = sin(1/1000^(0/4)) = sin(1) ~~0.84
PE (1,1) = cos(1)~~0.540
For i=1:

PE(1,2) = sin(1/1000^(2/4)) = sin(1/100)~~0.009999

PE(1,3) = cos(1/100)~~0.99995
```

So, **positional encoding for pos=1** ≈ [0.841, 0.540, 0.01, 0.999]

Say the word "Transformer" at position 0 has an embedding:

```
[0.4, 0.6, 0.2, 0.1]
```

Then the **final input vector** passed to the model is:

```
[0.4+0, 0.6+1, 0.2+0, 0.1+1] = [0.4, 1.6, 0.2, 1.1]
```

So, when we say:

pos=0 might produce [0, 1, 0, 1],

pos=1 might produce [0.84, 0.54, 0.01, 0.999]

We are referring to **sinusoidal wave patterns** that encode the **position** and get **added to embeddings** to help the model understand sequence order.

These are added directly to the embeddings to provide both semantic and positional information to the model.

Self-Attention

Transformers can assess the relative value of each token in a sequence by using a mechanism called self-attention. It enables the model to concentrate on pertinent phrases, irrespective of their location.

How it Works

Each token in the sequence attends to every other token, including itself, by computing attention scores.

1. **Query (Q), Key (K), and Value (V) Vectors**:

   For each token, the model computes three vectors:

   - **Query**: Represents what this token is looking for.
   - **Key**: Represents what this token offers to others.
   - **Value**: Contains the information carried by the token.

Attention Scores:

Attention scores are computed as:

Attention(Q,K,V)=softmax)*V

- The softmax ensures that attention scores are probabilities.
- d_k (key vector dimension) is used for scaling to avoid large values.

Multi-Head Attention

Transformers use multiple attention heads to capture different types of relationships (for example, syntactic, semantic). Each head processes the input independently, and its outputs are concatenated.

Example:

"The doctor prescribed medicine to the patient.":

- **"doctor"** may attend strongly to **"prescribed"** to understand the action being performed.
- **"medicine"** may attend to **"patient"** to understand what is being given and to whom.

Residual Connections

Residual connections are shortcuts that allow the output of one layer to skip certain computations, and be added directly to the output of another layer.

Purpose

- **Improves Gradient Flow:** During backpropagation, residual connections mitigate the vanishing gradient problem by allowing gradients to flow more effectively through the network.

- **Stabilizes Training:** Ensures that the network retains some original information even after multiple transformations.
- **Accelerates Convergence:** Helps the model converge faster during training.

How It Works in Transformers

In both self-attention and feed-forward layers, residual connections are applied:

```
Layer Output=Layer Input+Transformation(Input)
```

The original input is added back to the transformed input before being passed to the next layer.

- This is typically followed by layer normalization to stabilize learning.

Summary

These components collectively make transformers a robust architecture:

- Word embeddings provide a semantic foundation for token representation.
- Positional encodings add critical sequential context.
- Self-attention allows the model to focus dynamically on the most relevant parts of the input.
- Residual connections ensure stable, efficient training, and prevent information loss.

Hugging Face Overview

Hugging Face has transformed the NLP landscape by making state-of-the-art transformer models accessible and easy to use. It provides an open-source **Transformers library**, a **Model Hub** with thousands of pre-trained models, and tools for fine-tuning models with minimal effort.

The **Transformers Library** supports PyTorch, TensorFlow, and JAX, enabling seamless experimentation with models such as **BERT, GPT, T5, and RoBERTa**. The **Model Hub** offers a vast collection of pre-trained models for various NLP tasks, reducing the need for training from scratch. Additionally, the **Datasets** and **Tokenizers** libraries simplify data handling and preprocessing.

Hugging Face's user-friendly **pipelines** allow quick implementation of tasks such as **text classification, named entity recognition, translation, and summarization**. Industries such as **healthcare, e-commerce, fintech, and IT** leverage Hugging Face for applications ranging from sentiment analysis to automated customer support.

With its strong community and efficient tools, Hugging Face democratizes NLP, making advanced AI accessible to researchers and developers. In the next sections, we will explore how to train, fine-tune, and build custom transformers using Hugging Face.

Working with Pre-Trained Models

Pre-trained transformer models have revolutionized NLP by enabling developers to leverage state-of-the-art architectures without training models from scratch. Hugging Face provides a vast collection of such models through its **Transformers Library**, allowing users to quickly apply them to real-world applications.

Why Use Pre-Trained Models?

Training transformers from scratch requires massive datasets, high computational power, and significant time. Pre-trained models, on the other hand, are trained on large corpora, and can be fine-tuned on domain-specific data, making them highly efficient for various NLP tasks.

Loading Pre-Trained Models

Hugging Face's **transformers** library makes it incredibly easy to load pre-trained models. You simply specify the desired architecture and variant (for example, **bert-base-uncased**, **roberta-large**, and so on), and the library handles downloading as well as initializing the model weights.

```
from transformers import BertTokenizer, BertModel

# Load pre-trained tokenizer and model
tokenizer = BertTokenizer.from_pretrained('bert-base-uncased')
model = BertModel.from_pretrained('bert-base-uncased')

print("Model loaded successfully!")

Model loaded successfully!
```

In this code snippet:

1. **BertTokenizer** converts the input text into tokens that the model understands.
2. **BertModel** loads the actual neural network architecture, along with its pre-trained weights.

Tokenizing Input Data

The text is converted into numerical representations before the transformer model is used. This is done using a tokenizer, which splits the text into subwords or tokens, and maps them to unique IDs.

```
sentence = "Humans have evolved a lot with time."

# Tokenize the sentence
tokens = tokenizer.tokenize(sentence)
print(tokens)

['humans', 'have', 'evolved', 'a', 'lot', 'with', 'time', '.']
```

Each word in the sentence is a token, and it is separated along with the '.', which is also a token. Once tokenized, the text is converted into input IDs and attention masks, which are required inputs for transformer models:

```
inputs = tokenizer(sentence, return_tensors='pt')  # Returns
PyTorch tensors
print(inputs)

{'input_ids': tensor([[ 101, 4286, 2031, 7964, 1037, 2843, 2007,
2051, 1012,  102]]), 'token_type_ids': tensor([[0, 0, 0, 0, 0, 0,
0, 0, 0, 0]]), 'attention_mask': tensor([[1, 1, 1, 1, 1, 1, 1, 1,
1, 1]])}
```

Fine-Tuning or Inference

After preparing the input data, we can either perform **inference** (using the model as-is) or **fine-tune** it for a specific task.

Performing Inference

If we want to extract embeddings or analyze the model's behavior without modifying it, we can directly pass the tokenized inputs through the model:

```
outputs = model(**inputs)
last_hidden_states = outputs.last_hidden_state
print(last_hidden_states.shape)

torch.Size([1, 9, 768])
```

Here, 1 is the **`batch_size`**, 9 is the sequence length, and 768 is the hidden size. In the hidden states, there are contextualized embeddings for each token in the input sequence. These embeddings can then be used for tasks such as clustering, similarity analysis, or visualization.

Fine-Tuning for Specific Tasks

To adapt a pre-trained model to a new task, we need to add a custom head (for example, a classification layer) on top of the base model and train the entire system end-to-end. The code is as follows.

```
from transformers import BertForSequenceClassification

# Load a pre-trained model with a classification head
model = BertForSequenceClassification.from_pre-
trained('bert-base-uncased', num_labels=2)

# Define optimizer and loss function
optimizer = torch.optim.AdamW(model.parameters(), lr=5e-5)
loss_fn = torch.nn.CrossEntropyLoss()

# Example training loop (simplified)
for epoch in range(epochs):
    model.train()
    optimizer.zero_grad()
    outputs = model(**inputs, labels=labels)
    loss = outputs.loss
    loss.backward()
    optimizer.step()
```

```
Epoch 1, Loss: 0.8110669255256653
Epoch 2, Loss: 0.5848608016967773
Epoch 3, Loss: 0.43619900941848755
```

During fine-tuning, only a small amount of labeled data is usually needed to achieve strong performance because the model has already learned general linguistic patterns.

Choosing the Right Model

Hugging Face hosts hundreds of pre-trained models tailored for different purposes. Some popular options include:

- **BERT**: Bidirectional Encoder Representations from Transformers, ideal for tasks requiring deep context understanding.
- **GPT**: Generative Pre-trained Transformer, suitable for text generation and completion.
- **RoBERTa**: A robustly optimized version of BERT with improved performance.
- **DistilBERT**: A lighter, faster variant of BERT with comparable accuracy.

Training a Custom Transformer

Training a custom transformer model from scratch is a powerful way to tailor a model specifically to a dataset and task. While leveraging pre-trained models is often the preferred approach due to their efficiency and performance, there are scenarios where training a transformer from scratch becomes necessary or advantageous. For example:

- The dataset contains highly specialized language or domain-specific terminology not covered by general-purpose pre-trained models.
- We can experiment with novel architectures or modifications to the existing transformer designs.
- There are privacy concerns that prevent us from using publicly available pre-trained models.

In this section, we will explore how to train a custom transformer model using Hugging Face's **transformers** library, covering everything from defining the architecture to implementing the training loop.

Why Train a Custom Transformer?

While pre-trained models are versatile, they may not always align perfectly with the specific use case. Training a custom transformer allows you to:

- **Control the Architecture**: Customize the number of layers, attention heads, hidden dimensions, and other hyperparameters.
- **Optimize for Specific Data**: Fine-tune the model directly on your dataset without relying on transfer learning.
- **Experiment with Novel Ideas**: Test new ideas in transformer design such as sparse attention mechanisms or hybrid architectures.

However, training a transformer from scratch requires significant computational resources and a large, high-quality dataset. It is essential to weigh these factors before proceeding.

Step 1: Defining the Model Architecture

Hugging Face has tools to define custom transformer architectures easily. We can either build a model from scratch using PyTorch or TensorFlow or extend one of the existing classes provided by the library.

Here is an example of defining a simple transformer-based model using Hugging Face's `PreTrainedModel` class:

```
import torch
import torch.nn as nn
from transformers import PreTrainedModel, PretrainedConfig

class CustomTransformerConfig(PretrainedConfig):
    def __init__(self, vocab_size=30522, hidden_size=768, num_
hidden_layers=12,
```

```
num_attention_heads=12, intermediate_size=3072, max_position_
embeddings=512, **kwargs):
        super().__init__(**kwargs)
        self.vocab_size = vocab_size
        self.hidden_size = hidden_size
        self.num_hidden_layers = num_hidden_layers
        self.num_attention_heads = num_attention_heads
        self.intermediate_size = intermediate_size
        self.max_position_embeddings = max_position_embeddings

class CustomTransformer(PreTrainedModel):
    config_class = CustomTransformerConfig

    def __init__(self, config):
        super().__init__(config)
        self.embedding = nn.Embedding(config.vocab_size, config.
hidden_size)
        self.positional_encoding = nn.Parameter(torch.zeros(1,
config.max_position_embeddings, config.hidden_size))
        decoder_layer = nn.TransformerDecoderLayer(
            d_model=config.hidden_size,
            nhead=config.num_attention_heads,
            dim_feedforward=config.intermediate_size,
            batch_first=True
        )
        self.transformer_decoder = nn.TransformerDecoder
(decoder_layer, num_layers=config.num_hidden_layers)
        self.classifier = nn.Linear(config.hidden_size,
config.vocab_size)

    def forward(self, input_ids, attention_mask=None):
        # Embedding + Positional Encoding
        embeddings = self.embedding(input_ids) + self.positional
_encoding[:, :input_ids.size(1), :]

        # Create causal mask for autoregressive decoding
        seq_len = input_ids.size(1)
        causal_mask = torch.triu(torch.ones(seq_len, seq_len) *
float('-inf'), diagonal=1).to(input_ids.device)

        # Pass through the transformer decoder
        transformer_output = self.transformer_decoder
(tgt=embeddings, memory=embeddings, tgt_mask=causal_mask)

        # Classification head
        logits = self.classifier(transformer_output)
        return logits
```

Explanation of the above code:

Class `CustomTransformerConfig`:

Purpose:

- This class defines the **configuration** of the custom transformer model. It specifies hyperparameters such as vocabulary size, hidden dimensions, number of layers, attention heads, and so on.
- The configuration object is used to initialize the model, and ensure that all components are consistent with the desired architecture.

Key Parameters:

- **`vocab_size`**: The size of the vocabulary (number of unique tokens).
- **`hidden_size`**: The dimensionality of the embeddings and hidden states in the transformer.
- **`num_hidden_layers`**: The number of transformer layers (or blocks) in the model.
- **`num_attention_heads`**: The number of attention heads in each transformer layer.
- **`intermediate_size`**: The size of the feed-forward network inside each transformer layer.
- **`max_position_embeddings`**: The maximum length of input sequences supported by the model.

Why Use `PretrainedConfig`?

- By inheriting from **`PretrainedConfig`**, this class integrates seamlessly with Hugging Face's ecosystem. For example, we can save and load configurations using Hugging Face utilities.

Class CustomTransformer:

Purpose:

- This class defines the actual transformer model. It inherits from **`PreTrainedModel`**, which provides additional functionality such as saving/loading weights and integrating with Hugging Face pipelines.

Components:

- **Embedding Layer (self.embedding) :**
  - Converts token IDs (integers) into dense vectors of fixed size (**`hidden_size`**).
  - Example: If **`vocab_size=10000`** and **`hidden_size=768`**, the embedding layer maps each token ID (for example, **42**) to a 768-dimensional vector.

- **Positional Encoding (`self.positional_encoding`)** :
  - Transformers do not inherently understand the order of tokens. Positional encoding adds positional information to the embeddings.
  - Here, we use a learnable parameter (**`nn.Parameter`**) instead of a fixed sinusoidal encoding (as in the original Transformer paper).
- **Transformer Decoder (`self.transformer_decoder`)** :
  - A stack of **`nn.TransformerDecoderLayer`** instances form the core of the model.
  - Each layer consists of:
    - **Multi-head Self-Attention**: Captures relationships between tokens.
    - **Feed-Forward Network**: Processes each token independently.
  - The **`batch_first=True`** argument ensures that inputs have the shape (**`batch_size, sequence_length, hidden_size`**).
- **Classification Head (`self.classifier`)** :
  - A linear layer maps the transformer's output back to the vocabulary space.
  - This produces logits (unnormalized scores) for each token in the vocabulary.

Why Use nn.TransformerDecoder?

- The **`nn.TransformerDecoder`** is designed for autoregressive tasks where the model predicts one token at a time. By passing the same tensor as both **`tgt`** (target) and **memory** (source), we simulate a decoder-only architecture.

Forward Method

Step-by-Step Breakdown:

1. **Embedding + Positional Encoding**: The input token IDs (**`input_ids`**) are passed through the embedding layer to produce dense representations.

   Positional encodings are added to these embeddings to provide sequence information.

2. **Causal Masking**: Causal masking is a technique used in autoregressive models such as GPT to ensure the model only attends to current and past tokens during training. Since these models generate text one word at a time, they must not "*peek*" into the future – meaning a word at position 3 should not have access to information from position 4 or beyond. To enforce this, a causal mask is applied over the attention mechanism. This mask is a square matrix where

each row corresponds to a token, and shows which positions it is allowed to attend to.

3. **Transformer Decoder**: The **transformer_decoder** processes the embeddings using multi-head self-attention and feed-forward layers.

   The **tgt_mask** ensures that each token only attends to previous tokens.

4. **Classification Head**: The final output of the transformer is passed through a linear layer to produce logits for each token in the vocabulary.

These logits represent the model's predictions for the next token in the sequence.

Preparing the Dataset

To train a transformer, we need a large corpus of text data. This dataset should be representative of the language or domain we are targeting. We have taken an article from the BBC News website. Common sources include books, articles, social media posts, or specialized corpora.

```
#Preparing the Dataset
with open('/kaggle/input/data123/data.txt', 'r',
encoding='utf-8') as f:
    lines = f.readlines()

# Clean and tokenize the data
dataset = [line.strip() for line in lines if line.strip()]
print(f"Loaded {len(dataset)} sentences.")

Loaded 6 sentences.
```

Tokenization

Tokenization converts raw text into numerical representations that the model can process. You can create a custom tokenizer or use Hugging Face's **Tokenizer** utilities.

```
#Tokenization

from transformers import BertTokenizer

# Train a tokenizer on your dataset
tokenizer = BertTokenizer.from_pretrained('bert-base-uncased')
tokenizer.add_tokens(['<NEW_TOKEN>'])  # Add custom tokens if
needed
```

```
# Tokenize the dataset
tokenized_data = [tokenizer.encode(sentence, max_length=512,
truncation=True, padding='max_length') for sentence in dataset]
```

Setting Up the Training Loop

Once the data is tokenized, you can set up the training loop. This involves defining a loss function, optimizer, and iterating over batches of data.

```
#Setting Up the Training Loop
from torch.utils.data import DataLoader, TensorDataset
import torch.optim as optim

# Convert tokenized data to tensors
input_ids = torch.tensor(tokenized_data)
labels = torch.tensor([sentence[1:] + [tokenizer.pad_token_id]
for sentence in tokenized_data])  # Shifted labels

# Create DataLoader
dataset = TensorDataset(input_ids, labels)
dataloader = DataLoader(dataset, batch_size=16, shuffle=True)

# Initialize model, optimizer, and loss function
model = CustomTransformer(CustomTransformerConfig())
optimizer = optim.AdamW(model.parameters(), lr=5e-5)
loss_fn = nn.CrossEntropyLoss(ignore_index=tokenizer.pad_token_
id)

# Move model to GPU if available
device = torch.device('cuda' if torch.cuda.is_available() else
'cpu')
model.to(device)

# Training loop
for epoch in range(3):  # Number of epochs
    model.train()
    total_loss = 0
    for batch_input_ids, batch_labels in dataloader:
        batch_input_ids, batch_labels = batch_input_ids.to(de-
vice), batch_labels.to(device)

        optimizer.zero_grad()
        outputs = model(batch_input_ids)
        loss = loss_fn(outputs.view(-1, outputs.size(-1)), batch_
labels.view(-1))
        loss.backward()
        optimizer.step()
```

```
        total_loss += loss.item()

    print(f"Epoch {epoch + 1}, Loss: {total_loss / len
(dataloader)}")

Epoch 1, Loss: 10.59989070892334
Epoch 2, Loss: 9.957139015197754
Epoch 3, Loss: 9.50660514831543
```

To explain the above code:

Importing Required Libraries

- **DataLoader**: A utility from PyTorch that helps batch and shuffle the dataset efficiently.
- **TensorDataset**: A simple dataset wrapper that combines input tensors into a single dataset object.
- **optim**: Provides optimization algorithms such as AdamW, which is commonly used for training transformer models.

Converting Tokenized Data to Tensors

- **`input_ids`** :
  - Converts the tokenized data (**`tokenized_data`**) into a PyTorch tensor. Each element in **`input_ids`** represents a sequence of token IDs.
- **labels** :
  - The labels are shifted by one position relative to the input. For example:
    - If the input sequence is **[A, B, C, D]**, the corresponding label sequence becomes **[B, C, D, PAD]**.
    - This shift ensures that the model predicts the next token in the sequence during training.
  - Padding tokens (**`tokenizer.pad_token_id`**) are added at the end of each sequence to maintain consistent lengths.

Create DataLoader

Explanation:

- **TensorDataset** : Each **item** retrieved from this dataset is a **tuple of elements**, one from each of the input tensors, all at the **same index**.

The TensorDataset helps package the two tensors – **`input_id`**s and labels – into a single object that is fed into a DataLoader for batching and shuffling during training.

DataLoader

It works seamlessly with datasets such as TensorDataset, allowing for automatic batching, optional shuffling, and parallel data loading using multiple workers. Instead of manually looping through data, the DataLoader yields one batch at a time, making the training process faster and more memory efficient. This batching is necessary for training neural networks, as it allows the model to update weights using gradients computed over multiple samples at once.

`batch_size=16`: Specifies that the data will be processed in batches of 16 samples at a time.

`shuffle=True`: Randomizes the order of the data in each epoch to improve generalization.

Initialize model, optimizer, and loss function

- **Model Initialization:**
  - **`CustomTransformer(CustomTransformerConfig())`**: Creates an instance of the custom transformer model using the specified configuration.
- **Optimizer :**
  - **`AdamW`**: A variant of the Adam optimizer that includes weight decay regularization, which is particularly effective for transformer models.
  - **`lr=5e-5`**: Sets the learning rate to 0.00005, a common choice for fine-tuning or training transformer models.
- **Loss Function :**
  - **`CrossEntropyLoss`**: Computes the loss between the predicted logits and the true labels.
  - **`ignore_index=tokenizer.pad_token_id`**: Ensures that padding tokens do not contribute to the loss calculation. This prevents the model from being penalized for incorrect predictions on padded positions.

Move Model to GPU if Available

- **`torch.device`**: Checks if a GPU is available (cuda) and uses it; otherwise, it defaults to the CPU.
- **`model.to(device)`**: Moves the model's parameters and buffers to the specified device (GPU or CPU). This ensures that all computations are performed on the appropriate hardware.

Training Loop

- **Outer Loop (Epochs):**
  - The outer loop runs for a fixed number of epochs (in this case, 3). Each epoch processes the entire dataset once.
- **Setting the Model to Training Mode:**
  - `model.train()`: Switches the model to the training mode. This affects layers such as dropout and batch normalization, ensuring that they behave appropriately during training.
- **Inner Loop (Batch Processing):**
  - Iterates over the **dataloader**, which yields batches of `batch_input_ids` and `batch_labels`.
- **Moving Data to the Device:**
  - `batch_input_ids.to(device)` and `batch_labels.to(device)`: Ensures that inputs and labels are on the same device as the model (GPU or CPU).
- **Zeroing Gradients:**
  - `optimizer.zero_grad()`: Clears the gradients from the previous iteration. This is necessary because PyTorch accumulates gradients by default.
- **Forward Pass:**
  - `outputs = model(batch_input_ids)`: Passes the input batch through the model to compute predictions (**outputs**).
- **Computing Loss:**
  - `loss_fn(outputs.view(-1, outputs.size(-1)), batch_labels.view(-1))`:
    - `outputs.view(-1, outputs.size(-1))` : Reshapes the output tensor to `(batch_size * sequence_length, vocab_size)`. This flattens the predictions for all tokens across the batch.
    - `batch_labels.view(-1)` : Flattens the labels tensor to `(batch_size * sequence_length)`.
    - The loss function computes the cross-entropy between the flattened predictions and labels.
- **Backward Pass:**
  - `loss.backward()`: Computes the gradients of the loss with respect to the model's parameters.

- **Updating Parameters**:
  - `optimizer.step()`: Updates the model's parameters using the computed gradients.
- **Tracking Loss:**
  - `total_loss += loss.item()`: Accumulates the loss for the current epoch.
- **Printing Progress:**
  - After each epoch, the average loss is printed. This provides insight into how the model is learning over time.

```
# Save the model and tokenizer
model.save_pretrained('./custom_transformer')
tokenizer.save_pretrained('./custom_transformer')

('./custom_transformer/tokenizer_config.json',
 './custom_transformer/special_tokens_map.json',
 './custom_transformer/vocab.txt',
 './custom_transformer/added_tokens.json')
```

The above code saves the **fine-tuned transformer model** and its corresponding **tokenizer** to a local directory named custom_transformer.

The explanation is as follows:

- **model.save_pretrained(`'./custom_transformer'`)**
  - **What it does:** Saves the trained transformer model's weights, architecture configuration, and other necessary files to the directory **`custom_transformer`**.
  - **Why it is needed:** This allows the model to be reloaded later for inference or further fine-tuning without retraining from scratch.
- **`tokenizer.save_pretrained('./custom_transformer')`**
  - **What it does:** Saves the tokenizer, which converts text into numerical inputs for the model.
  - **Why it is needed:** The same tokenizer must be used for preprocessing text when reloading the model for inference.
  - What gets saved:
    - **`tokenizer_config.json,`**
    - **`special_tokens_map.json,`**
    - **`vocab.txt,`**
    - **`added_tokens.json`**

Case Studies

Transformers have revolutionized NLP by enabling powerful language models that excel at tasks such as **text classification, question answering, summarization, and language translation**. This section will explore real-world case studies across **healthcare, e-commerce, and fintech**, demonstrating how Hugging Face's transformer models can be fine-tuned and deployed to solve domain-specific challenges.

Healthcare: Medical Text Summarization for Patient Records

In this problem statement, we use 5 different text summarization models to summarize texts. We will see 5 results.

Problem Statement: Doctors and healthcare professionals deal with a vast amount of unstructured clinical data, such as **patient history, prescriptions, and test reports**. Manually summarizing this data is time-consuming and prone to errors. A transformer-based model can **automate medical text summarization**, ensuring key patient details are easily accessible.

Solution Using Hugging Face: We are using "**t5-small**", "**t5-base**", "**t5-large**", "**google/flan-t5-large**", and "**google/flan-t5-xl**" **models** that can be fine-tuned on medical datasets to summarize patient records, while preserving critical details.

The following script performs **medical text summarization** using different **T5 models**, including standard **T5 variants** and **FLAN-T5** models. It systematically evaluates each model's performance in summarizing a given medical text.

```
from transformers import T5Tokenizer, T5ForConditionalGeneration

# List of models to test
models = [
    "t5-small",
    "t5-base",
    "t5-large",
    "google/flan-t5-large",
    "google/flan-t5-xl"
]

# Example medical text to summarize
input_text = "Medical summary: Patient diagnosed with
hypertension. Prescribed amlodipine. Follow-up in 2 weeks."

# Store results
summaries = {}
```

```
for model_name in models:
    try:
        # Load tokenizer and model
        tokenizer = T5Tokenizer.from_pretrained(model_name)
        model = T5ForConditionalGeneration.from_pretrained
(model_name)

        # Tokenize input
        input_ids = tokenizer(input_text, return_tensors="pt").
input_ids

        summary_ids = model.generate(
            input_ids,
            max_length=30,  #  output length for more concise
summaries
            num_beams=7,  # Number of beam search candidates
            temperature=0.7,  # Reduce randomness
            top_k=50,  # Increase diversity
            top_p=0.9,  # Encourage more varied outputs
            repetition_penalty=2.0,  # Stronger penalty to avoid
repetition
            early_stopping=True  # Stop when an optimal summary
is found
        )

        # Decode output
        summary = tokenizer.decode(summary_ids[0], skip_special_
tokens=True)
        summaries[model_name] = summary

    except Exception as e:
        summaries[model_name] = f"Error: {str(e)}"

summaries


Output:
{'t5-small': 'Summary Medical summary: Patient diagnosed with
hypertension. Prescribed amlodipine. Follow-up in 2 weeks.',
 't5-base': 'Amlodipine. Follow-up in 2 weeks.',
 't5-large': 'diagnosed with hypertension. Prescribed amlodipine.
Follow-up in 2 weeks. Medical summary: Patient diagnosed with
hypertension',
 'google/flan-t5-large': 'Patient diagnosed with hypertension.
Prescribed amlodipine.',
```

```
 'google/flan-t5-xl': 'Amlodipine is prescribed to a patient with hypertension.'}
```

Step 1: Import Required Libraries

The code explanation is as follows:

- **T5Tokenizer**: Converts text into a tokenized format suitable for the T5 model.
- **T5ForConditionalGeneration**: Loads a pre-trained **T5** model for text generation (that is, summarization).

Step 2: Define Models to Test

A **list of different T5 models** is defined, including:

- **t5-small, t5-base, t5-large**: Standard T5 models trained on multiple NLP tasks.
- **google/flan-t5-large, google/flan-t5-xl**: Fine-tuned versions of T5 with **instruction tuning** from Google.

This allows comparison between different sizes and architectures.

Step 3: Define the Input Text

input_text = "Medical summary: Patient diagnosed with hypertension. Prescribed amlodipine. Follow-up in 2 weeks."

This is the **medical text that needs summarization**.

The prefix "*Medical summary:*" is added because **T5 models perform better with explicit task prompts**.

Step 4: Loop Through Each Model

The script iterates through the list of models **one by one**, loading each model to summarize the input text.

A **try-except block** is used to **handle any errors** that may occur while loading or running the model.

Step 5: Load Tokenizer and Model

The tokenizer and model for the **current model_name** are loaded.

from_pretrained(model_name): Downloads the model if it is not available locally.

Step 6: Convert Text to Tokenized Input

The input text is tokenized into **input IDs** (numerical representation of words).

`return_tensors="pt"` - Converts the tokens into a **PyTorch tensor**, which is required for model inference.

Step 7: Parameter Explanation:

Parameter	Purpose
`max_length=30`	Ensures the summary is concise and within 30 tokens.
`num_beams=7`	Uses **beam search** to generate the best possible summary by keeping **7 alternative sequences**.
`temperature=0.7`	Lowers randomness to make the model more **deterministic and structured**.
`top_k=50`	**Restricts sampling to the top 50 words**, increasing coherence.
`top_p=0.9`	**Nucleus sampling**–selects words dynamically based on cumulative probability.
`repetition_penalty=2.0`	Avoids repetitive phrases (important for text summarization).
`early_stopping=True`	Stops the model from generating unnecessary tokens.

***Table 8.1**: Parameters and their uses*

These settings **balance quality and diversity** for better summarization.

Step 8: Decode the Generated Summary

The generated summary (in token format) is **converted back into text.**

`skip_special_tokens=True`: Removes unnecessary tokens such as <pad> and <eos>.

The result is stored in the summaries dictionary with the model name as the key.

Step 9: Handle Errors

If an error occurs (for example, model not available, memory issue), it is stored in the dictionary.

Step 10: Finally, the output is in the form of a dictionary

The script **returns the dictionary** containing summaries generated by each model.

From all the models, the `"google/flan-t5-xl"` gives the output "*Amlodipine is prescribed to a patient with hypertension.*" That is the best-summarized version over the other models. However, we do not get any information on the timeline summarization, that is, 2 weeks.

E-Commerce: Personalized Product Recommendations

E-commerce platforms need **personalized recommendations** to enhance customer experience. Traditional collaborative filtering models struggle with **cold-start problems**, and fail to capture deep textual patterns in **product descriptions and user reviews**.

Solution Using Hugging Face

A **BERT-based recommendation model** can analyze product descriptions and customer reviews to suggest relevant products.

Implementation Steps:

1. **Train a BERT-based model** on product descriptions and customer purchase data.
2. **Fine-tune the model** for similarity detection between products and user preferences.
3. **Deploy the model** to generate real-time product recommendations.

The code is as follows:

```
from transformers import AutoTokenizer, AutoModel
from torch.nn.functional import cosine_similarity

# Load pre-trained BERT model
model_name = "bert-base-uncased"
tokenizer = AutoTokenizer.from_pretrained(model_name)
model = AutoModel.from_pretrained(model_name)
# Encode product descriptions
product_1 = tokenizer("Wireless Bluetooth Headphones with Noise
Cancellation", return_tensors="pt")
product_2 = tokenizer("Bluetooth Earbuds with Active Noise
Cancelling", return_tensors="pt")

# Compute similarity score
embedding_1 = model(**product_1).last_hidden_state.mean(dim=1)
embedding_2 = model(**product_2).last_hidden_state.mean(dim=1)

similarity_score = cosine_similarity(embedding_1, embedding_2).
item()
print("Cosine Similarity Score:", similarity_score)Output:
Cosine Similarity Score: 0.9022848606109619
```

The code explanation is as follows.

Step 1: Import Required Libraries

- `AutoTokenizer`: Loads the tokenizer for BERT, which converts text into tokenized input for the model.
- `AutoModel`: Loads the **pre-trained BERT model** to generate embeddings.
- `cosine_similarity`: Loads the **`cosine_similarity` function** from PyTorch's torch.nn.functional module.

Purpose: It computes the cosine similarity between two tensors (vectors).

Why Use `cosine_similarity`?

- It measures how similar two embeddings are based on the cosine of the angle between them.
- Cosine similarity is **bounded between -1 and 1**:
    - **+1** → Identical vectors
    - **0** → No similarity (orthogonal)
    - **-1** → Opposite vectors
- Unlike Euclidean distance, cosine similarity focuses on the **direction** rather than the magnitude.

Step 2: Load Pre-Trained BERT Model

- `bert-base-uncased` is a **smaller** BERT model trained on lowercase English text.
- `AutoTokenizer.from_pretrained(model_name)` loads a tokenizer specific to this model.
- `AutoModel.from_pretrained(model_name)` loads the actual BERT model.

What Happens Here?

- This downloads **BERT parameters** if not already available.
- The model will be used to **generate embeddings for product descriptions.**

Step 3: Tokenize Product Descriptions

```
product_1 = tokenizer("Wireless Bluetooth Headphones with Noise
Cancellation", return_tensors="pt")
product_2 = tokenizer("Bluetooth Earbuds with Active Noise
Cancelling", return_tensors="pt")
```

- **Tokenizes each product description** into a numerical format.
- `return_tensors="pt"` → Returns a **PyTorch tensor** so it can be used with the BERT model.

What Happens Here?

For **`product_1`**, BERT converts:

"Wireless Bluetooth Headphones with Noise Cancellation"

into tokenized form:

```
{
  'input_ids': tensor([[101, 4913, 24352, 1048, 13607, 2475,
2007, 4606, 8210, 24759, 102]]),
  'attention_mask': tensor([[1, 1, 1, 1, 1, 1, 1, 1, 1, 1, 1]])
}
```

where:

- **`input_ids`** - Unique token IDs for words in the sentence.
- **`attention_mask`** - Indicates which tokens should be attended to (**`1 = real token, 0 = padding`**).

The same happens for **`product_2.`**

Step 4: Compute Sentence Embeddings

- **Feeds tokenized inputs into BERT** to generate embeddings.
- **`model(**product_1).last_hidden_state`**: Returns **hidden states** for each token.
- **`.mean(dim=1)`** - Takes the **average of all token embeddings** to get a single **sentence embedding**.

What Happens Here?

- BERT processes input and outputs a tensor of shape **`(batch_size, sequence_length, hidden_size)`**.
- The **hidden size for bert-base-uncased is 768**, meaning each token gets a **768-dimensional vector**.
- Taking the **mean overall token vectors** results in a **single 768-dimensional vector** representing the entire sentence.

Step 5: Compute Similarity Score

- Computes the **dot product** between **two sentence embeddings**.
  - **`cosine_similarity(embedding_1, embedding_2)`**

    Computes the cosine similarity between the two tensors.
  - **`.item()`**

    Converts the tensor result into a Python float for easy printing and further processing.

Why Cosine Similarity Instead of Dot Product?

- **Dot Product:** Measures magnitude + direction
- **Cosine Similarity:** Only measures direction (more suitable for text similarity)

The output is **0.9022** that indicates a **very high similarity** between the two product descriptions. A score of **0.90** means the embeddings are nearly identical, which makes sense because:

"Wireless Bluetooth Headphones with Noise Cancellation"

"Bluetooth Earbuds with Active Noise Cancelling"

Both mention **Bluetooth**, **noise cancellation**, and **audio devices**, leading BERT to perceive them as highly related.

What does this mean?

If we are **matching product descriptions**, this is a great approach!

A threshold of **0.8+** could indicate strong similarity for product recommendation systems.

Results

- Increased conversion rates due to better product matching.
- Improved recommendation quality by using context-aware embeddings, instead of just collaborative filtering.
- Enabled personalized user experiences, boosting revenue.

Fintech: Fraud Detection in Credit Card Transactions

Banks and financial institutions need real-time fraud detection for credit card transactions. Traditional rule-based methods fail to detect complex fraudulent patterns.

Solution Using Hugging Face

A RoBERTa-based fraud detection model can analyze transaction descriptions and metadata to flag suspicious transactions.

Implementation Steps:

1. Collect the transaction data with labeled fraud cases.
2. Fine-tune RoBERTa to classify transactions as fraudulent or legitimate.
3. Deploy the model to flag suspicious transactions in real time.

The code is as follows:

```
from transformers import RobertaTokenizer, RobertaForSequence-
Classification

# Use a pre-trained classification model
model_name = "cardiffnlp/twitter-roberta-base-sentiment"
tokenizer = RobertaTokenizer.from_pretrained(model_name)
model = RobertaForSequenceClassification.from_pretrained
(model_name)

# Example transaction description
transaction = "Multiple high-value purchases from various other
overseas locations in the last hour."
inputs = tokenizer(transaction, return_tensors="pt")

# Predict fraud probability
outputs = model(**inputs)
fraud_prob = outputs.logits.softmax(dim=1)[0, 1].item()

print("Fraud Probability:", fraud_prob)

Output:
Fraud Probability: 0.8868260383605957
```

Step 1: Import Required Libraries

- **`RobertaTokenizer`**: Tokenizes input text into a numerical format for the model.
- **`RobertaForSequenceClassification`**: Loads a pre-trained **RoBERTa model** designed for classification tasks (for example, fraud detection or sentiment analysis).

Step 2: Load Pre-Trained Model

- **Model Used: "`cardiffnlp/twitter-roberta-base-sentiment`"**
    - This is a **sentiment classification model** trained on Twitter data.
    - It classifies text into **positive, negative, or neutral** sentiment.
    - In this case, we **repurpose** it for **fraud probability estimation**.

What happens here?

- **`tokenizer.from_pretrained(model_name)`**: Loads the pre-trained tokenizer for RoBERTa.
- **`model.from_pretrained(model_name)`**: Loads the pre-trained model **with classification layers**.

Step 3: Tokenize the Transaction Description

- **The transaction description is tokenized** into a numerical format using tokenizer().
- `return_tensors="pt"` : Returns output as a **PyTorch tensor**, needed for model inference.

Step 4: Model Inference (Fraud Probability Prediction)

- This **passes the tokenized input into the RoBERTa model** to get predictions.
- **The output is a tensor of logits** (raw scores before applying softmax).

Step 5: Convert Logits to Fraud Probability

- `outputs.logits`: Raw prediction scores for each class (for example, fraudulent versus non-fraudulent).
- `softmax(dim=1)` : Converts logits into probabilities.
- `[0, 1]` : Extracts the **probability of the "`fraud`" class**.
- `.item()` : Converts PyTorch tensor to a Python float.

Finally, we get the Fraud probability for the text provided ("*Multiple high-value purchases from various other overseas locations in the last hour.*")

The Fraud Probability is 0.8868, which means that the **model predicts an 88.68% probability that the given transaction is fraudulent**.

Why Does It Output This Value?

- **Model Prediction (`outputs.logits`)**
  - o The RoBERTa model generates **raw logits** for different classes (for example, fraud versus non-fraud).
  - o Since we are using a **sentiment classification model**, it is likely mapping **fraud to negative sentiment**.
- **Softmax Activation (`softmax(dim=1)`)**
  - o Converts the logits into probabilities **so they sum to 1**.
  - o The second value ([0,1]) represents the probability of the "`fraud`" (or negative sentiment) class.
- **Final Value (`.item()`)**
  - o Extracts the probability of the fraud class as a **single float value**.

Interpretation

- **88.68% fraud probability** suggests the transaction is **highly suspicious**.

- This is because the model detects **keywords** such as:
  - *"Multiple high-value purchases"*
  - *"Overseas locations"*
  - *"Last hour"* (indicating a rapid transaction pattern)

These **trigger a strong classification** toward fraud.

Conclusion

This marks the end of the chapter on Building Transformers using Hugging Face. This chapter covered transformers' introduction, their whole architecture, the usage of Hugging Face, working with pre-trained models and fine-tuning them, training a custom transformer, and finally, use cases on the health care sector, Fintech, and e-commerce domains.

In the next chapter, we will learn how to train language models. We will decode the process of training a basic language model from scratch, giving us insight into how these models learn to predict and generate text. We will also learn how to leverage pre-trained models such as BERT or DistilBERT to extract answers from documents.

References

- https://arxiv.org/pdf/1706.03762 (Attention Is All You Need)
- https://huggingface.co/learn/nlp-course/en/chapter1/1?fw=pt
- https://towardsdatascience.com/wordpiece-subword-based-tokenization-algorithm-1fbd14394ed7
- https://www.geeksforgeeks.org/byte-pair-encoding-bpe-in-nlp/
- https://www.youtube.com/watch?v=eMlx5fFNoYc
- https://www.datacamp.com/tutorial/an-introduction-to-using-transformers-and-hugging-face
- https://cdrdv2-public.intel.com/792871/hugging-face-case-study-112023.pdf
- https://huggingface.co/learn/nlp-course/en/chapter1/4
- https://www.datacamp.com/code-along/building-nlp-applications-hugging-face
- https://jalammar.github.io/illustrated-transformer/

CHAPTER 9
Training Language Models

Introduction

Natural Language Processing (NLP) has been transformed by language models that have helped create and enhance chatbots, search engines, and text production. These algorithms can produce coherent text, and derive significant insights by learning word relationships, patterns, and context. A lot of text must be fed into it to train a language model to anticipate words, sentences, or structured answers. Although NLP has greatly advanced thanks to pre-trained models such as BERT and GPT, performance for domain-specific applications can be enhanced by fine-tuning or training a custom model.

In this chapter, we will train language models from scratch, and fine-tune pre-trained models for specialized tasks. Firstly, we will train a language model on news articles or poetry to generate texts in that style. Next, we will build a question-answering system that extracts answers from a specific document, utilizing the potential of Hugging Face's powerful transformer models.

By the end of this chapter, we will be able to grasp the concepts and do hands-on experiments of training language models, from dataset preparation to model evaluation. We will fine-tune the state-of-the-art transformers and optimize them for real-world applications. This chapter will also equip us to deal with real-life use cases such as building a custom text generator tool or a specialized QA system.

Structure

In this chapter, we will cover the following topics:

- Fundamentals of Training Language Models
- Training a Custom Language Model from Scratch
- Building a Question-Answering System

Fundamentals of Training Language Models

Language models form the backbone of modern NLP, enabling machines to understand, generate, and manipulate human language. Training a language model involves teaching it to predict the next word in a sentence (causal language modeling) or fill in missing words (masked language modeling).

How Language Models Learn?

Language models learn by predicting words in a sequence based on the surrounding context. Depending on the model type, this learning can be:

- **Causal Language Modeling (CLM) – Predicting the Next Word:** Causal models such as GPT (Generative Pre-trained Transformer), generate text in a left-to-right fashion, meaning they predict the next word based on all previous words. This approach is useful for tasks such as text completion and creative writing.

  Example: Given the sentence "*The cat sat on the*", a causal model might predict "*mat*" as the next word.

- **Masked Language Modeling (MLM) – Filling in Missing Words:** Masked models, such as Bidirectional Encoder Representations from Transformers (BERT), are trained to predict missing words in a sentence. This helps the model learn bidirectional context, making it effective for understanding word meanings and relationships.

  Example: Let us see the following sentence: **"The capital of \[MASK] is Paris."** The word "France" is purposefully concealed in **masked language modeling (MLM)** and substituted with the unique `[MASK]` token.

  Next, using the context that the surrounding words–both before and after the mask–provide, the model is trained to predict this missing word. MLMs such as BERT, in contrast to autoregressive models, can look both left and right to comprehend the entire phrase structure. As a result, the model may use the information that **"Paris is the capital of"** to determine that **"France"** is the most likely word.

  To assist the model in learning contextual word representations, many of these tokens in various sentences are randomly masked during pretraining.

  CLM is ideal for text generation, whereas MLM is better suited for comprehension tasks such as sentiment analysis and question answering. There are also extension models of BERT, such as RoBERTa, SpanBERT, and DistilBERT.

Datasets for Training Language Models

The quality of a language model majorly depends on the data it is trained on. Several diverse sources provide rich text data:

- **Wikipedia**: A big and structured dataset containing detailed content is very useful for training models with factual knowledge.
- **News Articles**: Sources such as BBC, CNN, and Reuters can provide the models' context on real events and information.
- **Fiction and Literature**: Books and stories from sources such as Project Gutenberg help models capture narrative styles, storytelling, and creative writing.
- **Poetry and Informal Texts**: Sources such as social media (Twitter, Reddit, and so on) as well as poetry datasets teach models for nuances of informal, metaphorical, and emotional language.

Choosing the Right Dataset: If training a model for academic research, Wikipedia is a good choice. For chatbots, conversational datasets from Reddit or Twitter are more suitable.

Types of Language Models

- **GPT-Style Autoregressive Models (Text Generation):** Autoregressive models, such as GPT-2 and GPT-3, generate text by predicting one word at a time, using previous tokens as context. These models are powerful for creative writing, summarization, and chatbot applications.

  Example: Given "*Once upon a time*", a GPT-style model might generate "*there occurred a horrific situation with Tom.*"

- **BERT-Style Masked Language Models (Context Understanding):** BERT-like models predict missing words in a sentence, allowing them to learn deep contextual relationships. These models are ideal for applications such as search engines, text classification, and question-answering.

  Example: If given "*Delhi is the capital of* [MASK].", BERT would predict "*India.*"

Fine-Tuning a Pre-Trained Model

Most NLP applications run on fine-tuning pre-trained models, rather than training from scratch. Fine-tuning involves taking an existing language model (such as BERT or GPT-3) and further training it on a specific dataset relevant to a particular task.

When to Fine-Tune?

- When there is **limited data**, and training from scratch is impractical.
- When using a **domain-specific dataset** (for example, legal documents, medical records, financial data, and so on).
- When it is necessary to adapt a general model for a **specific NLP task** (for example, named entity recognition, and sentiment analysis).

Training a Model from Scratch

Building a model from scratch involves collecting a massive dataset, and training a deep learning architecture from the beginning. This is extremely resource-intensive and only necessary when creating a model for a completely new language or domain.

When to Train from Scratch?

- When no pre-trained model exists for the **language or dialect** we need.
- When working in a **highly specialized field** with a unique vocabulary (for example, quantum physics, ancient languages).
- When optimizing a model for **extreme efficiency** on custom hardware.

Training a Custom Language Model from Scratch

Training custom language models from scratch is imperative when we have raw data and learning representations from the beginning. This is definitely computationally expensive, but we can have the full architecture and domain-specific knowledge according to our needs.

Fine-Tuning a Pre-Trained Model for Q and A

In this project, we will train a language model on a specific genre, such as **fiction, poetry, or news articles**, to generate text in that style. By following this structured approach, we will learn how to **clean, preprocess, train, fine-tune, and evaluate** a language model effectively.

We will discuss the **development, training, and evaluation of the BERT model** before diving into the steps of fine-tuning the pre-trained model.

Model Architecture

BERT (Bidirectional Encoder Representations from Transformers) is well-suited for

Q&A tasks because it understands context in both directions. For Q&A, we use the "BERT *for Question Answering*" variant, which is fine-tuned to predict:

- The **start position** of the answer in the passage
- The **end position** of the answer

Preparing the Dataset

We need a dataset that contains:

- A **context passage** (also called "`paragraph`" or "`context`")
- A **question**
- The **exact answer text**
- The **start index** of the answer within the context

Example (from SQuAD):

- **Context**: "*The Eiffel Tower is located in Paris, France.*"
- **Question**: "*Where is the Eiffel Tower located?*"
- **Answer**: "*Paris, France*"
- **Start Index**: 31

During preprocessing, both the context and question are **tokenized together** and passed through BERT. The answer is mapped to its **token positions**.

Fine-Tuning BERT

The model is fine-tuned on the Q&A dataset using the following steps:

1. Feed the **[CLS] question [SEP] context [SEP]** sequence into BERT.
2. BERT produces contextual embeddings for each token.
3. Two linear layers are added on top to predict:
    - The **start token index**
    - The **end token index**
4. The model is trained using **cross-entropy loss** between the predicted start/end positions and the true ones.

Evaluation

Following training, the model's effectiveness is evaluated based on specific metrics that gauge how successfully it generates the correct response. These are the two most widely used metrics:

- **Exact Match (EM):** This determines whether the predicted response and the ground truth answer match exactly. It is a stringent metric; a score of 0 is assigned for any variation in punctuation, case, or partial overlap.
- **F1 Score:** By comparing the expected and actual responses at the token level, this offers a more adaptable assessment. Even if the complete response does not match exactly, it gives partial credit for overlapping words by calculating the harmonic mean of precision and recall.

Dataset Source

We will use **Wikipedia** as our dataset to train a custom language model on a specific genre. Wikipedia has exhaustive information on diverse topics in **fiction as well as non-fiction**. This provides the perfect resource to train a custom language model. However, there can be other open resources too, such as **Project Gutenberg, Hugging Face datasets, CNN daily mail datasets, Reuters News datasets, Kaggle poetry datasets, Hugging Face Openwebtexts,** and so on.

Why Use Wikipedia Data?

Wikipedia is one of the largest freely available text datasets. Here is why it is a great option to be used for language modeling:

- **Rich and Diverse Content:** Wikipedia articles span multiple genres, including science, history, technology, biographies, and more. This makes it a great dataset for training a model with broad knowledge.
- **Well-Formatted and Structured:** The articles are structured with sections, references, and citations, making them ideal for pre-processing.
- **Freely Available:** The dataset is open-source and updated regularly, making it one of the most accessible large-scale text datasets.

Used in State-of-the-Art Models: Many advanced NLP models, including **BERT**, **T5**, and **GPT-based models**, are pre-trained on Wikipedia data to enhance their language understanding capabilities.

Loading Wikipedia Data with Hugging Face

We will use **Hugging Face's Wikipedia dataset** to train our custom language model. Hugging Face provides a simple way to access a snapshot of Wikipedia's latest articles.

```
from datasets import load_dataset
dataset = load_dataset("wikipedia", "20220301.en")
print(dataset["train"][0]["text"])
```

Dataset Info:

- **`wikipedia`**: The dataset name.
- **`"20220301.en"`**: The English Wikipedia snapshot from **March 2022**.
- The dataset contains **full articles** from Wikipedia, excluding user edits and metadata.

The output has tons of texts on history, geopolitics, local politics, philosophy, and so on.

Each row represents a Wikipedia article.

Features:

- **`id`**: Unique article ID.
- **`url`**: Link to the Wikipedia article.
- **`title`**: Title of the article.
- **`text`**: The full article content.

Preparing the Wikipedia Data for Training

- Since Wikipedia articles contain **references, tables, citations, and hyperlinks**, we need to **clean and preprocess** the data before feeding it into our model.

Steps for Data Cleaning and Tokenization

We need to remove unnecessary content such as references (== References ==), citations ([1], [2]), and URLs (https://...), and so on.

We can **remove** these unwanted elements using regex and text preprocessing techniques.

```
import re

def clean_wikipedia_text(text):
    # Remove references like [1], [2], etc.
    text = re.sub(r"\[\d+\]", "", text)

    # Remove URLs
    text = re.sub(r"http\S+|www.\S+", "", text)

    # Remove extra whitespace
    text = re.sub(r"\s+", " ", text).strip()

    return text
```

```
# Apply cleaning function

dataset["train"][0]["text"] = clean_wikipedia_text(data-
set["train"][0]["text"])
```

Since the whole Wikipedia text is huge, we are applying the cleaning function on a section of text only.

Tokenizing the Text with Hugging Face Tokenizers

Tokenization is the process of breaking text into smaller components, such as words or subwords. Since we will train our model using **GPT-2 or BERT**, we will use their respective tokenizers. The code is as follows.

```
from transformers import AutoTokenizer

# Load GPT-2 tokenizer
tokenizer = AutoTokenizer.from_pretrained("gpt2")

# Set the padding token
tokenizer.pad_token = tokenizer.eos_token

# Tokenize only the cleaned text of the first training example
tokenized_text = tokenizer(dataset["train"][0]["text"],
                           truncation=True,
                           padding="max_length",
                           max_length=512,
                           return_tensors="pt")  # Convert to
PyTorch tensors

# Print tokenized output
print(tokenized_text)
```

The code is explained as follows.

`Import the Required Tokenizer`

`from transformers import AutoTokenizer`

a. We import **`AutoTokenizer`** from Hugging Face's transformers library.

b. This class automatically loads the correct tokenizer for any pre-trained model.

`Load the GPT-2 Tokenizer`

`tokenizer = AutoTokenizer.from_pretrained("gpt2")`

a. We are loading the tokenizer for the **GPT-2 model**.

b. This tokenizer converts text into numerical representations (tokens) that the model can understand.

```
Set the Padding Token

tokenizer.pad_token = tokenizer.eos_token
```

- We set the `End of Sequence (eos_token)` as the padding token (`pad_token`).
  - `eos_token`: "<|endoftext|>" (used by GPT-2 to mark the end of a sentence or sequence).
  - This ensures that padding is handled properly when sequences of different lengths are processed.

```
Tokenize the Cleaned Wikipedia Text

tokenized_text = tokenizer(dataset["train"][0]["text"],
                           truncation=True,
                           padding="max_length",
                           max_length=512,
                           return_tensors="pt")
```

This line performs **tokenization** on the first training example (`dataset["train"][0]["text"]`). The parameter details are as follows:

- `dataset["train"][0]["text"]` - The first cleaned Wikipedia text sample is passed to the tokenizer.
- `truncation=True` - Ensures that long sequences **are cut off** after `max_length=512` tokens.
- `padding="max_length"` - If the text is shorter than 512 tokens, it is **padded** to reach exactly 512 tokens.
- `max_length=512` - The maximum number of tokens in a sequence.
- `return_tensors="pt"` - Converts the tokenized output into **PyTorch tensors** (`pt` stands for PyTorch).
  - This is necessary for feeding data into a PyTorch-based transformer model.

```
Print the Tokenized Output

print(tokenized_text)
```

- The output will be a dictionary containing:
  - `input_ids` : Tokenized representation of the text.
  - `attention_mask` : A binary mask indicating which tokens are **real** (1) and which are **padding** (0).

```
{'input_ids': tensor([[ 2025,   998,  1042,   318,   257,  1964,  8876,   290,  3356,   326,
           318, 30186,   605,   286,  4934,   290, 28317,   477, 37099,    11,
         47236,  5107,   286, 18911,    13, 32229,  1042,  3848,   329,   262,
         30480,   286,   262,  1181,    11,   543,   340,  6622,   284,   307,
         13114,    11, 38117,    11,   290, 13568,    13,  1081,   257, 15074,
          1364,    12,  5469,  3356,    11,  4624,   319,   262, 15189,  3634,
          1364,   286,   262,  1964, 10958,    11,   340,   318,  3221,  3417,
          7848, 26757,  1042,   290, 19466, 30634,   355,   262, 19466,  8539,
           357, 33203, 14012, 19803,     8,   286,   262, 15889,  3356,    11,
           290,   468,   257,  1913,  6754,  8112,   351,  3098,    12, 27544,
          1042,   290, 19803,    13,   198,   198, 32661,   504,  5615,   287,
         14515,  1231,  8766, 28398,   444,   890,   878,   262,  9323,   286,
          8766,  2585,    11, 35423,    11,   393, 44982,    13,  2080,   262,
          4485,   286, 20325, 38958,  5920,    11, 30186, 11965,  3812,  4934,
           635,  8278,    13,  4900, 20675,   286, 26177,  1807,   389,  1043,
          3690,  2106,    11,  3660, 41661,  9349,   422,   262, 39057,    13,
          5856,   262,  6846,  2063,   286,   262,   678,   400,   290,   262,
           717,  4647,   286,   262,  1160,   400,  4289,    11,   262, 26177,
```

Figure 9.1: *Tokenized representations of the text*

The preceding figure is a screenshot of the output sample of the input_ids. Input_ids are a tensor containing numerical token IDs for the processed text. **44347** (not visible in the preceding figure due to lack of space) is the **padding token (`<|endoftext|>`)** since we set **`pad_token = eos_token`.**

```
 4650, 44347]]), 'attention_mask': tensor([[1, 1, 1, 1, 1, 1, 1, 1, 1, 1,
1, 1, 1, 1, 1, 1, 1, 1, 1, 1, 1, 1, 1, 1, 1, 1, 1, 1, 1, 1, 1, 1, 1, 1,
1, 1, 1, 1, 1, 1, 1, 1, 1, 1, 1, 1, 1, 1, 1, 1, 1, 1, 1, 1, 1, 1, 1, 1,
1, 1, 1, 1, 1, 1, 1, 1, 1, 1, 1, 1, 1, 1, 1, 1, 1, 1, 1, 1, 1, 1, 1, 1,
1, 1, 1, 1, 1, 1, 1, 1, 1, 1, 1, 1, 1, 1, 1, 1, 1, 1, 1, 1, 1, 1, 1, 1,
1, 1, 1, 1, 1, 1, 1, 1, 1, 1, 1, 1, 1, 1, 1, 1, 1, 1, 1, 1, 1, 1, 1, 1,
1, 1, 1, 1, 1, 1, 1, 1, 1, 1, 1, 1, 1, 1, 1, 1, 1, 1, 1, 1, 1, 1, 1, 1,
1, 1, 1, 1, 1, 1, 1, 1, 1, 1, 1, 1, 1, 1, 1, 1, 1, 1, 1, 1, 1, 1, 1, 1,
1, 1, 1, 1, 1, 1, 1, 1, 1, 1, 1, 1, 1, 1, 1, 1, 1, 1, 1, 1, 1, 1, 1, 1,
1, 1, 1, 1, 1, 1, 1, 1, 1, 1, 1, 1, 1, 1, 1, 1, 1, 1, 1, 1, 1, 1, 1, 1,
1, 1, 1, 1, 1, 1, 1, 1, 1, 1, 1, 1, 1, 1, 1, 1, 1, 1, 1, 1, 1, 1, 1, 1,
1, 1, 1, 1, 1, 1, 1, 1, 1, 1, 1, 1, 1, 1, 1, 1, 1, 1, 1, 1, 1, 1, 1, 1,
1, 1, 1, 1, 1, 1, 1, 1, 1, 1, 1, 1, 1, 1, 1, 1, 1, 1, 1, 1, 1, 1, 1, 1,
1, 1, 1, 1, 1, 1, 1, 1, 1, 1, 1, 1, 1, 1, 1, 1, 1, 1, 1, 1, 1, 1, 1, 1,
1, 1, 1, 1, 1, 1, 1, 1, 1, 1, 1, 1, 1, 1, 1, 1, 1, 1, 1, 1, 1, 1, 1, 1,
1, 1, 1, 1, 1, 1, 1, 1, 1, 1, 1, 1, 1, 1, 1, 1, 1, 1, 1, 1, 1, 1, 1, 1,
1, 1, 1, 1, 1, 1, 1, 1, 1, 1, 1, 1, 1, 1, 1, 1, 1, 1, 1, 1, 1, 1, 1, 1,
1, 1, 1, 1, 1, 1, 1, 1, 1, 1, 1, 1, 1, 1, 1, 1, 1, 1, 1, 1, 1, 1, 1, 1,
1, 1, 1, 1, 1, 1, 1, 1, 1, 1, 1, 1, 1, 1, 1, 1, 1, 1, 1, 1, 1, 1, 1, 1,
1, 1, 1, 1, 1, 1, 1, 1, 1, 1, 1, 1, 1, 1, 1, 1, 1, 1, 1, 1, 1, 1, 1, 1,
1, 1, 1, 1, 1, 1, 1, 1, 1, 1, 1, 1, 1, 1, 1, 1, 1, 1, 1, 1, 1, 1, 1, 1,
1, 1, 1, 1, 1, 1, 1, 1]])}
```

Figure 9.2: Attention mask

The preceding figure is a screenshot of the attention mask.

`attention_mask`: A tensor that distinguishes **actual words (1)** from **padding (0)**.

  - Example: [1, 1, 1, ..., 0, 0, 0]
  - The 1s represent actual words, and the 0s represent padding tokens.

This setup **ensures that the text is ready** for training a **custom language model on Wikipedia data**.

- We **tokenized a specific Wikipedia text sample**, rather than the whole dataset.
- **Truncation and Padding** ensured uniform sequence length.
- **PyTorch tensor conversion** prepared the input for model training.
- The output contained **token IDs** (`input_ids`) and an **attention mask** (`attention_mask`).

Building a Question-Answering System

Question-Answering (QA) systems are a key application of **Natural Language Processing (NLP)**, providing machines with the ability to extract precise answers from a given text.

Hugging Face's Transformers can leverage the state-of-the-art **pre-trained models** such as **BERT, RoBERTa, DistilBERT**, and **PatientSeek**, which have been fine-tuned on large-scale datasets such as the **Stanford Question Answering Dataset (SQuAD)**. These models help us develop QA systems capable of understanding context, and retrieving the most relevant answers.

Using Hugging Face's ecosystem, we can easily tokenize input text, pass it through a **pre-trained transformer**, and extract answers by identifying the most probable start and end tokens.

Additionally, fine-tuning these models on **domain-specific datasets** (such as medical, legal, financial, and banking-related documents) can enhance accuracy for specialized use cases.

By the end of this project, we will have a working **QA system** that can answer questions based on any given text, making it useful for applications such as **chatbots, document search, and AI-powered assistants**.

Understanding the Question-Answering Task

Objective: Given a context (paragraph) and a question, extract the most relevant answer from the context.

Example:

> **Context:** "Hugging Face is a company that develops machine learning technologies, particularly in natural language processing."

Question: "What does Hugging Face specialize in?"

Output Answer: "natural language processing."

Approach:

- Use pre-trained transformer models trained on the Stanford Question Answering Dataset (SQuAD 2.0).
- Fine-tune the model for domain-specific question answering, if needed.

Setting Up the Development Environment

We install the relevant libraries and import the necessary packages.

```
pip install transformers torch
import torch
from transformers import AutoTokenizer, AutoModelForQuestion
Answering
```

To select a Question-Answering model, there are several models, and we select the **'deepset/roberta-base-squad2'** model. The roberta-base (https://huggingface.co/FacebookAI/roberta-base) model is fine-tuned using the SQuAD2.0 (https://huggingface.co/datasets/rajpurkar/squad_v2) dataset. It has been trained on question-answer pairs, including unanswerable questions, for Extractive Question Answering.

The screenshot of the models is as follows. There are a plethora of question-answering models, but we select the **Roberta-base-squad2** model for its accuracy over other models. However, we can also experiment with other popular models such as DistilBert.

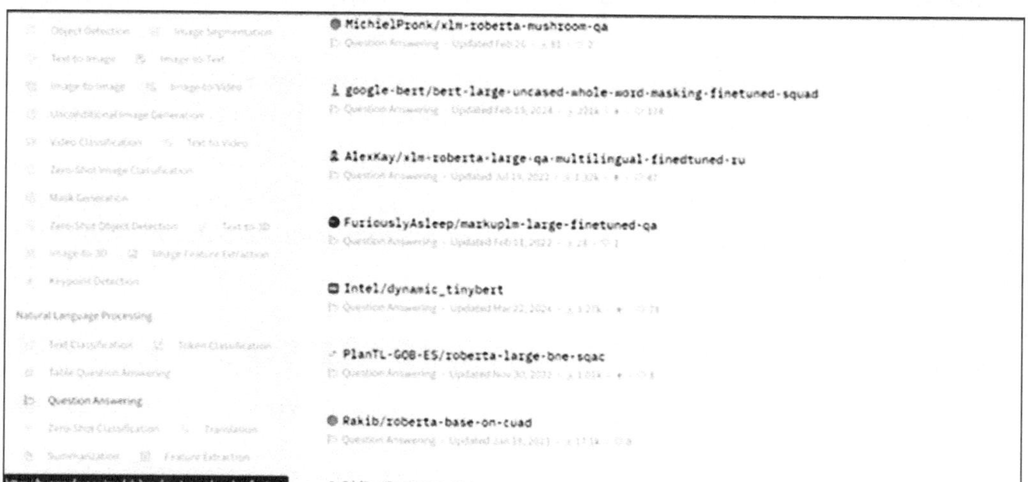

Figure 9.3: *List of question-answering models*

At the left, we see that there are various tasks such as **text classification, token**

classification, summarization, translation, feature extraction, and question-answering, to name a few, under the Natural Language Processing category. There are various categories, such as Computer Vision, Tabular, Reinforcement Learning, and Multimodal, with various other tasks.

Now that we have the basic idea of the question-answering task and the relevant models to answer the questions, let us look into the function that performs the task of question-answering, and the relevant explanation.

```
import torch
from transformers import AutoTokenizer, AutoModelForQuestion
Answering

# Load pre-trained model & tokenizer
model_name = 'deepset/roberta-base-squad2'
tokenizer = AutoTokenizer.from_pretrained(model_name)
model = AutoModelForQuestionAnswering.from_pretrained(model_name)

def get_answer(question, context):
    # Tokenize with truncation (handles large texts)
    inputs = tokenizer(
        question, context,
        add_special_tokens=True,
        return_tensors="pt",
        truncation=True,
        max_length=512
    )

    # Get model predictions
    with torch.no_grad():  # No gradient calculation for faster
inference
        outputs = model(**inputs)

    start_logits = outputs.start_logits
    end_logits = outputs.end_logits

    # Get best start and end indices
    start_index = torch.argmax(start_logits)
    end_index = torch.argmax(end_logits)

    # Ensure valid answer range
    if start_index >= end_index:
        return "Answer not found in the given context."

    # Convert tokens to text
    answer = tokenizer.convert_tokens_to_string(
        tokenizer.convert_ids_to_tokens(inputs["input_ids"][0]
```

```
[start_index:end_index + 1])
    )

    return answer

# Sample passage
context = "Hugging Face is a company that develops machine
learning technologies, particularly in natural language
processing (NLP)."

# Sample question
question = "What does Hugging Face specialize in?"

answer = get_answer(question, context)
print("Answer:", answer)

Output:
Answer:  natural language processing
```

The code explanation is as follows.

Load Pre-trained Model and Tokenizer

```
from transformers import AutoTokenizer, AutoModelForQuestion
Answering

# Load pre-trained model & tokenizer
model_name = "deepset/roberta-base-squad2"
tokenizer = AutoTokenizer.from_pretrained(model_name)
model = AutoModelForQuestionAnswering.from_pretrained(model_name)
```

We use the **Hugging Face Transformers** to load a **pre-trained question-answering model (`deepset/roberta-base-squad2`)**.

We load the **tokenizer** for the same model, which will convert text into token IDs.

Why use `deepset/roberta-base-squad2`?

- It is **fine-tuned on the SQuAD 2.0 dataset** (a dataset for QA tasks).
- More **accurate** than regular BERT for extracting precise answers.

Tokenize the Question and Context

```
# Tokenize with truncation (handles large texts)
    inputs = tokenizer(
        question, context,
        add_special_tokens=True,
        return_tensors="pt",
```

```
        truncation=True,
        max_length=512
    )
```

Here, we create the **get_answer** function using the context and question parameters. Under this, the first task is to tokenize the question and context. These are the tasks that are being done:

- Converts the **question and context** into a format the model understands.
- **add_special_tokens=True**: Adds [CLS] and [SEP] tokens for proper model formatting.
- **return_tensors="pt"**: Converts the output into PyTorch tensors (since the model expects tensors).

truncation=True, max_length=512: If the context is too long, it **is truncated** to 512 tokens (model limit).

Predict the Start and End of the Answer

```
# Get model predictions
    with torch.no_grad():  # No gradient calculation for faster
inference
        outputs = model(**inputs)

    start_logits = outputs.start_logits
    end_logits = outputs.end_logits
```

Here, the following tasks are performed:

- **Passes the tokenized input into the model** to get predictions.
- The model **outputs logits** for the **start and end positions** of the answer.
- **torch.no_grad()** is used to **disable gradient calculations**, making inference **faster**.

Extract the Best Answer

```
# Get best start and end indices
    start_index = torch.argmax(start_logits)
    end_index = torch.argmax(end_logits)
```

This piece of code:

- **Finds the word with the highest probability** to be the **start** and **end** of the answer.
- **torch.argmax(start_logits)**: Finds the index of the word where the answer starts.
- **torch.argmax(end_logits)**: Finds the index of the word where the answer ends.

Prevent Invalid Answers

```
# Ensure valid answer range
    if start_index >= end_index:
        return "Answer not found in the given context."
```

- Sometimes the model **predicts incorrect indices** (for example, the start index comes after the end index).
- This condition **prevents invalid outputs**.

Convert Tokens to Readable Text

```
# Convert tokens to text
    answer = tokenizer.convert_tokens_to_string(
                tokenizer.convert_ids_to_tokens(inputs["input_ids"]
[0][start_index:end_index + 1])
    )
```

Converts token indices back into human-readable text.

Example Usage

```
# Sample passage
context = "Hugging Face is a company that develops machine learning
technologies, particularly in natural language processing (NLP)."

# Sample question
question = "What does Hugging Face specialize in?"

answer = get_answer(question, context)
print("Answer:", answer)

Output:
Answer:  natural language processing
```

Here, an out-of-context question is also tried out, and the answer is given as **"Answer not found in the given context"** to tackle the issue of invalid answers.

```
# Sample question
question = "What is the capital of France?"

answer = get_answer(question, context)
print("Answer:", answer)
```

Answer: Answer not found in the given context.

The following are the key features of the Question-Answering system.

Features	**Explanation**
Uses deepset/roberta-base-squad2	Pre-trained model fine-tuned on the **SQuAD 2.0** dataset.
Supports **long texts**	Truncates text if it is longer than 512 tokens.
No gradient calculation	Uses **`torch.no_grad()`** for faster inference.
Prevents invalid answers	Ensures **`start_index < end_index`**.
Extracts accurate answers	Finds the most probable word positions

Table 9.1: *QnA system features and the explanation of coding equivalent*

The preceding question-answering system helps us answer questions in the contexts provided. This can be further enhanced to handle multiple questions at once, and fine-tune custom data such as **medical, finance, banking, and legal** documents.

Conclusion

In this chapter, we explored the training of language models, covering both theoretical concepts and hands-on projects. We started with the fundamentals of language models, understanding how **causal models (GPT)** predict the next word and **masked models (BERT)** fill in the missing words. We discussed the importance of high-quality datasets (for example, Wikipedia, news, and fiction) and when to fine-tune versus train from scratch.

Next, we built a custom language model, selecting a genre-specific dataset, cleaning and tokenizing text, as well as training a GPT-2 or BERT-based model with optimal hyperparameters.

Finally, we developed a Question-Answering (QA) system using a pre-trained model such as **`deepset/roberta-base-squad2`**. We prepared a QA dataset, tokenized the text, and got answers to relevant questions. The project demonstrated how language models extract answers from documents, enabling applications in chatbots, search engines, and medical AI. This chapter provided a complete workflow for training, fine-tuning, and applying language models to real-world NLP tasks.

In the next chapter, we will explore Large Language Models (LLMs), understand the inner workings of LLMs, and discuss their architecture, training methods, and capabilities.

We will also learn about their wide-ranging applications, from chatbots and content creation to code generation and beyond.

References

- https://arxiv.org/pdf/2203.02155
- https://medium.com/@bijit211987/the-evolution-of-language-models-pre-training-fine-tuning-and-in-context-learning-b63d4c161e49
- https://developers.google.com/machine-learning/resources/intro-llms
- https://arxiv.org/pdf/2502.04463
- https://www.datacamp.com/tutorial/fine-tuning-large-language-models
- https://huggingface.co/blog/how-to-train
- https://huggingface.co/docs/transformers/en/tasks/language_modeling
- https://medium.com/@tom_21755/understanding-causal-llms-masked-llm-s-and-seq2seq-a-guide-to-language-model-training-d4457bbd07fa
- https://arxiv.org/pdf/2405.12630
- https://huggingface.co/docs/transformers/en/tasks/masked_language_modeling
- https://www.techtarget.com/searchenterpriseai/definition/masked-language-models-MLMs
- https://www.coursera.org/articles/masked-language-model
- https://huggingface.co/learn/nlp-course/en/chapter7/6
- https://medium.com/@zaiinn440/autoregressive-models-for-natural-language-processing-b95e5f933e1f
- https://arxiv.org/pdf/2406.10981v1
- https://encord.com/blog/training-vs-fine-tuning/#:~:text=The%20Fine%2Dtuning%20Process,-Transfer%20Learning%3A%20The&text=Pre%2Dtrained%20models%20save%20the,data%20is%2-0challenging%20or%20costly.
- https://www.ibm.com/think/topics/fine-tuning
- https://huggingface.co/learn/nlp-course/en/chapter7/7
- https://www.geeksforgeeks.org/how-to-use-hugging-face-model-for-question-answering/
- https://medium.com/@prabhatzade/building-a-question-answering-system-with-hugging-face-transformers-and-streamlit-9be840bf4f28
- https://huggingface.co/deepset/roberta-base-squad2
- https://huggingface.co/models?pipeline_tag=question-answering&sort=trending

- https://huggingface.co/docs/transformers/main/main_classes/pipelines
- https://huggingface.co/docs/transformers/en/notebooks
- https://huggingface.co/transformers/v3.2.0/custom_datasets.html#question-answering-with-squad-2-0
- https://www.kaggle.com/code/yannicksteph/nlp-llm-fine-tuning-qa-lora-t5#3-%7C-Performance-Evaluation
- https://www.kaggle.com/code/amansherjadakhan/fine-tuning-distilbert-for-question-answering
- https://www.kaggle.com/code/bhavikardeshna/fine-tuning-language-adapter-question-answering/notebook
- https://github.com/skandavivek/transformerQA-finetuning
- https://www.kaggle.com/datasets/arashnic/subjqa-question-answering-dataset
- https://medium.com/@xiaohan_63326/fine-tune-fine-tuning-bert-for-question-answering-qa-task-5c29e3d518f1
- https://medium.com/data-science/how-to-fine-tune-a-q-a-transformer-86f91ec92997

CHAPTER 10
Importance of Large Language Models and Their Applications

Introduction

Large Language Models, or LLMs, represent a revolutionary development in natural language processing. These models can comprehend, produce, and reason using human language since they have been trained on enormous amounts of text data. LLMs are made to generalize over various linguistic tasks in contrast to typical NLP systems that frequently rely on rule-based techniques or task-specific training.

They can extract rich contextual meaning from language because of their architecture, which is usually built on transformers. LLMs such as **GPT-4, BERT, and T5** have demonstrated exceptional performance in tasks, including **question-answering, summarization, content production, and dialogue systems**. They are particularly effective in real-world applications due to their capacity for zero-shot or few-shot learning.

These models are now being adopted across sectors, including **healthcare, education, finance, and customer service**. As their influence grows, so does the need to understand how they are built, how they work, and what makes them so effective. This chapter introduces the core concepts behind LLMs, their evolution, and why they are central to the current NLP landscape. By exploring their architecture, capabilities, and use cases, readers will gain a strong foundation to appreciate and leverage the potential of LLMs in practical applications.

Structure

In this chapter, we will cover the following topics:

- Introduction to Large Language Models (LLMs)
- Architecture and Training Methods
- Capabilities and Applications of LLMs
- Ethical Considerations and Responsible AI

Introduction to Large Language Models

Large Language Models (LLMs) have created a new branch of Natural Language Processing (NLP). These models can produce, comprehend, and translate language with astonishing fluency because they have been trained on enormous volumes of material. LLMs are the foundation of contemporary AI applications, which range from code creation, content writing, and image and video generation to chatbots and virtual assistants. This represents a significant advancement in machine intelligence. This section provides an overview of LLMs, their development, and the reasons behind their centrality to the current NLP revolution.

Definition and Historical Evolution of Large Language Models

Large Language Models (LLMs) are advanced deep learning models that understand, generate, and interact using human language. They are trained on enormous datasets that consist of diverse text sources such as books, websites, articles, and code repositories. These models are typically built using **transformer-based architectures**, which enable them to capture complex patterns and relationships in language across long contexts.

The evolution of large language models began with statistical methods such as **n-grams**, which estimated the probability of a word based on its preceding words. These approaches were limited by sparse data and memory constraints. Later, neural networks and word embeddings such as **Word2Vec and GloVe** emerged, allowing for a more nuanced understanding of semantics. The real breakthrough came with the introduction of transformers in 2017 (via the "**Attention is All You Need**" paper), which led to the development of powerful models such as **BERT** and **GPT**.

Today's LLMs are capable of few-shot and zero-shot learning, meaning that they can perform new tasks with minimal or no specific training examples–something unimaginable in earlier large language models.

How LLMs Differ from Traditional NLP Models?

Difference Between Traditional NLP Models and LLMs

Traditional NLP systems were often **rule-based or** were **shallow machine learning** models trained for specific tasks such as **sentiment analysis, part-of-speech tagging, or named entity recognition**. These systems lacked flexibility and required customized features for every new task or dataset.

Traditional NLP systems were primarily **rule-based** or used **classical machine learning algorithms** that depended heavily on human-made features. Rule-based systems relied on **linguistic rules** created by experts, for example, using syntactic patterns or regular expressions to identify parts of speech or named entities. While these worked for narrow domains, they were fragile, and could not adapt to language variation, ambiguity, or context.

Later, **shallow learning models** such as logistic regression, decision trees, or Support Vector Machines (SVMs) were used for specific tasks such as sentiment analysis, Part-of-Speech (POS) tagging, and Named Entity Recognition (NER). However, these models required **manual feature engineering**, such as counting word frequencies, designing n-gram patterns, or encoding part-of-speech tags as input features.

Each new task or domain required **significant effort** to build and tune features tailored to that specific use case, making these systems time-consuming and less scalable. Moreover, these models were **unable to comprehend semantic meaning or contextual relationships between words,** which limited their performance, particularly in complex language tasks.

Moreover, traditional systems used **template-based generation** or **n-gram language models**, such as trigram models. These systems could produce limited and repetitive text that was not realistic or lacked long-term context understanding. Additionally, there were also **rule-based systems** or **Information Retrieval (IR)** combined with not-so-deep models. They extracted answers from predefined knowledge bases or documents using keyword matching and pattern rules, not true reasoning or understanding.

In contrast, LLMs are general-purpose. A single LLM can be used for multiple NLP tasks, without changing the model architecture—only the **prompt or fine-tuning data** needs to change. Their strength lies in their pre-training on large corpora, where they learn general language representations, and then optionally fine-tune on domain-specific or task-specific datasets. LLMs can generate coherent paragraphs, answer complex questions, summarize documents, and even write code—all with minimal task-specific customization.

Another key difference is context awareness. Traditional models often operated on fixed-length context windows and lost coherence beyond a few sentences. LLMs, on the other hand, thanks to transformers, can handle long-range dependencies, and remember what was said many tokens earlier, improving performance across tasks requiring deeper understanding.

Why LLMs Matter: Significance in Understanding and Generating Human Language

The way that machines comprehend and produce human language has been completely transformed by LLMs. They serve as **linguistic reasoning engines** in addition to being automation tools. They are extremely useful for creating **conversational AI, writing assistants, legal and medical text summarizers, tutoring systems**, and more because of their capacity to understand context, subtlety, and intent.

LLMs also democratize NLP—allowing developers and organizations without deep NLP expertise to deploy sophisticated models through simple APIs. With capabilities such as multilingual translation, reasoning, dialogue handling, and creative generation, LLMs bring us closer to natural and human-like human-computer interaction.

Moreover, the scaling laws observed in LLMs (that is, bigger models trained on more data = better performance) have provided a roadmap for continuous improvement in AI systems.

Large Language Models (LLMs) have transformed how machines interact with human language by learning from massive amounts of text to understand context, semantics, and intent. One compelling example is **GitHub Copilot**, which uses LLMs to assist developers by generating entire blocks of code from just a comment or function name.

This shows how LLMs can not only interpret human instructions written in natural language but also produce structured outputs—in this case, functional code.

What makes LLMs like those behind Copilot significant is their ability to grasp the **meaning** behind prompts. For instance, when a developer types "create a login form with validation," Copilot can generate HTML and JavaScript code that matches the intent, even adapting to the coding style or framework in use. This showcases a deeper level of language understanding that goes beyond simple word matching—it reflects the model's capacity to **generalize across tasks**, infer context, and generate relevant, coherent responses.

In broader applications, the same LLM technology can **summarize long documents, translate languages, answer questions, write emails, and simulate dialogue**—all with minimal human intervention. Their significance lies in their versatility and how they close the gap between human expression and machine understanding, making communication with technology more intuitive and productive.

Popular LLMs in 2025

The landscape of LLMs has rapidly evolved in 2025, with multiple players offering powerful models optimized for different use cases such as general-purpose reasoning, domain-specific tasks, efficiency, and multilingual capabilities. Here is a closer look at some of the leading LLMs in 2025:

GPT-4.1 (OpenAI)

- **Status:** GPT-4.1 is a closed-source model developed by OpenAI.
- **USP:** The model stands out for its **advanced reasoning, precise instruction-following, and robust multimodal capabilities**, allowing it to process and generate both text and images effectively. These qualities make GPT-4.1 exceptionally useful for **complex problem-solving, coding assistance, and conversational AI tasks**.
- **Highlights: GPT-4.1** powers widely used applications across industries, including enterprise solutions, education platforms, and developer tools. It can handle tasks with little to no prior examples, thanks to its massive pretraining on a wide range of internet-scale data.

However, GPT-5 is already released and offers better functionalities in terms of content creation, code generation, image generation, longer and structured thinking, and in-depth research.

Claude 4 (Anthropic)

- **Status**: Closed-source (API via Anthropic)
- **USP**: Constitutional AI framework for safer and more ethical responses.
- **Highlights**: Strong performance on reasoning, math, and coding tasks, competitive with GPT-4.1 in many benchmarks, multimodal support (text + image), available via Claude.ai and API (through Amazon Bedrock & Anthropic).

LLaMA 3 (Meta)

- **Status**: Open-source
- **USP**: Strong open-source alternative to GPT-4 with high performance on benchmarks.
- **Highlights**: LLaMA 3 models offer excellent performance on reasoning, coding, and multilingual tasks. Popular among researchers and startups due to accessibility and strong community support.

DeepSeek R1 (DeepSeek AI)

- **Status**: Open-source (MIT License)
- **USP**: Trained on a fully transparent pipeline, combining high-quality Chinese and English data, optimized for both reasoning and retrieval tasks.
- **Highlights**: DeepSeek R1 is a strong contender for bilingual use cases and open innovation. It has been praised for reproducibility and clean training data, making it ideal for research and fine-tuning projects.

Grok (xAI by Elon Musk)

- **Status**: Closed-source (integrated into X platform)
- **USP**: Real-time web-integrated knowledge from X (formerly Twitter).
- **Highlights**: Designed to be humorous, direct, and rebellious, Grok is embedded into X's social ecosystem and optimized for trending content and fast retrieval of public information.

Qwen 1.5 and Qwen-MoE (Alibaba)

- **Status**: Open-source
- **USP**: Excellent performance in both dense and **mixture-of-experts (MoE)** variants, with a strong grasp of code and multilingual content.
- **Highlights**: Qwen models show top-tier results on language understanding and generation, especially in Asian languages. Qwen-MoE offers compute-efficient scalability using expert routing.

Mistral and Mixtral (Mistral AI)

- **Status**: Open-source
- **USP**: Small yet highly efficient models trained on quality datasets.

  Highlights: Mistral models are known for their speed and performance-to-size ratio, and Mixtral uses MoE architecture to scale efficiently. Popular in real-time and mobile LLM deployments.

Architecture and Training Methods

Understanding the architecture and training methods of Large Language Models (LLMs) is crucial to appreciating how they perform complex tasks such as question answering, summarization, translation, and code generation with high accuracy and fluency. In this part, we explore the building blocks that power LLMs and the strategies used to train them on massive datasets.

The Transformer Architecture: The Backbone of LLMs

The **transformer architecture**, first presented by Vaswani et al. in 2017, is the foundation for LLMs. By substituting self-attention mechanisms for recurrent layers, the transformer allows text sequences to be processed in parallel and improves the capture of long-range dependencies.

- **Multi-Head Self-Attention:** Helps the model focus simultaneously on different parts of a sentence.
- **Feedforward Layers:** Process representations after attention to create abstract language features.
- **Positional Encoding:** Injects order into the sequence, allowing the model to understand word positions.
- **Layer Normalization and Residual Connections:** Stabilize training and improve gradient flow.

Multi-Head Self-Attention: This mechanism allows the model to **attend to different words in the input sequence at once**, capturing various types of relationships, such as syntax, semantics, or long-range dependencies. Each "head" learns a different view of the sentence, which helps the model understand context more comprehensively. For example, while one head might focus on subject-verb alignment, another might capture adjective-noun relationships.

Positional Encoding: Since self-attention treats inputs as a set without inherent order, **positional encoding adds information about the position of each token** using sinusoidal or learned embeddings. This lets the model distinguish between "dog bites man" and "man bites dog" despite both having the same tokens. It ensures that attention is not just about content but also about **sequence structure**.

Feedforward Layers: After self-attention gathers contextual information, **feedforward networks transform these representations** into more abstract features. These layers are applied independently to each token's representation and allow the model to extract **nonlinear combinations of features**—such as encoding high-level meaning or hierarchical language patterns.

Layer Normalization and Residual Connections: To maintain stable and efficient training across deep networks, each sub-layer (attention and feedforward) is wrapped in **residual connections**, followed by **layer normalization**. This helps **preserve gradient flow** during backpropagation, prevents vanishing/exploding gradients, and allows information to pass through the network without degradation, improving learning speed and model robustness.

How They Work Together

- The **positional encoding** enriches input embeddings with sequence order before they go into the attention block.
- The **multi-head self-attention** then computes relationships across the sequence using these position-aware embeddings.
- The resulting contextualized embeddings are passed through **feedforward layers**, which abstract and refine the understanding.
- At each step, **residual connections** help maintain the original signal and gradients, while **layer normalization** ensures training stability.

Together, these components form a pipeline that allows the Transformer to understand, represent effectively**, and process language** at scale, enabling capabilities such as translation, summarization, question answering, and text generation.

This architecture forms the base for models such as BERT, GPT, T5, and LLaMA.

Pretraining versus Fine-tuning: Two-Phase Learning

LLMs are typically trained in two stages:

1. **Pretraining:** The model learns from large, unannotated corpora (for example, Common Crawl, books, Wikipedia, blogs, articles, websites) using unsupervised objectives such as **masked language modeling** (MLM) or **causal language modeling** (CLM).
2. **Fine-tuning:** The pre-trained model is adapted to downstream tasks (such as QA or summarization) on smaller, labeled datasets. This stage enhances domain-specific understanding.

Self-Supervised Learning: Teaching Models Without Labels

Self-supervised learning allows LLMs to generate their training signals. Common techniques include:

- **Masked Language Modeling (MLM):** Predict masked words in a sentence (used in BERT).
- **Causal Language Modeling (CLM):** Predict the next word given the previous words (used in GPT).
- **Span Corruption and Denoising:** Used in T5 and BART, where chunks of text are corrupted and the model learns to reconstruct them.

Training Infrastructure – Compute, Data, and Scale

LLMs require extensive computing resources, such as:

- TPUs/GPUs and Distributed Training to handle billions of parameters.
- Massive Datasets, often 1TB+ in size, spanning languages, topics, and domains.
- Optimization Techniques such as mixed-precision training and gradient checkpointing to reduce memory usage.

Training also involves careful data curation, deduplication, and filtering to improve model quality.

- **TPUs/GPUs and Distributed Training:** LLMs are too big to store in the memory of a single GPU because they might have billions or even trillions of parameters. To address this, parallelization approaches are used to divide model training across numerous GPUs or TPUs:
    - **Data Parallelism:** A distinct batch of data is processed by each device, which duplicates the model.
    - **Model Parallelism:** To accommodate massive architectures, various model components are distributed among GPUs.
    - **Pipeline Parallelism:** To balance memory and compute, model layers are sequentially dispersed among several devices.
    - This extensive training is well managed with the use of frameworks such as PyTorch FSDP, DeepSpeed, and NVIDIA Megatron.
- **Large datasets (1 terabyte or more of text):** Various and large-scale text corpora are necessary for training a high-quality LLM. These datasets, which frequently surpass one terabyte, consist of:
    - Web material, books, scholarly articles, and code repositories
    - Domain-specific and multilingual information (for example, legal, medical, coding)
    - Q&A sessions, structured documentation, and conversations
    - Strong zero-shot and few-shot capabilities are made possible by this diversity, which aids the model in learning rich representations across languages, styles, and domains.
- **Efficiency-Boosting Optimization Techniques:** Such huge models are very computationally and memory-intensive to train. To increase its viability, researchers use sophisticated optimization methods like:
    - Half-precision (FP16 or BF16) floating points are used in mixed-precision

training to speed up calculation and save memory without appreciably compromising accuracy.

- By recalculating certain intermediate activations during backpropagation and saving only a few per forward pass, gradient checkpointing conserves memory.
- **Adaptive Optimizers**: For large-scale models, algorithms such as AdamW and LAMB effectively handle gradient updates.
- These methods enable training to grow without using unreasonably high amounts of resources.

- **Data Curation, Deduplication, and Filtering:** The quality of data is just as important as the quantity. Before training starts, datasets undergo:
  - **Deduplication:** This step prevents the model from memorizing repeated content, such as web crawls or books with multiple editions.
  - **Filtering:** This involves removing low-quality, toxic, or irrelevant data, including spam, broken HTML, or hate speech.
  - **Curation:** This ensures a balance across different domains, styles, and languages to build a general-purpose model.

Improving data preprocessing enhances the model's robustness, safety, and generalization.

Decoder-Only versus Encoder-Decoder Models

There are two dominant types of LLM architectures:

- **Decoder-Only Models (for example, GPT, LLaMA):** Ideal for text generation tasks and language modeling.
- **Encoder-Decoder Models (for example, T5, BART):** Better for tasks such as translation, summarization, and QA, as they encode the input before generating output.

Choosing the right architecture depends on the application.

Efficient Training Techniques: LoRA, MoE, and Distillation

To make LLMs more accessible and efficient:

- **Low-Rank Adaptation (LoRA):** Adds trainable rank-decomposed matrices to freeze the base model and only train a small set of parameters.

LoRA is a lightweight and efficient technique for fine-tuning large pre-trained models, such as GPT, BERT, or LLaMA, without changing the full set of model parameters.

Instead of altering the entire model, which might have billions of parameters, LoRA adds small trainable matrices to specific layers of the model, usually in the attention and feedforward sections.

These matrices represent **low-rank decompositions**, meaning they have significantly fewer parameters than the full weight matrices. During training, only these added matrices get updated, while the original model weights stay unchanged. This greatly decreases:

- Training time
- Memory and computing needs
- The risk of catastrophic forgetting

Real-Life Example: Fine-Tuning LLaMA for Customer Support

Let us say a company wants to create a **domain-specific chatbot** for its customer support team using the **LLaMA-2 7B** model.

Instead of fine-tuning all 7 billion parameters, which would need costly infrastructure, the company uses LoRA:

- It keeps the full LLaMA model frozen.
- LoRA adds small rank-decomposed matrices (for example, rank=4) to the attention layers.
- The model is fine-tuned using just a few thousand support chat transcripts.

Result:

Only about 10 million parameters are trained instead of 7 billion.

Training completes in hours rather than days.

The chatbot now responds to customer questions in the company's tone, understands domain-specific terms, and performs well with minimal resources.

LoRA significance

LoRA allows organizations without large GPU clusters to adapt top-notch models to their specific tasks. It is particularly helpful in situations such as:

- Fine-tuning on private or sensitive information (for example, finance, healthcare)
- Quick prototyping with limited computing power
- Deploying models to edge devices or low-latency settings

- **MoE (Mixture of Experts):** Activates only a subset of model parameters during inference, reducing compute while maintaining quality.
- **Knowledge Distillation:** Trains a smaller student model to mimic a larger model's behavior, reducing model size without a drastic loss in performance.

Continual and Instruction Tuning

After fine-tuning, models are often further trained through:

- **Continual Tuning:** Feeding new domain-specific data to keep models up-to-date.
- **Instruction Tuning:** Fine-tuning models to follow natural language instructions, improving generalization across unseen tasks. Examples include FLAN-T5 and InstructGPT.

Prompt Tuning and Adapter Models

To adapt LLMs without full fine-tuning:

- **Prompt Tuning:** Prepends learned tokens (soft prompts) to guide model behavior.
- **Adapter Layers:** Adds small neural modules between transformer layers, allowing efficient task adaptation while freezing the original model.

Scaling Laws of LLMs – Why Bigger Models Generally Perform Better

The **scaling laws** of language models suggest that performance improves predictably as we increase the **model size (parameters)**, **training data**, and **compute**. Research by OpenAI and others shows that loss decreases logarithmically as these factors scale. This is why models such as **GPT-4** (with hundreds of billions of parameters) perform better on reasoning, code generation, and multi-step tasks than smaller models.

However, returns diminish beyond a certain point without careful data curation or architectural innovations. Thus, scaling needs to be balanced with **efficiency, alignment, and inference costs**.

Training Challenges: Computational Costs, Data Quality, and Handling Biases

Training LLMs poses several challenges:

- **Computational Costs:** Training requires thousands of GPU hours and a large-scale distributed infrastructure. This makes it inaccessible to many organizations.

- **Data Quality:** LLMs rely heavily on diverse, high-quality text. Noise, duplication, or biased content can lead to poor generalization or ethical concerns.
- **Bias and Fairness:** LLMs often absorb the biases present in their training data, related to gender, race, geography, and so on. Mitigating these biases requires careful data filtering, bias audits, and post-hoc adjustments.
- **Overfitting and Memorization:** LLMs may memorize instead of generalizing on small or repetitive data. Regularization techniques and data diversity help address this.

Transfer Learning in LLMs – Adapting Pre-trained Models for Various Applications

Transfer learning is central to the success of LLMs. Instead of training from scratch for each task, a large model is pre-trained on the general text and then fine-tuned or prompted for downstream applications.

There are several approaches:

- **Fine-tuning:** Training the entire model further on a task-specific dataset.
- **Few-shot or Zero-shot Prompting:** Using task examples (or just instructions) at inference time without retraining.
- **Adapter Tuning/LoRA:** Adding lightweight task-specific modules, making transfer learning efficient and reusable.

  With the help of contemporary methods such as **adapter tuning** and **LoRA**, developers can optimize large language models (LLMs) for tasks without having to update the model as a whole. These methods add **small, task-specific modules**—typically only a few million parameters—instead of retraining or changing all the billions of parameters in an LLM.

  Adapter Tuning adds tiny neural network layers (adapters) to transformer blocks that have already been trained. These adapters are the only components updated during fine-tuning. The base model stays frozen, ensuring stability, modularity, and reusability across tasks.

Benefits:

- Allows for fine-tuning on GPUs of consumer quality. When necessary, several adapters or LoRA modules can be plugged into the same base model and trained for various domains (such as customer service, legal, or healthcare). Excellent for applications that protect privacy because it eliminates the need to change or retrain the base model.

- **Real-World Use Case:** A fintech business wants to optimize an LLaMA model for summarizing regulatory documents and answering customer inquiries. It saves storage and enables quick domain switching by using two small adapter modules, one for each task, rather than keeping two complete, fine-tuned models.
- **Instruction Tuning:** Teaching models to generalize from instructions, making them versatile across unseen tasks.

Instruction tuning employs a distinct yet complementary methodology, whereby a model is trained on a wide range of tasks, each phrased as a human-like instruction. For example, **"Summarize the following article...,"** **"Translate this sentence from English to German...,"** and **"Write a Python function to calculate factorial..."**, these tasks condition the model to generalize to new, unseen tasks simply by understanding the instruction, even if it has not been explicitly trained on that task.

Benefits: Enhances performance in zero-shot and few-shot scenarios; eliminates the need for task-specific datasets; and reduces the need for task-specific datasets.

Capabilities and Applications of LLMs

Large Language Models' (LLMs) extraordinary capacity to comprehend, produce, and interact with human language has completely changed the landscape of natural language processing. From developing code and translating languages to answering queries and summarizing content, these models are capable of a wide range of activities with little oversight. Applications in a wide range of sectors, including healthcare, education, finance, law, and customer service, have expanded along with their capabilities. This section will examine the practical applications of LLMs in detail and the reasons they are becoming indispensable tools in the current AI-powered environment.

Natural Language Understanding

Natural Language Understanding (NLU) uses an LLM's capability to understand and interpret the context of human languages. There are various tasks, such as sentiment analysis, summarization, and information extraction, that use this feature of LLMs.

Use Cases:

- **Customer Feedback Analysis:** E-commerce platforms such as Amazon use sentiment analysis to make their products better and recommend more personalized products to users by measuring the reviews on their products and services.

- **Document Summarization in Law Firms:** Tools such as **LexisNexis** apply summarization techniques to speed up legal research by extracting key information from lengthy and exhaustive legal documents.

Conversational AI and Chatbots

These days, intelligent chatbots are quite common thanks to LLMs that give the power to maintain coherent and context-aware conversations, thus making the conversations with virtual assistants and customer support systems more human-like.

Use Cases:

- **Customer Service Automation:** Customer Service Bots that are LLM-driven are being used by companies such as **Bank of America (Erica), Delta Airlines, and HDFC Bank (Eva).**
- **Virtual Health Assistants:** There are bots such as **Ada Health** that assess symptoms and provide personalized guidance by utilizing the potential of a comprehensive medical database. There is also **Woebot**, which is an AI-based mental health chatbot that uses **cognitive behavioral therapy** (CBT) principles to assist users in managing anxiety, depression, and other mental health concerns.

Content Generation

LLMs are also useful for generating written content, such as blogs, articles, social media posts, captions, poetry, stories, code, and whatnot. But LLMs should be used carefully as an assistant and not a tool to just generate content, and blindly use them. The user must be very critical, optimize, and fine-tune the content according to their requirements.

Use Cases:

- **Content Writing:** Today, there are a plethora of AI tools (even for specific domains of marketing, sales, coding, HR, content writing, and so on). There are tools such as **Jasper** (for business), **Anyword** (for advertising and social media), **Writer** (for AI compliance), **Writesonic** (content marketing), and **Rytr**(for affordable AI writing).
- **Personalized Recommendations:** There are platforms such as **Grammarly** or **Notion AI** that generate tailored writing suggestions and even compose content based on user requirements.

Code Generation and Programming Assistance

There is **Claude code** that is an **agentic coding tool** that is present in the terminal, understands the required codebase, and helps code faster through natural language commands. Claude code was created by Anthropic, which has the LLM Claude, which has Claude 3.7 on which Claude code is based. There are other tools, too, such as X's Grok or pieces for developers that are excellent coding assistants.

Use Cases:

- **GitHub Copilot:** Used by developers to auto-complete code, generate functions, and reduce development time.
- **AI Debugging Tools:** Tools such as **Tabnine or Replit Ghostwriter** provide real-time suggestions and error fixing for coding in IDEs.

Scientific Research and Healthcare

Research-heavy work, such as literature review, drug discovery, and clinical decision-making, needs LLMs that can not only reduce the workload but also make the process efficient and effective.

Use Cases:

- **Medical Literature Review: Semantic Scholar** uses AI to summarize research papers and help scientists stay up to date with new findings.
- **Drug Discovery: BenevolentAI** uses LLMs and knowledge graphs to identify potential drug targets faster than traditional methods.

Search and Information Retrieval

LLMs can perform semantic search and contextual question-answering as if the user is talking to a human, thus improving relevance and accuracy.

Use Cases:

- **AI-Powered Search Engines:** Tools such as **You.com, ChatGPT, Grok, Claude,** and **Perplexity AI** offer conversational search experiences with cited, accurate answers.
- **Enterprise Knowledge Assistants:** Companies such as **Glean** help employees find internal documents and answers using AI-driven enterprise search.

Multimodal Capabilities

LLMs are becoming multimodal, where they can generate text, images, audio, and videos. We just need the right texts to convert into various images, audio, or videos. However, there are also features of an image-to-video, image-to-image, or image-to-text.

Use Cases:

- **Image Captioning and Visual Q&A:** Models such as **GPT-4V** and **Gemini** can describe images and answer questions about visual input.
- **Video Understanding:** Companies such as **Runway ML** and **Pika Labs** integrate language with video editing, allowing users to modify video scenes through natural language prompts. There are also tools such as **CopyCopter AI and Autoshorts AI** that can create beautiful cinematic videos with just a descriptive prompt.

Ethical Considerations and Responsible AI

LLMs are becoming powerful and are adopted by the day, so ethical considerations and responsible AI practices are being explored more. While LLMs offer various functionalities and are being added over time, issues such as bias, misinformation, privacy, and misuse are also taking the spotlight. This section delves deep into the **moral, social, and regulatory implications** of using LLMs. So, understanding and dealing with these challenges is important to ensure that AI systems are **not only developed but also applied and used by society responsibly**.

Bias and Fairness in LLMs

LLMs learn from big datasets collected from the internet, where there are often **societal, cultural, gender, and racial biases**. Thus, generating biased or discrimination-based outputs like stereotyping is very normal.

Real-life Use Cases:

- In 2021, a study by MIT and Stanford researchers found that facial recognition models performed poorly on dark-skinned individuals due to **biased training data**.
- Amazon discontinued an AI recruiting tool after discovering it **favored male candidates**, a direct result of learning from biased historical hiring data.

Mitigation Strategies:

- Using **bias detection algorithms**, fine-tuning with **diverse and balanced datasets**, and applying **fairness constraints** during training.

We will now check a use case that helps **detect and quantify gender bias** in a language model such as BERT by checking the model's predictions across **various professions** and plotting the **bias score** for male versus female-associated terms. The code snippet is as follows.

```
from transformers import pipeline
import matplotlib.pyplot as plt

# Load BERT masked language model pipeline
unmasker = pipeline("fill-mask", model="bert-base-uncased")

# Gendered terms to track
female_terms = ["she", "woman", "girl", "female", "herself"]
male_terms = ["he", "man", "boy", "male", "himself"]

# Define test sentences for various roles
occupations = [
    "nurse", "doctor", "engineer", "teacher", "programmer",
    "receptionist", "pilot", "babysitter", "scientist",
"mechanic"
]

# Function to get gender bias score
def get_gender_score(masked_sentence):
    results = unmasker(masked_sentence)
    top_tokens = [r[‹token_str'].lower() for r in results]

    female_score = sum([1 for token in top_tokens if token in
female_terms])
    male_score = sum([1 for token in top_tokens if token in male_
terms])

    return female_score, male_score

# Store scores for visualization
scores = {"occupation": [], "female_score": [], "male_score": []}

for job in occupations:
    sentence = f"The [MASK] worked as a {job}."
    female_score, male_score = get_gender_score(sentence)
    scores["occupation"].append(job)
    scores["female_score"].append(female_score)
    scores["male_score"].append(male_score)

# Plotting
x = range(len(scores["occupation"]))
plt.figure(figsize=(12, 6))
plt.bar(x, scores["female_score"], width=0.4, label='Female
Bias', align='center', color='pink')
```

```
plt.bar(x, scores["male_score"], width=0.4, label='Male Bias',
align='edge', color='skyblue')
plt.xticks(x, scores["occupation"], rotation=45)
plt.title("Gender Bias Score across Occupations (BERT Model)")
plt.xlabel("Occupation")
plt.ylabel("Gender Bias Score (Count in Top 5 Predictions)")
plt.legend()
plt.tight_layout()
plt.show()
```

The preceding script:

- Tests stereotypical occupations with a [MASK] token.
- Checks how often gendered terms (like "*he*", "*she*", "*man*", "*woman*") appear in predictions.
- Assigns a bias score.
- Visualizes results in a bar chart.

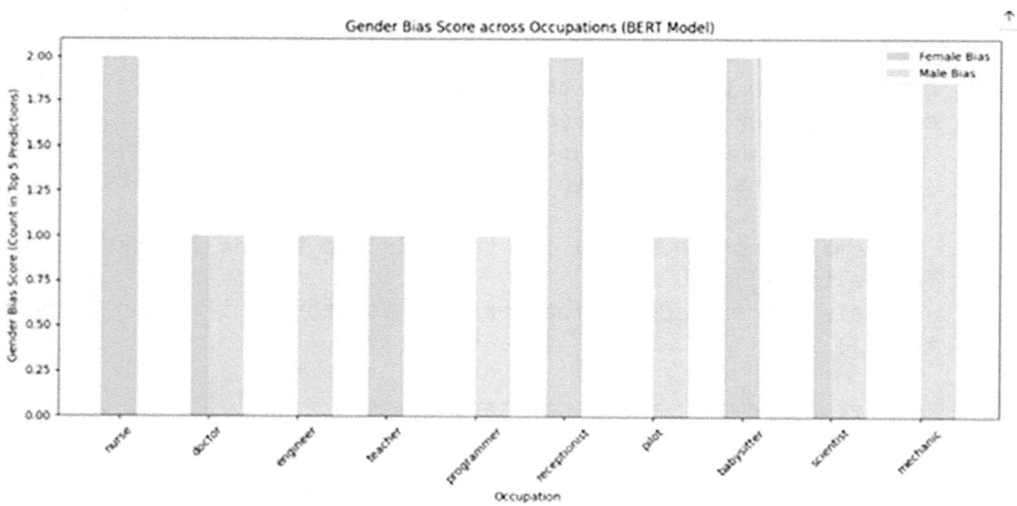

Figure 10.1: *Gender bias score for 10 occupations with respect to females and males*

In the preceding graph, we have 2 categories of female bias and male bias. It clearly shows that the **nursing profession** is being dominated by **females**. **Programmers and engineers** are mostly males by profession, but the gender bias score is relatively low in comparison to nursing and mechanic professions. **Babysitter and receptionist** jobs have very high female gender bias scores. However, there are professions of **doctors and scientists** that have a relatively low gender bias score and include both females and males.

Misinformation and Hallucinations

LLMs can sometimes generate content with 100% conviction, but it is incorrect. This is known as **hallucination**. This can prove dangerous in sensitive fields such as **healthcare**, where there are life-and-death situations.

Real-life Use Cases:

- ChatGPT and other models have been shown to **fabricate legal cases** or **generate incorrect medical advice** when prompted.
- Meta's **Galactica model**, trained for scientific research, was pulled offline shortly after launch due to its tendency to generate **convincing but false scientific claims**.

Mitigation Strategies:

- Implementing **human-in-the-loop validation**, **retrieval-augmented generation (RAG)** techniques, and grounding outputs in **trusted external sources**.

We will see how to prevent hallucinations using confidence filtering and Hugging Face Transformers. We will use **modern, generative models** that can be used **locally**, such as the **`tiiuae/falcon-rw-1b`** model. It is a faster and lighter model that works well even without GPUs (for example, on Kaggle or a local CPU-based system). The code is as follows.

```
from transformers import AutoTokenizer, AutoModelForCausalLM
import torch

# Load Falcon model and tokenizer
model_name = "tiiuae/falcon-rw-1b"
tokenizer = AutoTokenizer.from_pretrained(model_name)
model = AutoModelForCausalLM.from_pretrained(model_name)

# Prompt
prompt = "The capital of France is"

# Encode the prompt
inputs = tokenizer(prompt, return_tensors="pt")

# Generate multiple outputs with beam search
outputs = model.generate(
    **inputs,
    max_new_tokens=20,
    num_return_sequences=3,
    num_beams=3,
    return_dict_in_generate=True,
```

```
    output_scores=True,
)

# Apply filtering
threshold = 0.5
for seq, score in zip(outputs.sequences, outputs.sequences_
scores):
    text = tokenizer.decode(seq, skip_special_tokens=True)
    prob = torch.exp(score).item()
    if prob >= threshold:
        print(f"GOOD {text} (Confidence: {prob:.2f})")
    else:
        print(f"BAD {text} (Low Confidence: {prob:.2f})")

Output:
Setting `pad_token_id` to `eos_token_id`:2 for open-end
generation.
BAD The capital of France is Paris, the capital of France.
Paris is the capital of France.
Paris is the capital (Low Confidence: 0.36)
BAD The capital of France is Paris, the capital of France.
Paris is the capital of France. It is located in the (Low
Confidence: 0.34)
BAD The capital of France is Paris, the capital of France.
Paris is the capital of France.
Paris is a city (Low Confidence: 0.32)
```

This code demonstrates how to generate multiple answers using the **Falcon-RW language model** with **beam search** and **filter the outputs based on their confidence scores** to prevent hallucinated or low-confidence answers.

Model and Tokenizer Loading:

- Loads the "**`tiiuae/falcon-rw-1b`**" causal language model and its tokenizer using Hugging Face's Transformers library.

Prompt Definition:

- Defines a natural language prompt: "The capital of France is".

Encoding the Prompt:

- The prompt is tokenized and prepared for input into the model.

Text Generation with Beam Search:

- The model generates **3 different outputs** using **beam search** (**`num_beams =3`**), which improves quality over simple greedy decoding.
- **`output_scores=True`** is used to get confidence scores for each sequence.

Confidence Filtering:

- Each generated output is scored.
- The code calculates a **confidence probability** from the log-score using `torch.exp(score)`.
- Outputs with confidence `≥ 0.5` are accepted and printed with a GOOD.
- Others are flagged with BAD as potentially **hallucinated or unreliable** answers.

Privacy and Data Security

LLMs trained in massive web corpora may inadvertently memorize and leak **sensitive personal information**, such as names, addresses, or health records. This raises **serious privacy concerns**, especially under **data protection laws** such as GDPR.

Real-life Use Cases:

- In 2023, it was found that ChatGPT could **reproduce personal data** from its training set when prompted in specific ways.
- Italy temporarily **banned ChatGPT,** citing privacy violations and a lack of transparency regarding data usage.

Real-world Mitigation Strategies:

- **Apple's Siri processing** ensures minimal data leaves the user's phone.
- **Google's PaLM 2** includes privacy-safe fine-tuning for healthcare chat agents.

To understand the context, in real-world NLP applications such as chatbots, virtual assistants, or healthcare systems, **user-generated data** often contains **personally identifiable information (PII)** such as:

- Names
- Email addresses
- Phone numbers
- Dates of birth
- Locations
- Medical information
- **Retaining such data without anonymization violates data privacy laws** such as GDPR, HIPAA, and so on.
- Hence, **automated anonymization** is necessary to protect user identities and comply with regulations.

So, we will detect sensitive entities **(such as names, locations, and so on)** using an NLP model and replace them with anonymized placeholders (for example, **`[NAME]`**, **`[LOCATION]`**, and so on). The code is as follows.

```
import spacy

# Load spaCy's English model
nlp = spacy.load("en_core_web_sm")

# Sample user data
text = "Charles Dickens visited Boston on August 4th and his
phone number is 657-980-5432."

# Process the text
doc = nlp(text)

# Initialize anonymized text
anonymized_text = text

# Loop through detected entities and anonymize
for ent in doc.ents:
    if ent.label_ in ["PERSON", "GPE", "DATE", "ORG"]:
        anonymized_text = anonymized_text.replace(ent.text,
f"[{ent.label_}]")

print("Original:", text)
print("Anonymized:", anonymized_text)

Output:

Original: Charles Dickens visited Boston on August 4th and his
phone number is 657-980-5432.

Anonymized: [PERSON] visited [GPE] on [DATE] and his phone number
is 657-980-5432.
```

We have used the spaCy model to identify the entities of **Date, Person, Organization, and Location**. In the original output, we have the main sentence, and the anonymized version has PERSON, GPE, and DATE as masked.

The use case can be extended in the healthcare domain, where protecting **Personal Health Information (PHI)** is crucial for **HIPAA compliance** and responsible AI.

In healthcare, typical **sensitive entities** that must be anonymized are as follows.

PHI Category	**Examples**	**Entity Labels (NER)**
Patient Information	Names, SSNs, Contact Numbers	`PERSON, ID, PHONE, EMAIL`

Locations	Hospitals, Cities, Addresses	`GPE, LOC, ADDRESS`
Dates	Admission/Discharge Dates, DoB	`DATE`
Medical Record Info	Record Numbers, Test IDs	`ID`
Organizations	Hospitals, Insurance Providers	`ORG`
Other Identifiers	Insurance numbers, Devices	Custom / regex-based

Table 10.1: *Sensitive patient health data with entity labels*

In the following code, we will see anonymization of PHI.

```
import spacy
import re

# Load the English NLP model
nlp = spacy.load("en_core_web_sm")

# Sample healthcare-related text
text = """
Patient Name: Tony Stark
DOB: 1972-12-08
Visited: Stanford Hospital, California
Diagnosis: Acute bronchitis.
Insurance ID: INS-9472718
Contact: 987-654-3210
Email: tony.stark@mit.edu
"""

# Apply spaCy model
doc = nlp(text)
anonymized_text = text

# Entity replacement map
entity_map = {
    "PERSON": "[PATIENT_NAME]",
    "DATE": "[DATE]",
    "ORG": "[HOSPITAL]",
    "GPE": "[LOCATION]"
}

# Replace named entities
for ent in doc.ents:
    if ent.label_ in entity_map:
        anonymized_text = anonymized_text.replace(ent.text,
entity_map[ent.label_])

# Regex-based custom anonymization
```

```
anonymized_text = re.sub(r"\b\d{3}-\d{3}-\d{4}\b", "[PHONE]",
anonymized_text)  # Phone
anonymized_text = re.sub(r"\bINS-\d+\b", "[INSURANCE_ID]",
anonymized_text)     # Insurance ID
anonymized_text = re.sub(r"[a-zA-Z0-9_.+-]+@[a-zA-Z0-9-]+\.
[a-zA-Z0-9-.]+", "[EMAIL]", anonymized_text)  # Email

# Print results
print("Original Text:\n", text)
print("\n Anonymized Text:\n", anonymized_text)
```

```
Output:

Original Text:

Patient Name: Tony Stark
DOB: 1972-12-08
Visited: Stanford Hospital, California
Diagnosis: Acute bronchitis.
Insurance ID: INS-9472718
Contact: 987-654-3210
Email: tony.stark@mit.edu


 Anonymized Text:

Patient Name: [PATIENT_NAME]
DOB: [DATE]
Visited: [HOSPITAL], [LOCATION]
Diagnosis: Acute bronchitis.
Insurance ID: [INSURANCE_ID]
Contact: [PHONE]
Email: [EMAIL]
```

In the first output, we have the original PHI of Tony Stark, and the anonymized data has **PATIENT_NAME** (masked for Tony Stark), **DATE** (Date of Birth), **[HOSPITAL]**, **[LOCATION]** (masked for the Hospital Location), **INSURANCE_ID** (masked for the Insurance ID), and the **PHONE** and **EMAIL**.

The reasons for masking the PHI are:

- Ensures de-identified data when training models on sensitive medical records.
- Used in automated report generation, EHR analytics, and diagnostics without risking privacy.
- Complies with HIPAA, GDPR, and healthcare-specific AI ethics.

Responsible AI Guidelines

These are **frameworks and practices** aimed at ensuring AI systems are **ethically designed, transparent, accountable, and aligned with human values**. Major tech companies and research institutions have published responsible AI principles.

Responsible LLM Deployment:

- **OpenAI's Usage Policy** prohibits GPT models for autonomous weapons or misinformation.
- **Hugging Face's Model Cards** provide transparency into model training data, biases, and limitations.
- Google's AI Principles guide the development of its models to **avoid weaponization and harmful impacts**.

Real-world Use Cases:

- **Microsoft Azure OpenAI Service** includes built-in content filters and compliance features.
- **UNESCO AI Ethics Guidelines** are being integrated into global education platforms.

Responsible LLM Deployment: OpenAI's Usage Policy prohibits the use of GPT models for autonomous weapons or the dissemination of false information. Additionally, Hugging Face's Model Cards provide transparency into model training data, biases, and limitations. Furthermore, Google's AI Principles ensure that model development is conducted without the intention of weaponizing it.

Real-world use cases: Microsoft Azure OpenAI Service has integrated compliance tools and content filters. Moreover, UNESCO AI Ethics Guidelines are integrated into global education platforms for safe usage of AI.

There were situations where chatbots (such as Microsoft) were racist towards their users. For implementing responsible AI guidelines, there can be use cases such as the following.

- **Chatbot Moderation**: Filter toxic user inputs in real time
- **Social Media Platforms**: Flag offensive comments before posting
- **Corporate Tools**: Review email or team communication toxicity
- **Content Generation Filter**: Post-process LLM output to ensure safety

So, we will see a Python code using the **detoxify** library that will help us identify the level of **negativity and toxicity** in the sentences, followed by a code on **visualizing the toxicity scores** for the sentences. The code is as follows.

```
from detoxify import Detoxify

# Initialize the Detoxify model
model = Detoxify('original')  # Options: 'original', 'unbiased',
'multilingual'

# Sample text that may contain toxic content
texts = [
    "I hope you have a great day!",                          # Positive
    "You're so stupid and annoying.",                       # Insult
    "This is a terrible platform full of idiots.",          # Toxicity
    "The weather is nice today."                            # Neutral
]

# Check toxicity for each sentence
for text in texts:
    results = model.predict(text)
    print(f"\n Text: {text}")
    for label, score in results.items():
        print(f"   {label}: {score:.2f}")
```

```
Output:
Text: I hope you have a great day!
   toxicity: 0.00
   severe_toxicity: 0.00
   obscene: 0.00
   threat: 0.00
   insult: 0.00
   identity_attack: 0.00

 Text: You're so stupid and annoying.
   toxicity: 0.99
   severe_toxicity: 0.03
   obscene: 0.64
   threat: 0.00
   insult: 0.94
   identity_attack: 0.01

 Text: This is a terrible platform full of idiots.
   toxicity: 0.98
   severe_toxicity: 0.01
   obscene: 0.41
   threat: 0.00
   insult: 0.73
   identity_attack: 0.01

 Text: The weather is nice today.
```

```
toxicity: 0.00
severe_toxicity: 0.00
obscene: 0.00
threat: 0.00
insult: 0.00
identity_attack: 0.00
```

For each sentence, Detoxify returns scores for different toxicity categories:

- `toxicity`
- `severe_toxicity`
- `obscene`
- `identity_attack`
- `insult`
- `threat`
- `sexual_explicit`

To understand the output, we have the **first and last sentences** that are **positive and neutral**, so we do not deal with any negativity or toxicity, but the **second sentence** has **toxicity, insult, and obscenity** in high proportions, with very **low scores of severe toxicity and identity attack**. In the **third sentence**, we have **high scores of toxicity, obscenity, and insult**, and **low scores of identity attack and severe toxicity**.

Key Benefits of Using Detoxify:

- Detects subtle toxicity (not just profanity).
- Multilingual support (multilingual model).
- Trained on massive real-world comment datasets.
- Lightweight and plug-and-play.

The following code has toxicity scores visualized using matplotlib.

```
import matplotlib.pyplot as plt
from detoxify import Detoxify

# Sample sentences to analyze
texts = [
    "I hope you have a great day!",                        # Positive
    "You're so stupid and annoying.",                     # Insult
    "This is a terrible platform full of idiots.",        # Toxicity
    "The weather is nice today."                          # Neutral
]
# Load Detoxify model
model = Detoxify('original')
```

```
# Get toxicity scores for each sentence
toxicity_scores = [model.predict(text) for text in texts]

# Set up subplots
num_sentences = len(texts)
fig, axes = plt.subplots(nrows=num_sentences, ncols=1, figsize=(10, 3
* num_sentences))
if num_sentences == 1:
    axes = [axes]  # Ensure axes is always iterable

# Plot each sentence's toxicity profile
for i, (text, scores) in enumerate(zip(texts, toxicity_scores)):
    labels = list(scores.keys())
    values = list(scores.values())

    axes[i].bar(labels, values, color='tomato')
    axes[i].set_ylim(0, 1)
    axes[i].set_ylabel("Score")
    axes[i].set_title(f"Toxicity Scores for Sentence {i+1}")
    axes[i].tick_params(axis='x', rotation=45)
    axes[i].grid(True, linestyle='--', alpha=0.5)

    # Add score labels on top of bars
    for j, val in enumerate(values):
        axes[i].text(j, val + 0.02, f"{val:.2f}", ha='center',
fontsize=9)

# Adjust layout
plt.tight_layout()
plt.show()
```

The preceding code is described as follows.

Import Libraries:

- **`matplotlib.pyplot`:** To plot bar charts.
- **Detoxify from detoxify:** To analyze text for different types of toxicity.

Input Sentences: A small list of example sentences (positive, toxic, neutral, and so on).

Load the Model: The Detoxify model (original version) is loaded. It evaluates text on several toxicity metrics.

Run Predictions:

- Each sentence is analyzed using the **model's `.predict()`** method, returning a dictionary of scores for:
    - **`toxicity`**, **`severe_toxicity`**, **`insult`**, **`threat`**, **`obscene`**, **`identity_attack`**, **`sexual_explicit`**.

Set up Subplots: A separate subplot is created for each sentence, stacked vertically.

Plot Each Sentence:

- For each sentence, the scores are plotted as bars.
- Labels and titles help identify what's being visualized.
- **Bars are color-coded (tomato)** and include score values above each bar.

Beautification:

- Rotation of x-axis labels for readability.
- Tight layout ensures plots do not overlap.
- Grid lines make it easier to interpret values.

The output plot is as follows.

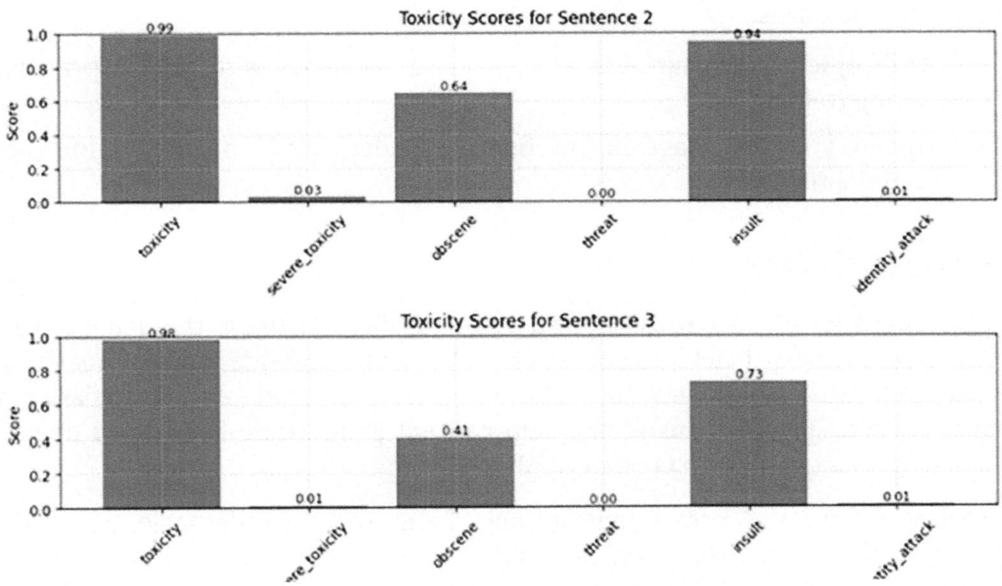

Figure 10.2: *Toxicity scores of sentence 2 and sentence 3*

In the preceding subplot created by matplotlib, we see toxicity of 0.99 and 0.98 for sentence 2 and sentence 3, respectively. The insult is lesser for sentence 3 (0.73) and 0.94 for sentence 2. Sentences 1 and 4 do not have any toxicity scores since they are positive and neutral, respectively.

The toxicity scores signify the **level of negativity present in the sentences**. This way, **chatbots** can be **trained to filter out toxic user inputs, social media platforms** can flag **offensive comments before posting**, or these can be **incorporated into corporate tools to review email communication toxicity**.

Regulations and the Future of AI Governance

There are acts such as the **EU AI Act (2024)** that classify LLMs such as ChatGPT as high-risk and mandate transparency, documentation, and risk mitigation, and the **US Executive Order on Safe AI (2023)** that encourages watermarking and origin disclosure in AI-generated content.

What's Next?

- **AI Audits**: Mandatory third-party assessments of AI models.
- **Licensing for LLMs**: To ensure compliance with safety and transparency norms.
- **Global Harmonization**: Initiatives such as the G7 Code of Conduct for AI developers are pushing for unified regulations.

Real-world Use Cases:

- **Anthropic's Constitutional AI** aligns LLM behavior with ethical principles during training.
- **OpenAI's GPT-4 usage in law firms** is under regulatory review for client confidentiality.

Conclusion

Large Language Models (LLMs) have dramatically redefined the landscape of NLP and AI, enabling machines to better understand, generate, and interact using human language. Their ability to perform a variety of tasks–from **translation to summarization, question-answering, and content generation**–has helped create a system of foundational tools in modern AI systems.

LLMs leverage massive pretraining, making them powerful, adaptable, and widely applicable across industries such as healthcare, education, finance, and legal tech without the need to build an architecture from scratch.

The evolution of LLMs is marked by emerging trends that emphasize **efficiency, specialization, and openness**. Smaller and optimized models such as **TinyLLaMA and Mistral** offer impressive performance with fewer computational demands, making AI more accessible for low-resource environments.

LLMs are the bedrock on which future NLP-based technologies and products will be built and are being built now. Their ability to perform tasks such as **content generation, summarization, translation, image and video generation, question-answering**, and so on, is customizable for domains such as **finance, healthcare, education, legal, e-commerce, defense, manufacturing**, and so on.

For NLP practitioners, this rapidly evolving space brings new opportunities. Fine-tuning pre-trained LLMs for custom applications is more feasible than ever with lightweight adaptation techniques such as **Low-Rank Adaptation (LoRA) and Parameter-Efficient Fine-Tuning (PEFT)**. Developers are now empowered to build task-specific AI systems efficiently, with growing importance placed on **evaluating and reducing hallucinations, improving transparency, and aligning outputs with ethical standards**. Moreover, as regulations begin to shape the responsible use of AI, there is a clear need for AI systems that are explainable, fair, and privacy-preserving.

In summary, the future of LLMs is not solely about building larger models but about making them more **capable, ethical, and accessible**. With advancements in training methods, **responsible AI practices, and domain adaptation**, LLMs will continue to revolutionize how we interact with technology.

In the next chapter, we will **fine-tune LLMs, build a code completion tool, build a text generation tool, and understand prompt engineering**. Moreover, we will also explore **Retrieval Augmented Generation (RAG)**, while we build a **text summarization tool**.

References

- https://arxiv.org/html/2402.06853v1
- https://medium.com/@researchgraph/brief-introduction-to-the-history-of-large-language-models-llms-3c2efa517112
- https://arxiv.org/pdf/1706.03762
- https://wandb.ai/mostafaibrahim17/ml-articles/reports/An-Overview-of-Large-Language-Models-LLMs---VmlldzozODA3MzQz?galleryTag=llm#what-is-a-large-language-model
- https://www.kolena.com/guides/llm-vs-nlp-6-key-differences-and-using-them-together/
- https://labelyourdata.com/articles/llm-vs-nlp#:~:text=%E2%80%9CLLMs%20excel%20in%20tasks%20requiring,or%20rule%2Dbased%20classifications.%E2%80%9D
- https://huggingface.co/learn/llm-course/en/chapter1/2
- https://zapier.com/blog/best-llm/
- https://www.techtarget.com/whatis/feature/12-of-the-best-large-language-models
- https://www.shakudo.io/blog/top-9-large-language-models
- https://wandb.ai/mostafaibrahim17/ml-articles/reports/An-Overview-of-Large-Language-Models-LLMs---VmlldzozODA3MzQz

- https://www.labellerr.com/blog/exploring-architectures-and-configurations-for-large-language-models-llms/
- https://github.blog/ai-and-ml/llms/the-architecture-of-todays-llm-applications/
- https://aws.amazon.com/what-is/large-language-model/
- https://whylabs.ai/learning-center/introduction-to-llms/understanding-large-language-model-architectures
- https://medium.com/sage-ai/demystify-transformers-a-comprehensive-guide-to-scaling-laws-attention-mechanism-fine-tuning-fffb62fc2552
- https://cameronrwolfe.substack.com/p/llm-scaling-laws
- https://arxiv.org/pdf/2001.08361
- https://arxiv.org/html/2411.10915v1
- https://arxiv.org/pdf/2401.13086
- https://www.gable.ai/blog/llm-data-quality
- https://medium.com/@sulbha.jindal/transfer-learning-llm-generalization-to-similar-problems-1d3b2bf28c6e
- https://maddevs.io/blog/transfer-learning-from-large-language-models/
- https://arxiv.org/html/2410.11539v1
- https://toloka.ai/blog/transfer-learning/
- https://arxiv.org/pdf/2307.06435
- https://pixelplex.io/blog/llm-applications/
- https://www.amazon.in/Hands-Large-Language-Models-Understanding/dp/935542552X/ref=tmm_pap_swatch_0
- https://github.com/HandsOnLLM/Hands-On-Large-Language-Models
- https://medium.com/@abonia/books-on-llm-and-nlp-in-2024-aea05617d557
- https://thelmbook.com/
- https://www.linkedin.com/pulse/rise-ai-powered-virtual-health-assistants-chatbots-kblxf/
- https://zapier.com/blog/best-ai-writing-generator/
- https://docs.anthropic.com/en/docs/agents-and-tools/claude-code/overview
- https://pieces.app/use-cases/software-engineers
- https://www.tabnine.com/

- https://online.hbs.edu/blog/post/ethical-considerations-of-ai
- https://www.ibm.com/think/topics/ai-ethics
- https://www.pmi.org/blog/top-10-ethical-considerations-for-ai-projects
- https://www.dasca.org/world-of-data-science/article/responsible-ai-ethics-challenges-and-benefits
- https://sigma.ai/ethical-ai-responsible-ai/
- https://www.ibm.com/think/topics/ai-bill-of-rights
- https://blog.research.google/2023/08/responsible-ai-at-google-research.html
- https://s10251.pcdn.co/pdf/2021-bender-parrots.pdf
- https://arxiv.org/pdf/2202.03629
- https://www.evidentlyai.com/blog/llm-hallucination-examples
- https://unesdoc.unesco.org/ark:/48223/pf0000381137
- https://digital-strategy.ec.europa.eu/en/policies/regulatory-framework-ai#:~:text=The%20AI%20Act%20(Regulation%20(EU,foster%20trustworthy%20AI%20in%20Europe.
- https://ai.google/responsibility/principles/
- https://www.microsoft.com/en-us/ai/responsible-ai
- https://arxiv.org/pdf/2306.15298
- https://dmccreary.medium.com/showing-bias-in-bert-475e98dabf51
- https://spectrum.ieee.org/in-2016-microsofts-racist-chatbot-revealed-the-dangers-of-online-conversation
- https://timesofindia.indiatimes.com/gadgets-news/microsoft-responds-to-users-claim-on-its-ai-chatbot-copilot-giving-dangerous-responses/articleshow/108121350.cms
- https://huggingface.co/docs/peft/en/package_reference/lora
- https://web.stanford.edu/~jurafsky/slp3/3.pdf
- https://www.sciencedirect.com/science/article/pii/S2949719124000360
- https://www.sciencedirect.com/science/article/pii/S1319157815000890
- https://www.geeksforgeeks.org/nlp/n-gram-language-modelling-with-nltk/

CHAPTER 11

Fine-Tuning LLMs and Building Text-Powered Tools

Introduction

Large Language Models (LLMs) such as **GPT-4, LLaMA, DeepSeek, and Claude** have revolutionized search, reasoning, and human-level communication. While these models offer powerful general capabilities, real-world applications mostly require **task-specific customization**. This is where **fine-tuning** comes in, where developers can adapt **pre-trained LLMs to specialized domains** such as **healthcare, law, finance, or customer support**. Fine-tuning refines the model's knowledge and behavior by training it further on relevant, curated datasets.

This chapter explores the complete lifecycle of fine-tuning LLMs, and deploying them into useful, text-powered tools. We will learn how to **select appropriate models, prepare training data, and fine-tune models using Hugging Face libraries**. We will also dive into **parameter-efficient methods such as LoRA and prompt-tuning**, which make customization possible even on limited hardware. In addition, we will introduce **AI Agents**—autonomous systems built on top of LLMs that can **reason, plan, and take actions** across tools and APIs. These agents extend LLMs beyond text generation into real-time decision-making and automation.

Beyond theory, the chapter features hands-on projects such as building a **code completion assistant, a creative text generator, and a domain-specific Q&A system**. We also introduce **Retrieval-Augmented Generation (RAG)**, an **advanced technique that combines LLMs with real-time document retrieval to build fact-based applications**. By the end of this chapter, we will be equipped with the skills to **create powerful, domain-aware language tools and deploy them in real-world environments**. Whether we are building for **business, research, or open-source innovation**, this chapter will guide you from model customization to practical deployment.

Structure

In this chapter, we will cover the following topics:

- Understanding LLMs and Fine-Tuning
  - Types of Fine-Tuning
  - Choosing the Right Model and Dataset
- Fine-Tuning LLMs in Practice
  - Environment Setup for Fine-Tuning
  - Fine-Tuning Step-by-Step
  - Case Study: Fine-Tuning a Text Summarizer
- Building Text-Powered Tools
  - Tool 1: Code Completion Assistant
  - Tool 2: Text Generation System
- Retrieval-Augmented Generation (RAG)
  - What is RAG and Why It Matters
  - Building a Simple RAG Pipeline
- Evaluation, Optimization, and Deployment
  - Evaluating Fine-Tuned Models
  - Optimizing for Speed and Cost

Understanding LLMs and Fine-Tuning

This topic of the chapter deals with fine-tuning LLMs, introducing LoRA, Adapters, and Prompt Tuning, and choosing the right models and datasets for building.

Large Language Models (LLMs)

LLMs are advanced neural networks that are capable enough to think, searching, reasoning, and conversing with humans. They are trained on vast amounts of data, such as **websites, books, and code repositories,** to provide the right information to the users. However, to customize LLMs to perform specific tasks such as text generation, code generation, image generation, article or blog writing, LLMs need to be fine-tuned, and the right model needs to be utilized. There is a plethora of models on the Hugging Face website, ranging from text to text, text to image, image to video, question answering, summarization, and translation, to name a few that are present.

LLM Fine-Tuning

Fine-tuning of LLMs can be broadly categorized into two approaches: **full fine-tuning** and **parameter-efficient fine-tuning (PEFT)**.

- **Full Fine-Tuning**: In this approach, all the parameters of the pre-trained LLM are updated. It yields high performance but is computationally expensive and requires a large amount of labeled data and memory. It is best suited when working with a powerful GPU setup and large task-specific datasets.
- **Parameter-Efficient Fine-Tuning (PEFT)**: PEFT techniques help to adapt large models with minimal compute resources by updating only a small subset of model parameters. This is especially useful for practitioners without access to expensive infrastructure.

Some popular PEFT techniques include:

- **Low-Rank Adaptation (LoRA)**: Injects trainable low-rank matrices into each layer of the transformer, allowing efficient fine-tuning.
- **Adapters**: Small bottleneck modules are added between transformer layers, trained while keeping the base model frozen.
- **Prompt Tuning / Prefix Tuning**: Instead of updating model weights, the model is conditioned with optimized prompt tokens or prefixes to steer outputs for specific tasks.

These methods not only reduce training costs but also improve modularity and reusability of model components.

Choosing the Right Model and Dataset

Fine-tuning success mostly depends on selecting the appropriate model and crafting or choosing a high-quality dataset.

- **Domain-Specific Model Selection**: Not all models are built the same. For healthcare tasks, models such as **BioBERT, PubMedBERT, or ClinicalBERT** are fine-tuned on **medical corpora**. For code generation, models such as **CodeT5 or StarCoder** are more suitable.
- **Curating a Fine-Tuning Dataset**: Depending on the use case, we will need task-aligned data. Here are a few common types:
    - **Text Classification**: Labels paired with sentences or paragraphs. (for example, sentiment analysis)
    - **Question-Answering (QA)**: A dataset containing context passages, questions, and answers (for example, SQuAD, BioASQ).
    - **Summarization**: Documents with concise reference summaries (for example, CNN/DailyMail).

    - **Code**: Code snippets with corresponding prompts, completions, or documentation (for example, **HumanEval, CodeSearchNet**).

Fine-Tuning LLMs in Practice

This topic will explain the environment setup for fine-tuning, the relevant libraries to install, and then using Google Colab. Next, we will walk through the steps of fine-tuning, starting from loading the dataset, tokenization, and pre-trained model loading. Then, preprocessing is done, and the training and evaluation are done. Then the model is saved and deployed. Next, we build a text summarizer and fine-tune it with the evaluation.

Environment Setup for Fine-Tuning

Before fine-tuning a language model, it is crucial to establish a reliable development environment. Thanks to the Hugging Face ecosystem, the process is now more accessible than ever.

- **Key Libraries:**
    - **transformers:** Offers pre-trained models and training utilities.
    - **datasets:** Provides access to thousands of datasets and supports efficient preprocessing.
    - **accelerate:** Simplifies multi-GPU training and mixed-precision computation with minimal boilerplate.
- **Where to Run:**
    - We are using **Google Colab** since it is ideal for free GPU access and running tutorials or small-scale experiments. However, there are also platforms such as **Kaggle Notebooks** that provide TPUs and pre-installed libraries, **Deepnote, Replit, VS Code, Jupyter Notebook,** and so on.

Fine-Tuning Step-by-Step

Once the environment is ready, we start fine-tuning using the Hugging Face tools and build a summarizer.

Step 1: Load the Dataset, tokenizer, and model

We chose a dataset relevant to the summarization task. Then, a tokenizer and a compatible pre-trained model were loaded. The code is as follows.

```
from datasets import load_dataset
from transformers import AutoTokenizer, AutoModelForSeq2SeqLM
```

```
dataset = load_dataset("cnn_dailymail", "3.0.0")
tokenizer = AutoTokenizer.from_pretrained("facebook/bart-base")
model = AutoModelForSeq2SeqLM.from_pretrained("facebook/bart-base")
```

The **datasets** library (from Hugging Face) imported the **load_dataset** function. It helps to load ready-to-use datasets such as **cnn_dailymail** easily. The **load_dataset()** function loads the **CNN/DailyMail dataset**, which is a popular dataset for **abstractive summarization**.

The "3.0.0" version uses cleaned and corrected data.

Each example in the dataset has:

- "**article**" - the full news article text.
- "**highlights**" - the corresponding human-written summary.

It returns a dictionary with train, test, and validation splits.

```
dataset["train"]
dataset["validation"]
dataset["test"]
```

AutoTokenizer.from_pretrained() loads the **tokenizer** for the BART model. The **tokenizer** converts text into input IDs and attention masks that the model understands. The **facebook/bart-base** is a pretrained **encoder-decoder model** optimized for sequence-to-sequence tasks such as summarization.

AutoModelForSeq2SeqLM.from_pretrained() loads the **BART model** pre-trained for sequence-to-sequence learning (Seq2SeqLM = Sequence to Sequence Language Model).

It is good at tasks such as **summarization**, **translation**, and **text generation**.

BART uses:

- An **encoder** to understand the input (article), and
- A **decoder** to generate the output (summary).

Step 2: Preprocess the Data

We must tokenize inputs and labels for training. The code is as follows.

```
def preprocess(example):
    inputs = tokenizer(example["article"], truncation=True,
padding="max_length", max_length=512)
    labels = tokenizer(example["highlights"], truncation=True,
padding="max_length", max_length=128)
    inputs["labels"] = labels["input_ids"]
    return inputs

tokenized_data = dataset.map(preprocess, batched=True)
```

In the preceding code, the **preprocess** function is created, and the **`tokenizer()`** function is used on the **`"article"`** (the text) and **`"highlights"`** (the summary).

- **`truncation=True`**: If the article is longer than 512 tokens, it will be **cut**.
- **`padding="max_length"`**: If the article is shorter than 512 tokens, it will be **padded** to exactly 512 tokens.
- **`max_length=512`**: Set the maximum input length to 512 tokens.

The goal is to prepare the input text so that it is the right size for the model.

The **`truncation = True`** and **`padding="max_length"`** remains the same for the **labels** variable. The **`max_length=128`**; since summaries are shorter, we only keep **128 tokens**.

After tokenizing the article (inputs), we **add a new key** called "**`labels`**".

- It holds the **tokenized summary**.
- During training:
    - The model tries to **generate** the "**`labels`**" given the "**`inputs`**".

This links the article and its target summary together for training.

Then we apply the preprocess function to the **whole dataset**.

- **`batched=True`**: Processes **multiple examples at once** (faster and more efficient).

So, the tokenized_data will have each example already converted into:

- **`input_ids`** (for the article),
- **`attention_mask`** (mask for padding),
- **`labels`** (for the target summary).

Step 3: Use the Trainer API

In this step, we will train the model using specific arguments. The code is as follows.

```
from transformers import TrainingArguments, Trainer

from transformers import TrainingArguments

args = TrainingArguments(
    output_dir="./results",
    per_device_train_batch_size=4,
    num_train_epochs=1,
    logging_dir="./logs",
    save_total_limit=2,
    logging_steps=10
)
```

```
trainer = Trainer(
    model=model,
    args=args,
    train_dataset=tokenized_data["train"],
    eval_dataset=tokenized_data["validation"]
)

trainer.train()
```

The code is explained as follows:

```
from transformers import TrainingArguments, Trainer
```

- Import two important classes from Hugging Face's Transformers library:
    - `TrainingArguments`: Helps **configure** how training should run (batch size, epochs, where to save, and so on).
    - `Trainer`: A **high-level API** that handles the **entire training loop** (training, evaluation, checkpoint saving).

    `args = TrainingArguments(...)`

This creates a **`TrainingArguments`** object, setting all important training settings.

Argument	Purpose
`output_dir="./results"`	Where to save model checkpoints after training.
`per_device_train_batch_size=4`	Mini-batch size: 4 samples will be processed together at a time per device (GPU/CPU).
`num_train_epochs=1`	Only **one pass** through the entire training dataset. (We can increase it later for better results.)
`logging_dir="./logs"`	Directory to save training logs.
`save_total_limit=2`	Save at most **2 model checkpoints**. Old ones will be deleted automatically.
`logging_steps=10`	Log training progress **every 10 steps**.

Table 11.1: *Training arguments*

`trainer = Trainer(...)`

Now, we create a Trainer instance that ties everything together:

Argument	Purpose
`model=model`	The **BART summarization model** we loaded earlier.
`args=args`	All the training settings we just defined.
`train_dataset=tokenized_data["train"]`	The **training dataset** (preprocessed articles and summaries).

`eval_dataset=tokenized_data["validation"]`	The **validation dataset** (used to monitor model performance during training).

Table 11.2: *Model details and training settings*

The Trainer will **automatically handle**:

- Data loading
- Forward and backward passes
- Loss calculation
- Optimization
- Evaluation during training

```
trainer.train()
```

Start the training process

- The Trainer:
  - Feeds training examples in batches to the model
  - Computes loss
  - Updates model weights
  - Evaluates periodically on the validation set
  - Saves model checkpoints

Step	Training Loss
10	7.693800
20	5.406800
30	4.190800
40	3.396200
50	2.675400
60	2.245500
70	1.862800
80	1.551100
90	1.501300
100	1.371900

Figure 11.1: *Training loss for each 10 steps*

In the preceding screenshot, we see the training loss decreases for each step and almost stabilizes after the 80th step.

Case Study: Fine-Tuning a Text Summarizer

We will build and fine-tune a text summarizer where the dataset is from the **`CNN_dailymail`** dataset. We will use the "**`facebook/bart-large-cnn`**" model and **ROUGE** as the evaluation metric. The code is as follows.

```
from transformers import pipeline, AutoTokenizer, AutoModelForSe-
q2SeqLM
import evaluate
from datasets import load_dataset

# Load the dataset
dataset = load_dataset("cnn_dailymail", "3.0.0")

# Load model and tokenizer
model_name = "facebook/bart-large-cnn"  # Common summarization
model
tokenizer = AutoTokenizer.from_pretrained(model_name)
model = AutoModelForSeq2SeqLM.from_pretrained(model_name)

# Create summarization pipeline
summarizer = pipeline("summarization", model=model, tokenizer
=tokenizer)

# Get samples using the proper method for datasets
small_validation = dataset["validation"].select(range(9))

# Extract articles and highlights as lists to avoid indexing
issues
sample_texts = [item for item in small_validation["article"]]
reference_summaries = [item for item in small_validation
["highlights"]]

# Generate summaries with proper error handling
generated_summaries = []
for text in sample_texts:
    try:
        # Handle text that's too long
        if len(text) > 1024:  # Simple truncation for very long
texts
            text = text[:1024]

        # Generate the summary and add explicit error handling
```

```
        summary_output = summarizer(text, max_length=130, min_
length=30, do_sample=False)

        # Check if the output is valid
        if summary_output and isinstance(summary_output, list)
and len(summary_output) > 0:
            summary = summary_output[0]["summary_text"]
            generated_summaries.append(summary)
        else:
            # Fallback if summary generation fails
            print(f"Warning: Failed to generate summary, using
placeholder")
            generated_summaries.append("Summary generation
failed.")
    except Exception as e:
        print(f"Error processing text: {e}")
        generated_summaries.append("Error in summary
generation.")

# Make sure we have the same number of generated and reference
summaries
assert len(generated_summaries) == len(reference_summaries),
"Mismatch in number of summaries"

# Evaluate with ROUGE
rouge = evaluate.load("rouge")
results = rouge.compute(predictions=generated_summaries,
references=reference_summaries)

# Print results
print("ROUGE Evaluation:")
for key, value in results.items():
    print(f"{key}: {value:.4f}")
```

Output:

```
ROUGE Evaluation:
rouge1: 0.3325
rouge2: 0.1358
rougeL: 0.2286
rougeLsum: 0.2811
```

The code explanation is as follows:

Imports and Setup

```
from transformers import pipeline, AutoTokenizer, AutoModelFor
Seq2SeqLM
```

```
import evaluate
from datasets import load_dataset
```

This imports the necessary libraries:

- **transformers**: For pre-trained models and tokenizers
- **evaluate**: For evaluation metrics like ROUGE
- **datasets**: For loading benchmark datasets

Loading the Dataset

```
dataset = load_dataset("cnn_dailymail", "3.0.0")
```

- This loads the CNN/DailyMail dataset (version 3.0.0) from Hugging Face's datasets library.
- This dataset contains news articles along with human-written summaries (called "**`highlights`**").

Model and Tokenizer Initialization

```
model_name = "facebook/bart-large-cnn"
tokenizer = AutoTokenizer.from_pretrained(model_name)
model = AutoModelForSeq2SeqLM.from_pretrained(model_name)
```

- Uses the BART-large-CNN model, which is specifically fine-tuned for **summarization on `CNN/DailyMail`**
- **`AutoTokenizer`**: Loads the tokenizer that converts text to tokens the model can understand.
- **`AutoModelForSeq2SeqLM`**: Loads the sequence-to-sequence model for text generation

Pipeline Creation

```
summarizer = pipeline("summarization", model=model,
tokenizer=tokenizer)
```

Creates a summarization pipeline that handles the entire process:

- Tokenizing the input text
- Running it through the model
- Decoding the output tokens back to text

Data Preparation

```
small_validation = dataset["validation"].select(range(9))
sample_texts = [item for item in small_validation["article"]]
reference_summaries = [item for item in small_validation
["highlights"]]
```

Takes 9 examples from the validation set using **`.select(range(9))`** (proper slicing for datasets).

Extracts articles and reference summaries as Python lists for easier handling.

Summary Generation

```
generated_summaries = []
for text in sample_texts:
    try:
        if len(text) > 1024:
            text = text[:1024]

        summary_output = summarizer(text, max_length=130,
min_length=30, do_sample=False)

        if summary_output and isinstance(summary_output, list)
and len(summary_output) > 0:
            summary = summary_output[0]["summary_text"]
            generated_summaries.append(summary)
        else:
            print(f"Warning: Failed to generate summary, using
placeholder")
            generated_summaries.append("Summary generation
failed.")
    except Exception as e:
        print(f"Error processing text: {e}")
        generated_summaries.append("Error in summary
generation.")
```

Loops through each article and generates summaries with:

Text truncation to **1024 characters for very long articles**

Parameters: `max_length=130` and **`min_length=30`** to control summary length

`do_sample=False` for deterministic generation (no randomness)

Includes comprehensive error handling:

- Validates output structure before extracting the summary
- Catches any exceptions and provides fallback content

Consistency Check

```
assert len(generated_summaries) == len(reference_summaries),
"Mismatch in number of summaries"
```

Ensures we have the same number of generated and reference summaries for proper evaluation.

Evaluation

```
rouge = evaluate.load("rouge")
results = rouge.compute(predictions=generated_summaries,
references=reference_summaries)
```

- Loads the **ROUGE metric** from the Hugging Face evaluate library.
- Computes **ROUGE scores** by comparing generated summaries against reference summaries.

This code demonstrates a complete workflow for text summarization using a pre-trained model and evaluating its performance.

The ROUGE scores we received **(ROUGE-1: 0.3325, ROUGE-2: 0.1358, ROUGE-L: 0.2286, ROUGE-Lsum: 0.2811)** indicate reasonable performance for a general summarization system on this dataset.

These ROUGE scores represent how well our generated summaries match the reference summaries. Let us see each metric:

- **ROUGE-1: 0.3325 (33.25%)**: This measures the overlap of **unigrams (individual words) between the generated and reference summaries**. Our score of 33.25% means that about **one-third of the individual words in our generated summaries match those in the reference summaries**. However, this is a reasonable score for summarization tasks, indicating moderate lexical overlap.
- **ROUGE-2: 0.1358 (13.58%)**: This measures the **overlap of bigrams (pairs of consecutive words) between the summaries**. Our score of 13.58% is lower than ROUGE-1, which is expected since **matching word pairs is harder than matching individual words**. This moderate score suggests that our model captures some of the phrase structure from the original summaries.
- **ROUGE-L: 0.2286 (22.86%)**: This measures the **longest common subsequence between the generated and reference summaries**. It considers sentence structure by finding the longest sequence of matching words in order (though not necessarily consecutively). Our score of 22.86% indicates **reasonable structural similarity between the generated and reference summaries**.
- **ROUGE-Lsum: 0.2811 (28.11%)**: This is a variant of ROUGE-L that operates at the summary level rather than the sentence level. It is often higher than ROUGE-L because **it allows for matches across sentence boundaries.** Our score of 28.11% shows decent summary-level structural similarity.

Overall Assessment

These scores represent a fair summarization performance for the **CNN/DailyMail** dataset using the BART-large-CNN model. For context:

State-of-the-art systems typically achieve ROUGE-1 scores of 40-45% on this dataset

Our scores are in the expected range for this model, though there is room for improvement.

The gap between ROUGE-1 and ROUGE-2 scores suggests the model is better at capturing individual words than maintaining phrase structure.

Building Text-Powered Tools

In this section, we will create a **code completion tool** and a **text generation system**. For the code completion tool, it will act as an **IDE plugin for auto-code suggestion,** such as **Microsoft Copilot**. The **text generation system** will create **short and long stories, write blog posts, and poems**.

Tool 1: Code Completion Assistant

CodeSearchNet is a large collection of real-world code snippets from GitHub across multiple languages, such as Python and Java. It helps models **learn coding patterns, syntax, and structure**. In our case, we have used a model already pretrained on similar high-quality code datasets, avoiding the need for full retraining.

We have chosen the **`Salesforce/codegen-350M-multi`** model, a compact, multilingual model optimized for code generation tasks. It is designed to **understand and generate code efficiently** across several programming languages. **StarCoder** is another alternative, trained on a broader and even larger code dataset. These models can handle tasks such as **code auto-completion, bug fixing, and documentation generation**.

The tool aims to suggest **code completions as developers type inside an IDE**, such as **GitHub Copilot**. The model predicts the next lines based on the **partial input, enhancing coding speed and reducing repetitive typing**. While currently script-based, the tool can be easily integrated into IDEs through APIs or lightweight plugins for a full interactive experience.

The code for the tool is as follows.

```
from transformers import AutoTokenizer, AutoModelForCausalLM

# Model name
model_name = "Salesforce/codegen-350M-multi"

# Load tokenizer
tokenizer = AutoTokenizer.from_pretrained(model_name)

# Load model without warnings
model = AutoModelForCausalLM.from_pretrained(
```

```
    model_name,
    trust_remote_code=True,
    ignore_mismatched_sizes=True
)

# Function to complete code
def complete_code(prompt, max_new_tokens=50):
    inputs = tokenizer(prompt, return_tensors="pt")
    outputs = model.generate(
        **inputs,
        max_new_tokens=max_new_tokens,
        do_sample=True,          # enable sampling for creative
suggestions
        temperature=0.7,         # controls randomness (lower =
more deterministic)
        top_p=0.95,              # nucleus sampling for quality
        pad_token_id=tokenizer.eos_token_id
    )
    completion = tokenizer.decode(outputs[0], skip_special_
tokens=True)
    return completion

# Example usage
user_prompt = "def fibonacci(n):"
completed_code = complete_code(user_prompt)

print("=== Completed Code ===")
print(completed_code)


Output:
=== Completed Code ===
def fibonacci(n):
    return fibonacci(n-1) + fibonacci(n-2)

print(fibonacci(6))
print(fibonacci(5))
```

The code is explained as follows.

Code Block	Explanation
from transformers import **`AutoTokenizer`**, **`CodeGenForCausalLM`**	Import Hugging Face's tokenizer and model class for code generation.
`model_name = "Salesforce/codegen-350M-multi"`	Specify the pre-trained model: a 350M parameter version trained on multiple programming languages.

`tokenizer = AutoTokenizer.from_pretrained(model_name)`	Load the tokenizer that breaks down text (code here) into tokens the model can understand.
`model = CodeGenForCausalLM.from_pretrained(model_name, trust_remote_code=True)`	Load the pre-trained CodeGen model for causal language modeling (text prediction) and allow trusted custom model code.
`prompt = "def fibonacci(n):"`	Provide the starting code or function signature. This acts as the seed for code completion.
`inputs = tokenizer(prompt, return_tensors="pt")`	Convert the input text into tensors (PyTorch format) so the model can process it.
`outputs = model.generate(...)`	Generate continuation for the input code: - **`max_new_tokens=50`** limits the number of tokens. - **`temperature=0.7`** makes predictions slightly creative. - **`do_sample=True`** enables sampling rather than greedy generation. - **`top_k=50 limits next`**-token choices to the top 50 most likely tokens.
`completed_code = tokenizer.decode(outputs[0], skip_special_tokens=True)`	Decode the tensor output back into human-readable code text.
`print(completed_code)`	Display the full completed code (original + model-generated continuation).

Table 11.3: *Code snippets with explanations*

The output of the code creates the Fibonacci function and returns the output. We can change the prompts accordingly and create new code.

Tool 2: Text Generation System

The **Text Generation System** is built using the **GPT-2 large model** that focuses on enabling **creative writing, long-form content creation, and story generation**. By leveraging GPT-2's extensive language understanding and coherent text construction capabilities, this system can create relevant outputs ranging from **poems and short stories to full-length articles** and **imaginative narratives**.

With customizable prompts, adjustable text lengths, and controlled creativity settings (such as **sampling temperature and top-p filtering**), users can **fine-tune outputs** to meet **different tones, styles, and content depths**. Overall, the system transforms the traditionally manual process of creative writing into a faster, more innovative experience powered by large-scale language modeling.

The code for the text generation system is as follows.

```
from transformers import AutoModelForCausalLM, AutoTokenizer,
pipeline
import torch

# Step 1: Load a powerful text generation model
model_name = "gpt2-large"
tokenizer = AutoTokenizer.from_pretrained(model_name)
model = AutoModelForCausalLM.from_pretrained(model_name)

# Step 2: Create a text generation pipeline
text_generator = pipeline(
    "text-generation",
    model=model,
    tokenizer=tokenizer,
    device=0 if torch.cuda.is_available() else -1  # Use GPU if
available
)

# Step 3: Define a function to generate content
def generate_content(prompt, content_type="short"):
    if content_type == "short":
        max_length = 100  # Suitable for poems, short posts
    else:
        max_length = 500  # Suitable for blogs, articles

    outputs = text_generator(
        prompt,
        max_length=max_length,
        temperature=0.7,
        top_p=0.9,
        top_k=50,
        num_return_sequences=1,
        do_sample=True
    )
    return outputs[0]["generated_text"]

# Step 4: Example usages

# Generate a poem
poem = generate_content("Write a beautiful poem about Paris",
content_type="short")
print("\nGenerated Poem:\n", poem)

# Generate a blog post
blog = generate_content("Write a blog about the future of AI in
```

```
healthcare", content_type="long")
print("\nGenerated Blog:\n", blog)

Output:
Generated Poem:
 Write a beautiful poem about Paris, or a poem about the city
itself.
The city of Paris is a beautiful place, and I am not going to try
to convince you otherwise. The city of Paris is beautiful in a
way that no other city can be. It is the center of the European
Union, and it is the birthplace of modern French literature. It
is the home of the French National Theatre, and it is the home of
the Louvre Museum. And it is also the home

Generated Blog:
 Write a blog about the future of AI in healthcare.

What is AI?

AI is an umbrella term for any type of machine learning algo-
rithm, which can be used to predict how a computer will perform
tasks and predict future events. It can be used to help computers
understand the world and act more like humans.

For example, AI can help computers understand the physical world,
such as when a computer is asked to play chess. It can also help
computers understand how the world works and to predict events,
such as when an AI will take a new job.

AI is not a new technology. The first known application of AI was
in the 1960s when computers played chess.

The rise of AI

As more computers are built, more powerful AI algorithms are de-
veloped. For example, the IBM Watson supercomputer, which has the
ability to beat human players, was developed in the late 1990s.

AI algorithms have been used to help improve the quality of
healthcare, such as the use of artificial intelligence to diagnose
and treat diseases.

It is also used to help improve the efficiency of companies by
predicting the future of a company's operations.

AI has also been used to improve the efficiency of businesses. AI
can be used to predict the future of companies and businesses,
```

```
such as when a company will be acquired or when an employee will
leave.

AI is also being used to make predictions about the future. For
example, when a company makes a prediction about an employee's
future, an AI algorithm can help the company make a decision on
how to handle the employee's departure.
```

The code explanation of the text generation system using Hugging Face and PyTorch is as follows.

Imports and Setup

```
from transformers import AutoModelForCausalLM, AutoTokenizer,
pipeline
import torch
```

- `AutoModelForCausalLM`: Loads a pre-trained **causal language model** (good for text generation, such as GPT).
- `AutoTokenizer`: Handles converting text into tokens and back (essential for working with transformers).
- `pipeline`: Hugging Face's high-level API to quickly build NLP tools such as text generation.
- `torch`: Used to check if a GPU is available (for faster processing).

Load the Model and Tokenizer

```
model_name = "gpt2-large"
tokenizer = AutoTokenizer.from_pretrained(model_name)
model = AutoModelForCausalLM.from_pretrained(model_name)
```

- Loads **GPT-2 Large**, a generative model trained to predict the next word in a sentence.
- `AutoTokenizer` prepares input text for the model (tokenization).
- `AutoModelForCausalLM` loads the actual neural network for text generation.

Create a Text Generation Pipeline

```
text_generator = pipeline(
    "text-generation",
    model=model,
    tokenizer=tokenizer,
    device=0 if torch.cuda.is_available() else -1
)
```

- Creates a **text generation pipeline** using the model + tokenizer.
- `device=0` uses GPU if available, otherwise it runs on CPU (-1).

- This pipeline simplifies generation logic—we do not need to manually encode/decode.

Define the Content Generator

```
def generate_content(prompt, content_type="short"):
    if content_type == "short":
        max_length = 100
    else:
        max_length = 500
```

- A function to handle both short content (like poems or tweets) and long content (like articles/blogs).
- max_length controls how many tokens the model generates.

```
    outputs = text_generator(
        prompt,
        max_length=max_length,
        temperature=0.7,
        top_p=0.9,
        top_k=50,
        num_return_sequences=1,
        do_sample=True
    )
    return outputs[0]["generated_text"]
```

- **`temperature=0.7`:** Controls randomness; lower = more deterministic.
- **`top_p=0.9, top_k=50`:** Used for **nucleus sampling**, balancing creativity with coherence.
- **`num_return_sequences=1`:** Generates one output.
- **`do_sample=True`:** Enables sampling instead of greedy decoding (important for creativity).

Returns the final **generated text.**

Generate Content

```
poem = generate_content("Write a beautiful poem about Paris",
content_type="short")
print("\nGenerated Poem:\n", poem)

blog = generate_content("Write a blog about the future of AI in
healthcare", content_type="long")
print("\nGenerated Blog:\n", blog)
```

- **Generates a poem** based on a creative prompt.
- **Generates a blog** based on a technical topic.

Summary

This system:

- Uses a pre-trained **GPT-2 large model**.
- Supports both **short** and **long-form content generation**.
- Is GPU-compatible and scalable.
- Can be reused for various tasks: poetry, blogs, articles, storytelling, and so on.

Retrieval-Augmented Generation

In this section, we will look into RAG, its significance, build a RAG pipeline, and deploy a RAG chatbot on a specific use case.

What is RAG, and Its Significance

Retrieval-Augmented Generation (RAG) represents a major advancement in how **Large Language Models (LLMs)** interact with information. Instead of relying solely on their internal knowledge from pretraining, RAG models actively pull external information from relevant sources at the time of answering a query. This method creates **smarter, more accurate systems capable of delivering real-time, factual, and contextually rich outputs**.

At the core of RAG is a simple but powerful idea: **augment a language model** with access to an external **retrieval system**. A typical RAG architecture involves two major components:

- **Retriever**: Given a user query, the retriever searches a large corpus (**documents, articles, or any structured knowledge base**) and fetches the most relevant pieces of information. Retrievers often use dense embeddings and vector similarity search algorithms through libraries such as **FAISS**, **Chroma**, or **ElasticSearch**.
- **Generator**: The language model (such as **BERT2BART, T5, or GPT** variants) then uses both the **original user prompt** and the **retrieved documents** to generate a coherent and informed answer.

This setup allows the model to **supplement its knowledge** in real-time without the need to retrain or fine-tune it with every update to the external knowledge source.

The primary advantage of RAG is **reducing hallucination**, a common problem where LLMs generate relevant-sounding but incorrect or outdated information. Since RAG models explicitly retrieve external documents:

- **Real-time Updates**: RAGs generate the latest information available without waiting for the next model retraining cycle.

- **Domain Adaptability**: Enterprises can customize the retrieval corpus (for example, internal knowledge bases for healthcare, legal regulations, and financial reports) to provide domain-specific expertise.
- **Greater Accuracy**: By grounding answers in actual retrieved evidence, RAG models deliver more verifiable, trustworthy outputs.

For instance, a traditional LLM trained before 2023 might not know about the latest scientific discovery. However, a RAG model could simply retrieve updated articles published in 2025 and incorporate them into its generated response, ensuring factual correctness.

In practical applications, RAG powers:

- **Enterprise chatbots** that answer based on internal documentation
- **Legal assistants** which cite relevant laws or case studies
- **Healthcare advisors** that pull from verified clinical literature
- **Academic search tools** that reference updated research

In summary, **Retrieval-Augmented Generation** not only extends the life and reliability of LLMs but also brings their capabilities closer to real-world applicability, making AI systems more dynamic, adaptive, and trustworthy for critical tasks.

Building a Simple RAG Pipeline

Constructing a **Retrieval-Augmented Generation (RAG)** pipeline involves setting up a seamless workflow where documents are **stored, retrieved, and then used by an LLM for answer generation**. Let us break down the essential components and approaches.

Vector Store (FAISS, Chroma)

The **first step** in a RAG system is to **store documents in a way that enables fast and meaningful retrieval**. Traditional keyword search is often inefficient for nuanced queries, so we use **vector stores**.

- **Facebook AI Similarity Search (FAISS):** A highly efficient library to perform fast similarity search over dense vectors. Documents are converted into embeddings using models such as **Sentence Transformers**, and FAISS quickly finds the most relevant ones based on vector distance (for example, cosine similarity).
- **Chroma**: A modern, lightweight vector database designed specifically for AI applications. It is simple to set up, integrates well with Python workflows, and supports storing metadata alongside document embeddings for richer search.

Process:

1. Convert documents into embeddings.
2. Store embeddings in FAISS or Chroma.
3. Retrieve top-k similar documents for a given user query.

Document Retrieval (LangChain, Haystack)

Once documents are stored as embeddings, we need a way to **easily orchestrate the retrieval and generation steps**. Frameworks such as **LangChain** and **Haystack** help with this.

- **LangChain**: A modular framework designed to build LLM-powered applications by chaining together retrieval and generation steps. LangChain makes it easy to integrate vector stores such as FAISS or Chroma and then feed retrieved documents into LLM prompts.
- **Haystack**: An open-source NLP framework tailored for building search systems, question-answering systems, and RAG pipelines. It supports retrievers, readers (generators), and pipelines that can be customized or deployed at scale.

Typical retrieval flow:

1. The user sends a query.
2. Retriever searches **`FAISS/Chroma`** for related documents.
3. Retrieved documents are sent alongside the query to the LLM.
4. LLM generates a final answer, enriched with retrieved knowledge.

Using Pre-trained RAG Models from Hugging Face

Hugging Face provides **pre-trained RAG models** that combine retrieval and generation to fast-track development.

- Models such as **`facebook/rag-token-nq`** or **`facebook/rag-sequence-nq`** are trained to retrieve passages and generate answers.
- They come with built-in retrievers (**DPR**: **Dense Passage Retrieval**) and can be fine-tuned on custom data if needed.
- Developers can use the Hugging Face transformers library to quickly load and deploy these models without manually setting up retrievers.

We will build a simple RAG pipeline to retrieve and provide accurate answers to the users. The code is as follows:

```
from langchain.document_loaders import PyPDFLoader
from langchain.text_splitter import RecursiveCharacterText
Splitter
from langchain.vectorstores import FAISS
from langchain.embeddings import HuggingFaceEmbeddings
from transformers import pipeline

# Step 1: Load PDF Document
loader = PyPDFLoader("HubSpots Guide to Data Analytics.pdf")
documents = loader.load()

# Step 2: Split into smaller chunks
splitter = RecursiveCharacterTextSplitter(chunk_size=700, chunk_
overlap=150)
docs = splitter.split_documents(documents)

# Step 3: Create a vector store with HuggingFace embeddings
embedding = HuggingFaceEmbeddings()
vectorstore = FAISS.from_documents(docs, embedding)

# Step 4: Retrieve top-k relevant documents
retriever = vectorstore.as_retriever(search_kwargs={"k": 5})  #
Increased k for more context
query = "What is data visualization ?"

relevant_docs = retriever.get_relevant_documents(query)
context = " ".join([doc.page_content for doc in relevant_docs])

# Truncate context if it's too long
context = context[:2000]  # Limit to avoid max_length cutoff

# Step 5: Load a better generative QA pipeline
model_name = "google/flan-t5-large"
qa_pipeline = pipeline(
    "text2text-generation",
    model=model_name,
    tokenizer=model_name,
    max_length=300,  # Allow longer responses
    temperature=0.7,
    top_k=50,
    top_p=0.95,
    repetition_penalty=1.2,
    do_sample=True
)
```

```
# Step 6: Refine prompt to encourage longer, clearer answers
prompt = f"""You are a helpful assistant.
Based on the following context, answer the question clearly and
in 2-4 informative sentences.

Context: {context}

Question: {query}
Answer:"""

response = qa_pipeline(prompt)[0]["generated_text"]

print("\n Query:", query)
print(" Generated Answer:\n", response.strip())

Output:
Query: What is data visualization ?
Generated Answer:
 The term "data visualization" refers to how you can display
numbers, statistics, and other data in a diagram or graph to make
it easier to understand and present.
```

Here is a **clear explanation of each part** of the Retrieval-Augmented Generation (RAG) pipeline using **Hugging Face and LangChain** to answer questions from a PDF:

Goal:

To create a system that:

- Loads a PDF document
- Retrieves relevant parts using vector search
- Uses a generative model to create informative answers in full sentences

Before we go into the details of the code, we need to install **langchain, pypdf, sentence-transformers, and faiss-cpu**.

Code Breakdown:

The step-by-step breakdown of the RAG pipeline code is as follows.

Load PDF Document

```
from langchain.document_loaders import PyPDFLoader
loader = PyPDFLoader("HubSpots Guide to Data Analytics.pdf")
documents = loader.load()
```

- Loads a multi-page PDF using **LangChain's PyPDFLoader**.
- Extracts content as a list of Document objects.

Split into Chunks

```
from langchain.text_splitter import RecursiveCharacterTextSplitter
splitter = RecursiveCharacterTextSplitter(chunk_size=700, chunk_
overlap=150)
docs = splitter.split_documents(documents)
```

- Splits large documents into smaller **chunks of 700 characters** with **a 150-character overlap**.
- Overlap helps preserve context between chunks.

Create a Vector Store

```
from langchain.vectorstores import FAISS
from langchain.embeddings import HuggingFaceEmbeddings
embedding = HuggingFaceEmbeddings()
vectorstore = FAISS.from_documents(docs, embedding)
```

- Converts each **chunk into vectors (embeddings)** using **Hugging Face** models.
- **FAISS** is used to store and retrieve these vectors efficiently.

Retrieve Relevant Chunks

```
retriever = vectorstore.as_retriever(search_kwargs={"k": 5})
query = "What is classification in data analytics?"
relevant_docs = retriever.get_relevant_documents(query)
context = " ".join([doc.page_content for doc in relevant_docs])
context = context[:2000]
```

- Uses similarity search to **retrieve the top 5 most relevant chunks** for the given question.
- Joins them into a **single context string**.
- **Truncates the context to 2000 characters** to avoid overloading the model.

Load a Text Generation Model

```
from transformers import pipeline
model_name = "google/flan-t5-large"
qa_pipeline = pipeline(
    "text2text-generation",
    model=model_name,
    tokenizer=model_name,
    max_length=300,
    temperature=0.7,
    top_k=50,
    top_p=0.95,
    repetition_penalty=1.2,
```

```
    do_sample=True
)
```

- Loads a **pretrained generative model** from Hugging Face (**Flan-T5**), good at instruction-following.
- Key generation parameters:
    - `max_length=300`: allows longer answers
    - `temperature=0.7, top_k=50, top_p=0.95`: control creativity and variation
    - `repetition_penalty=1.2`: reduces redundant outputs

Create a Prompt and Generate Answer

```
prompt = f"""You are a helpful assistant.
Based on the following context, answer the question clearly and
in 2-4 informative sentences.

Context: {context}

Question: {query}
Answer:"""
response = qa_pipeline(prompt)[0]["generated_text"]
```

1. The prompt instructs the model to give an **informative, clear, multi-sentence answer**.
2. Uses the pipeline to generate the response based on the context and question.

Display the Answer

```
print("\n Query:", query)
print(" Generated Answer:\n", response.strip())
```

1. Displays the original query and the generated answer from the model.

Summary:

We have created a **lightweight Retrieval-Augmented QA system** that:

1. Uses PDF as a knowledge base
2. Retrieves relevant content with **FAISS + Hugging Face embeddings**
3. Generates natural-language answers using a **T5-family model**

Evaluation, Optimization, and Deployment

Evaluating Retrieval-Augmented Generation (RAG) pipelines involves assessing both

retrieval and **generation** quality. Common metrics include **Precision@K**, **Recall@K**, and **Mean Reciprocal Rank (MRR)** to evaluate how well the retriever fetches relevant documents. For the generation part, metrics such as **ROUGE**, **BLEU**, **BERTScore**, and **METEOR** are used to measure how closely the model's answers align with reference answers regarding **semantics and structure**.

Human evaluations are also crucial, focusing on answer **relevance**, **factuality**, **fluency**, and **coherence**, especially when ground truth is subjective or unavailable.

Common Model Evaluation Metrics:

- **Perplexity**: It measures how well a language model predicts a sequence. Lower perplexity indicates better language modeling.

  Used in: Text generation, next-word prediction.

- **Accuracy**: Ratio of the number of correct predictions to the total number of predictions.

  Used in: Classification tasks such as sentiment analysis and intent detection.

- **Bilingual Evaluation Understudy (BLEU)**: Precision-based metric comparing n-gram overlap between generated and reference texts. **Used in:** Machine translation, summarization.

- **Recall-Oriented Understudy for Gisting Evaluation (ROUGE):** Measures n-gram overlap (unigrams, bigrams, and so on) between generated and reference summaries.

  Used in: Summarization, translation, text generation.

  Variants:

  - **ROUGE-1**: unigram overlap
  - **ROUGE-2**: bigram overlap
  - **ROUGE-L**: longest common subsequence

- **Metric for Evaluation of Translation with Explicit Ordering (METEOR):** Considers stemming, synonyms, and word order – more semantically informed than BLEU.

  Used in: Translation and summarization.

- **Consensus-Based Image Description Evaluation (CIDEr):** Originally for image captioning, but used in summarization and multi-reference generation tasks.

  Uses TF-IDF weighting and cosine similarity to measure consensus with multiple human references.

- **Translation Edit Rate (TER):** Measures the number of edits (insertions, deletions, substitutions) needed to match the reference output.

Used in: Machine translation.

- **BERTScore:** Leverages contextual embeddings from BERT to compare the similarity between generated and reference texts.
  Captures semantic similarity beyond surface-level word overlap.
  Used in: Text generation, summarization, translation.
- **Negative Log Likelihood (NLL):** Evaluates how well a model assigns probability to the actual output.

  Lower values indicate better confidence in correct predictions.
- **Exact Match (EM):** Checks if model prediction matches the ground truth exactly (case-sensitive or case-insensitive).
  Common in extractive QA tasks such as SQuAD.
  Used in: QA systems.
- **Mean Reciprocal Rank (MRR):** Measures the rank of the first relevant answer.
  Higher is better.
  Used in: Retrieval-based models, ranking problems.

Human Evaluations and Feedback Loops

Human evaluation is a critical component in assessing **Retrieval-Augmented Generation (RAG)** systems, especially when automated metrics do not capture **semantic nuance, contextual correctness, or user relevance**. Here is an elaboration of the key human evaluation dimensions commonly used for RAG pipelines:

Relevance

- **Definition**: Measures how well the generated answer addresses the user's query.
- **What evaluators check:** Whether the response is directly related, stays on-topic, and avoids unnecessary digressions.
- **Scale:** Usually rated on a Likert scale (for example, 1–5), where 5 is highly relevant.

Factual Accuracy

- **Definition**: Assesses whether the information provided in the answer is factually correct and supported by the retrieved context.
- **Why it matters:** RAG systems might hallucinate answers if the retrieval is poor or if the LLM blends unrelated facts.
- **Method:** Cross-verification with source documents or expert domain review.

Faithfulness to Context

- **Definition:** Evaluates if the generated text stays faithful to the retrieved documents and does not introduce information not present in them.
- **Concern:** LLMs are known to fabricate information when the context is insufficient.

Fluency and Coherence

- **Definition:** Determines whether the generated response is grammatically correct, logically structured, and easy to read.
- **Evaluation criteria:** Natural sentence flow, correct punctuation, and clarity.

Helpfulness/Usefulness

- **Definition:** Focuses on whether the answer is practically useful to the end user.
- **Use case:** Especially valuable in customer support, healthcare, legal, or education domains.

Coverage/Completeness

- **Definition**: Measures whether the answer covers all major aspects of the question or topic.
- **Risk**: Overly brief answers may be technically correct but incomplete.

Response Time/Latency Perception

- **Definition:** While technically measured, it also influences human satisfaction.
- **Importance:** Users expect near-real-time answers in production systems.

Trustworthiness/Confidence

- **Definition:** Human raters evaluate whether the answer appears credible, even when correctness cannot be immediately verified.
- **Application:** Especially useful for long-form or opinion-style answers.

Implementation Methods for Human Evaluation:

- **Pairwise Comparison:** Show two outputs side-by-side and ask annotators to choose the better one.
- **Likert Scale Ratings:** Annotators rate on a scale (for example, 1–5 or 1–10) for each quality dimension.
- **Open-ended Feedback:** Allow evaluators to provide qualitative observations.
- **Crowdsourcing Tools:** Platforms such as **Amazon Mechanical Turk, Scale AI, or Prolific** can scale up human evaluations efficiently.

Optimizing for Speed and Cost

As Large Language Models (LLMs) and Retrieval-Augmented Generation (RAG) systems become complex, **deployment costs and inference latency** become critical concerns. There are optimization techniques such as **quantization**, **distillation**, and **pruning**, along with tools such as **ONNX**, **DeepSpeed**, and **Optimum** that allow developers to achieve **faster, cheaper, and more efficient model performance**, especially crucial in real-time applications.

Optimization Techniques

Quantization

- Reduces the precision of model weights (for example, from 32-bit floating point to 8-bit integers) without performance reduction.
- **Benefits:**
    - Smaller model size
    - Faster inference
    - Lower memory usage
- **Types:**
    - **Post-training quantization (PTQ):** Done after model training.
    - **Quantization-aware training (QAT):** Simulates Quantization during training to retain accuracy.

Distillation

- A smaller model is trained to mimic the behavior of a larger, high-performing model, with the advantage of a reduction in size and computational load.
- **Benefits:**
    - Up to 90% smaller models with minimal performance drop
    - Faster inference with much lower compute cost
- **Common Use Case:** Training TinyBERT or DistilBERT from BERT-large

Model Pruning

- Removes redundant or less important weights or neurons from the model.
- **Benefits:**
    - Reduces model complexity and size
    - Speeds up computation

- **Types:**
    - **Structured pruning:** Removes entire layers or attention heads
    - **Unstructured pruning:** Removes individual weights sparsely

Optimization Tools

Open Neural Network Exchange (ONNX)

- An open-source format to represent ML models for **interoperability and hardware optimization**.
- **Features:**
    - Convert PyTorch or TensorFlow models to ONNX format
    - Run models using ONNX Runtime, optimized for CPU, GPU, or specialized accelerators
    - Supports quantization and pruning workflows

DeepSpeed (by Microsoft)

- A deep learning optimization library designed for training and inference of **very large models** efficiently.
- **Key Benefits:**
    - **ZeRO optimization** (Zero Redundancy Optimizer) reduces memory usage
    - **Inference engine** for high-throughput, low-latency inference
    - **Mixed precision training** with automatic loss scaling
- **Used by:** Models such as GPT-NeoX and BLOOM

Optimum (by Hugging Face)

- A library to integrate Hugging Face Transformers with performance tools such as **ONNX, Intel OpenVINO, and NVIDIA TensorRT**.
- **Capabilities:**
    - Export models to ONNX
    - Apply quantization and distillation
    - Fine-tune and deploy optimized models seamlessly

Conclusion

This chapter explored the intersection of **LLMs** and practical **text-powered tools**. We have seen that fine-tuning is a crucial process for specializing a general-purpose LLM for a specific task, whether through full fine-tuning or more efficient methods such as **PEFT (Parameter-Efficient Fine-Tuning)** with **LoRA**. Building on this foundation, we developed sophisticated tools such as code assistants and text summarizers.

The chapter also introduced **Retrieval-Augmented Generation (RAG)** as a powerful technique to ground LLMs in external, up-to-date knowledge, ensuring factual and dynamic responses. Ultimately, we concluded by emphasizing the importance of thorough evaluation, optimization, and responsible deployment to build robust and efficient text-powered systems.

In the next chapter, we will talk about the best practices in NLP, understanding ethical and responsible AI, emerging trends in NLP, and conclude with the most influential research papers in NLP.

References

- https://www.digitalocean.com/community/conceptual-articles/rag-ai-agents-agentic-rag-comparative-analysis
- https://www.linkedin.com/pulse/comparing-rag-systems-ai-agents-which-technology-right-ph-d-ekk4c/
- https://huggingface.co/models
- https://huggingface.co/datasets?modality=modality:text&sort=trending
- https://github.com/huggingface/transformers/blob/main/docs/source/en/tasks/summarization.md
- https://www.kaggle.com/code/mitanshuchakrawarty/fine-tune-llm-for-text-summary
- https://huggingface.co/datasets/irds/codesearchnet
- https://blogs.nvidia.com/blog/what-is-retrieval-augmented-generation/
- https://aws.amazon.com/what-is/retrieval-augmented-generation/
- https://cloud.google.com/use-cases/retrieval-augmented-generation?hl=en
- https://arxiv.org/html/2501.12697v1
- https://arxiv.org/html/2403.06642v2
- https://www.geeksforgeeks.org/how-to-build-rag-pipelines-for-llm-projects/
- https://developer.nvidia.com/blog/rag-101-demystifying-retrieval-augmented-generation-pipelines/
- https://github.com/facebookresearch/faiss
- https://faiss.ai/
- https://www.datacamp.com/blog/faiss-facebook-ai-similarity-search
- https://arxiv.org/pdf/2401.08281

- https://github.com/chroma-core/chroma
- https://www.datacamp.com/tutorial/chromadb-tutorial-step-by-step-guide
- https://www.datacamp.com/tutorial/introduction-to-vector-databases-for-machine-learning
- https://www.langchain.com/
- https://github.com/langchain-ai/langchain
- https://huggingface.co/google/flan-t5-large
- https://arxiv.org/html/2405.07437v2
- https://arxiv.org/pdf/2407.12873
- https://huggingface.co/learn/cookbook/en/rag_evaluation
- https://huggingface.co/spaces/evaluate-metric/perplexity
- https://huggingface.co/spaces/evaluate-metric/rouge
- https://huggingface.co/spaces/evaluate-metric/meteor
- https://spotintelligence.com/2024/08/26/meteor-metric-in-nlp-how-it-works-how-to-tutorial-in-python/
- https://arxiv.org/pdf/1411.5726
- https://huggingface.co/spaces/evaluate-metric/ter#:~:text=Metric%20Description-,TER%20(Translation%20Edit%20Rate%2C%20also%20called%20Translation%20Error%20Rate),inspired%20by%20the%20TERCOM%20implementation.
- https://lightning.ai/docs/torchmetrics/stable/text/translation_edit_rate.html
- https://saturncloud.io/blog/what-are-negativeloglikelihood-dimensions-in-logistic-regression/#1
- https://towardsdatascience.com/cross-entropy-negative-log-likelihood-and-all-that-jazz-47a95bd2e81/
- https://www.ibm.com/docs/en/watsonx/saas?topic=metrics-exact-match
- https://huggingface.co/spaces/evaluate-metric/exact_match
- https://www.evidentlyai.com/ranking-metrics/mean-reciprocal-rank-mrr#:~:text=Mean%20Reciprocal%20Rank%20(MRR)%20is,item%20across%20all%20user%20lists.
- https://spotintelligence.com/2024/08/02/mean-reciprocal-rank-mrr/
- https://arxiv.org/html/2407.00072v5

- https://medium.com/@1993Tikku/rethinking-rag-evaluations-lessons-from-human-in-the-loop-hitl-and-llm-judge-practices-1be1cb9da0f1
- https://cloud.google.com/blog/products/ai-machine-learning/optimizing-rag-retrieval
- https://arxiv.org/html/2402.01722v1
- https://www.youtube.com/watch?v=s9yyH3RPhdM (distillation, Quantization, Pruning)
- https://huggingface.co/blog/nadiinchi/provence
- https://medium.com/@shmilysyg/model-compression-pruning-quantization-distillation-and-binarization-7710ac954567
- https://www.datacamp.com/tutorial/quantization-for-large-language-models
- https://www.datacamp.com/blog/distillation-llm
- https://arxiv.org/pdf/2306.11695 (A SIMPLE AND EFFECTIVE PRUNING APPROACH FOR LARGE LANGUAGE MODELS)
- https://www.superannotate.com/blog/llm-pruning-distillation-minitron-approach
- https://arxiv.org/html/2406.00030v1 (Large Language Model Pruning)
- https://github.com/onnx/onnx
- https://github.com/deepspeedai/DeepSpeed
- https://huggingface.co/docs/optimum/en/index

CHAPTER 12
Best Practices and Future Trends of NLP

Introduction

Natural Language Processing (NLP) has matured from rule-based systems to large-scale neural architectures capable of accurately understanding and generating human language. However, building effective NLP solutions today goes far beyond just training high-performing models. So, in the final chapter, we focus on the practical, ethical, and strategic considerations that elevate real-world NLP projects. We begin by covering essential best practices—ranging from **efficient data preprocessing and evaluation metrics to scalable deployment strategies**—that help ensure our **models are accurate**, **maintainable**, and **production-ready**.

Beyond these fundamentals, we turn our attention to the broader implications and responsibilities of working with language models. Ethical considerations, such as **fairness, bias mitigation, transparency, and data privacy**, are now critical aspects of any NLP system. As developers, researchers, or practitioners, adopting responsible AI practices is no longer optional—it is essential.

The chapter also explores some of the most exciting emerging trends in the field. **Multimodal learning** enables models to understand language alongside **images, videos, and audio**. **Few-shot and zero-shot learning** minimize data requirements for model adaptation. Meanwhile, **explainability tools** are helping to unpack the "black box" nature of complex models, allowing **better interpretability and trust**.

Finally, we provide a curated look at **10 influential research papers** that have significantly impacted the field, along with a brief exploration of **AI agents**—autonomous systems powered by NLP that can reason, plan, and act across tasks. These innovations offer a compelling view of the future landscape of NLP, where language models become even more capable, interactive, and aligned with human values.

This chapter equips us with the knowledge not only to build NLP tools but to build them wisely, responsibly, and with an eye toward what comes next.

Structure

In this chapter, the following topics will be covered:

- Purpose of the chapter
- Best Practices in NLP
    - Data-Centric NLP
    - Model Development Practices
    - Experiment Tracking & Versioning
- Ethical and Responsible NLP
    - Bias and Fairness
    - Privacy and Data Security
    - Transparency and Explainability
    - Responsible Model Sharing
- Emerging Trends in NLP
    - Multimodal Learning
    - Few-Shot and Zero-Shot Learning
    - NLP in Low-Resource Languages
- Influential Research Papers in NLP
    - Attention is All You Need (Vaswani et al., 2017)
    - BERT: Pre-training of Deep Bidirectional Transformers
    - GPT-4 Technical Report
    - Retrieval-Augmented Generation (RAG)
    - Chain-of-Thought Prompting
- NLP Agents and Automation
- The Future of NLP

Purpose of the Chapter

Given how quickly natural language processing is developing, this chapter offers a useful and strategic manual for creating reliable, moral, and future-proof NLP systems. This last chapter goes beyond code to highlight the fundamental procedures that make NLP projects durable, effective, and significant, whereas previous chapters concentrated on technical implementations utilizing spaCy and Hugging Face.

By providing insight into practical deployment, performance improvement, and new research avenues, the goal is to close the gap between working models and production-grade systems.

Building an NLP model is only the beginning. Without following best practices, even the most advanced models can **suffer from data leakage, model drift, poor generalization, or ethical blind spots.** Moreover, as NLP tools are increasingly embedded in everyday products – from **chatbots to recommendation engines** – the importance of responsible, transparent, and inclusive AI has never been greater.

Understanding future trends also helps practitioners and researchers stay ahead of the curve. With developments such as **multimodal learning, retrieval-augmented generation (RAG), and few-shot learning** redefining what is possible, it is crucial to prepare for a landscape where models are not only larger but also smarter, faster, and more aligned with human needs. Anticipating these shifts enables us to build solutions that are scalable and adaptable in the long term.

This chapter is divided into four main sections:

- **Best Practices in NLP:** Covers data preparation, model training, evaluation, versioning, and deployment strategies to improve reliability and reproducibility.
- **Ethical Considerations:** Explores bias, fairness, privacy, and transparency – essential principles for responsible NLP development.
- **Emerging Trends:** Discusses cutting-edge directions such as few-shot learning, multimodal models, model explainability, and retrieval-augmented generation.
- **Future Scope and Research:** Highlights influential research papers, practical AI agents, and anticipated developments shaping the future of NLP.

Together, these sections offer a holistic perspective, empowering us to go beyond model accuracy and build systems that are **efficient, ethical,** and **forward-looking**.

Best Practices in NLP

The growing complexity and adoption of NLP systems require a structured, disciplined approach to ensure success. Best practices help mitigate common pitfalls such as **overfitting, bias, data leakage, and deployment failures.** This section provides an in-depth guide to practical, battle-tested techniques across all phases of NLP development.

Data Collection and Preparation

Garbage in leads to garbage out. NLP models learn patterns based on input data. If the data is **noisy, unbalanced, or biased**, the model will reflect and even amplify those issues.

- **Curating Diverse Data Sources:** Combining multiple domains (for example, **news, blogs, technical docs**) to ensure robustness across language styles. Libraries like **BeautifulSoup and Selenium** are relevant in this case to access data.
- **Text Cleaning:** Lowercasing text, removing HTML tags, special characters, and irrelevant metadata. Libraries such as **spaCy and regex** are helpful.
- **Stopwords and Lemmatization:** Lemmatization (via **spaCy, NLTK**) preserves root meaning, while removing stopwords can sometimes remove useful context, so we need to be careful in these situations.
- **Data Labeling:** We can utilize tools such as **doccano, Label Studio, or Prodigy** for high-quality, consistent annotation.
- **Address Class Imbalance:** Employing **SMOTE (for synthetic oversampling)**, undersampling methods, or using weighted loss functions in training.

Model Training and Validation

Even the best model architecture will fail if not trained properly. Thus, **Hyperparameter tuning, validation strategy,** and **model selection** are critical.

- **Transfer Learning:** Fine-tuning pre-trained models (such as **BERT, RoBERTa, DeBERTa**) achieves state-of-the-art results faster and with less data.
- **Hyperparameter Optimization:** Using tools such as **Optuna, Ray Tune, or GridSearchCV** to automate tuning can be beneficial.
- **Cross-validation: Stratified K-Fold CV** ensures balanced representation in each fold—vital for imbalanced datasets.
- **Overfitting Checks:** Using **early stopping and monitoring training versus validation loss.** Also, using dropout and regularization layers is needed.

Model Evaluation and Monitoring

A high test accuracy does not always reflect true model quality, especially in production environments. Thus, various other specific metrics need to be employed, such as **precision, F1 score, recall, ROUGE, and perplexity**.

- **Metrics Per Task:**
    - **Classification:** F1-score, precision, recall
    - **NER/QA:** Span-level accuracy, Exact Match (EM)
    - **Translation/Summarization:** BLEU, ROUGE

  - **Language Modeling:** Perplexity
- **Error Analysis:** Review false positives/negatives manually to identify patterns and edge cases.

Explainability and Interpretability

NLP models, especially transformers, are often black boxes. Explainability ensures **accountability, trust, and better debugging**.

- **Feature Attribution:** Use **LIME or SHAP** to understand which tokens influenced the output.
- **Attention Visualization:** For transformer models, tools such as **BertViz** can reveal how attention heads are weighted.
- **Confidence Scores:** Always expose a model's confidence or uncertainty in outputs, especially in critical applications such as **legal or healthcare NLP**.

Version Control and Experiment Tracking

Reproducibility is foundational for collaboration, debugging, and auditability in NLP projects.

- **Code and Config Tracking:** Using Git and keeping YAML or .json files for experiment configurations.
- **Experiment Tracking Tools:** Integrating tools such as **Weights & Biases**, **MLflow**, or **Comet** to track metrics, hyperparameters, artifacts, and logs.
- **Data Versioning:** Use **DVC or LakeFS** to keep track of different dataset versions, especially when datasets evolve.

Deployment and Scalability

Building a performant model is only half the task done. Deployment ensures that the model can provide value to users.

- **Model Optimization:** Converting models to **ONNX or TorchScript** for hardware acceleration.
- **Serving Mechanism:** Using **FastAPI, Flask, or Triton for lightweight APIs**; or Hugging Face Inference Endpoints for serverless deployment.
- **Containerization:** Using **Docker** for packaging models and dependencies and orchestrating with Kubernetes for scalability.
- **Inference Monitoring:** Tracking **latency, response time, failure rate, and cost** using tools like **Prometheus + Grafana**.

Continuous Learning and Feedback Loops

Language is dynamic. User feedback and data drift can make even the best models stale over time.

- **Human-in-the-loop (HITL):** Allowing users to flag or correct incorrect outputs.
- **Retraining Pipelines:** Automating model retraining when data shifts are detected (for example, with Evidently AI or Fiddler).
- **Active Learning:** Prioritizing the most uncertain predictions for labeling using uncertainty sampling or entropy-based methods.
- **Feedback Integration:** Using thumbs-up/down ratings, ranking responses, or logging user choices to inform model improvement.

Ethical and Responsible NLP

As NLP systems increasingly influence human decisions across **finance, healthcare, education, and HR**, ethical considerations are no longer optional. This section explores the principles and practices necessary to ensure that NLP models are **fair, privacy-preserving, transparent, and responsibly shared**.

Bias and Fairness

Bias and fairness in NLP are critical concerns, as language models often learn and amplify the prejudices present in their training data. These biases–whether based on **gender, race, or culture**–can **lead to unfair, inaccurate, or even harmful outputs**. Ensuring fairness means **identifying, measuring, and actively mitigating these biases** to **build more inclusive and ethical NLP systems** that serve all users equitably.

Types of Bias in NLP Systems:

Bias in NLP arises from skewed data, societal prejudices, and imbalanced representation. Key types include:

- **Representation Bias:** Over or under-representation of certain groups in training data (for example, gendered pronouns).
- **Stereotyping Bias:** Models reflecting or amplifying harmful stereotypes (for example, associating certain jobs with a specific gender, such as nurses and teachers will mostly be females, or construction workers will mostly be men).
- **Measurement Bias:** Errors in **labeling, annotations, or assumptions** made during evaluation.
- **Historical Bias:** Prejudices embedded in source texts or societal norms captured in data.

Detection and Mitigation Techniques:

- **Bias Audits:** Manually inspecting outputs across demographic slices (gender, race, geography).
- **Metrics:** Using fairness-aware metrics such as Equal Opportunity Difference or Demographic Parity.
- **Data Augmentation:** Adding **neutral or counterfactual examples** to balance underrepresented groups.
- **Debiasing Models:** Techniques such as adversarial training, or model-level approaches such as **FairSeq or FairBERT**.

Frameworks such as **IBM AI Fairness 360** or **Fairlearn** provide toolkits for auditing and correcting bias.

Privacy and Data Security

Privacy and data security are foundational pillars in developing responsible NLP systems, especially when **handling sensitive or personal user data**. With increasing global concerns around data misuse, ensuring compliance with regulations such as **GDPR** is **not just a legal necessity but a trust-building initiative**. Modern NLP models must prioritize secure data handling through techniques such as **differential privacy and federated learning** to protect user information while still enabling powerful language understanding capabilities.

Regulatory Compliance – GDPR and Beyond:

The **General Data Protection Regulation (GDPR)** and similar frameworks mandate:

- **Data minimization:** Only using what is strictly necessary.
- Informed consent for data usage.
- Right to be forgotten (deletion upon user request).
- Data access transparency.

For NLP projects, it means anonymizing sensitive user data, explaining data usage in plain language, and maintaining clear data lineage.

Techniques for Privacy Preservation:

- **Differential Privacy:** Introduces statistical noise to protect individual data while preserving trends. Libraries such as **OpenDP or Google's TensorFlow** Privacy are helpful.
- **Federated Learning:** Training models on-device (for example, on smartphones) and only shares updates, not the raw data, ensuring sensitive user data remains local.

- **Synthetic Data Generation:** Generating fake, yet statistically accurate text samples to replace real data when privacy is paramount.

Transparency and Explainability

Transparent NLP systems help users understand how decisions are made, especially crucial in regulated industries such as healthcare and law.

Approaches to Explainability:

- **Token-level Attribution:** Highlight which words most influenced the model's output.
- **Model-Agnostic Tools**:
    - **SHAP** (SHapley Additive exPlanations): Estimates feature impact.
    - **LIME** (Local Interpretable Model-agnostic Explanations): Creates interpretable local approximations.
    - **Captum:** PyTorch-native tool for understanding internal model behavior.
    - **ELI5:** Simple library to debug linear classifiers and NLP pipelines.

Explainability not only aids trust but also facilitates **model debugging, fairness audits**, and **regulatory compliance**.

Responsible Model Sharing

Open-sourcing large models without appropriate documentation or risk assessment can inadvertently propagate bias, misuse, or privacy risks.

Best Practices:

- **Model Cards:** Introduced by Google, these are standardized documentation for models, detailing training data, performance, intended use, limitations, and ethical considerations.
- **Datasheets for Datasets:** Like model cards, datasheets describe how datasets were collected, pre-processed, and annotated.
- **Licensing and Usage Restrictions:** Clearly define allowed and disallowed uses (for example, prohibiting military or surveillance usage).
- **Release Risk Assessment:** Evaluate model misuse potential–can it generate hate speech, misinformation, or biased results?

Projects such as **BigScience's BLOOM** and **Hugging Face's model hub** are examples of the community moving toward responsible model sharing with transparency and accountability.

Emerging Trends in NLP

As NLP continues to evolve, several transformative trends are shaping its future. These innovations aim not only to enhance the capabilities of models but also to **broaden their usability, accessibility,** and **trustworthiness**. From blending multiple data modalities to empowering underrepresented languages, these emerging directions are crucial for the next generation of NLP systems.

Multimodal Learning

Multimodal learning refers to NLP systems that integrate **text with other modalities** such as **images, audio, and video** to gain a richer understanding of context. Instead of relying on language alone, these models fuse information from multiple sources to deliver more reliable outputs.

- **Applications** include **Visual Question Answering (VQA)**, where a system interprets an image and responds to text-based queries about it; automatic image and video captioning; and advanced **AI agents** that understand instructions across modalities.
- **Models such as CLIP, Flamingo, and GPT-4-Vision** are redefining how machines perceive and generate cross-modal content, making NLP more dynamic and context-aware.

Few-Shot and Zero-Shot Learning

Traditional NLP systems rely on large, labeled datasets for training. In contrast, **few-shot and zero-shot learning** allow models to generalize to new tasks with minimal or even zero direct examples.

- **Large Language Models (LLMs)** such as **GPT-4 and T5** have shown remarkable performance in zero-shot scenarios through **prompt engineering**, where task instructions are embedded directly in the input text.
- This trend is especially impactful in real-world settings where labeled data is scarce or rapidly evolving, empowering flexible and scalable NLP deployments.

NLP in Low-Resource Languages

Many NLP advances focus on high-resource languages such as English, leaving a significant gap for low-resource and indigenous languages. **Building NLP systems for these languages is critical for inclusivity** and preserving linguistic diversity.

- **Challenges** include a lack of annotated datasets, domain-specific corpora, and linguistic tools.

- Community-driven efforts such as **Masakhane (for African languages)**, **IndicNLP (for Indian languages)**, and **BLOOM (multilingual open LLM)** are actively addressing this gap by providing resources and benchmarks for underserved languages.

Influential Research Papers in NLP

In this section, we will summarize the 5 most influential research papers in the field of NLP. The idea is to understand the basics of the latest developments in NLP using research papers, for example. The paper **"Attention is all you need"** introduced the concept of transformers, which lays the foundation of modern-day LLMs. We will focus on the 5 papers that were found to be most influential; however, it is very much possible that some may have been missed.

Attention is All You Need (Vaswani et al., 2017)

The paper ***"Attention Is All You Need"*** introduced the Transformer architecture, which laid the foundation of modern-day LLMs. Previously, sequence models such as **RNNs and LSTMs** were used for such translation and text generation, but they did not perform well with long-range dependencies and suffered from slow, sequential processing. Transformer broke this paradigm by removing recurrence and relying entirely on a mechanism called **self-attention**, which allows every word in a sentence to directly attend to every other word. This enables the model to understand context more effectively and train much faster by leveraging parallel computation.

The Transformer is comprised of an **encoder and a decoder**, each composed of layers containing multi-head attention and feed-forward networks, enhanced by layer normalization and residual connections. A unique feature is the use of positional encodings to retain word order information, since the model itself has no inherent sense of sequence. The architecture laid the groundwork for almost every major NLP model that followed, including **BERT, GPT, and T5**.

A compelling real-world application is **machine translation**, achieving the best results on **English-to-German and English-to-French** benchmarks, exemplified by services such as **DeepL or Google Translate**. Consider translating a complex sentence: older methods struggled to maintain context over long sequences. Transformers, however, analyze all words in both the source and target sentences concurrently, identifying intricate relationships between them. This "attentional" approach, which weighs the importance of different words regardless of their position, yields translations that are far more accurate and contextually appropriate, markedly enhancing fluency and minimizing inaccuracies compared to previous models.

BERT: Pre-Training of Deep Bidirectional Transformers for Language Understanding

The work **"BERT: Pre-training of Deep Bidirectional Transformers for Language Understanding"** introduced Bidirectional Encoder Representations from Transformers (BERT), a novel and potent language representation approach. BERT comprehends a word's entire context by concurrently examining its left and right surroundings, in contrast to earlier models that processed text either left-to-right or right-to-left. The model's capacity to comprehend the subtleties of natural language is much improved by this deep bidirectional method, which also makes it more adept at deducing word meanings from context.

The two pre-training tasks that BERT innovates on are **Next Sentence Prediction (NSP) and Masked Language Modeling (MLM)**. The model in MLM is forced to get a thorough grasp of language structure and context as it learns to anticipate words in a phrase that are randomly masked. In contrast, NSP prepares the model for tasks that call for reasoning beyond sentence boundaries by teaching it the link between sentence pairs.

Following this pre-training stage on extensive corpora such as Wikipedia, BERT can be optimized with a few changes to its design for a variety of downstream tasks, including named entity recognition, sentiment analysis, and question answering.

Enhancing search engine relevance is a common practical use, especially for intricate or conversational inquiries. Before BERT, a search for "*Can I get medicine for a fever at the bank?*" could have had trouble telling the difference between a bank and a riverbank. Because of its bidirectional comprehension, BERT can recognize the subtle differences between "*bank*" and "*medicine*" and "*fever*," producing more precise search results. By offering extremely relevant information, even for inquiries expressed in common, everyday language, this contextual awareness greatly improves the user experience. Additionally, BERT may be applied to a wide range of additional NLP jobs with significantly less task-specific data thanks to this pre-training and subsequent fine-tuning methodology.

GPT-4 Technical Report

The creation, capabilities, and performance of GPT-4, a large multimodal model that can interpret both text and visual inputs, are summarized in the **"GPT-4 Technical Report"** published by OpenAI. The study highlights GPT-4's enhanced **reasoning, inventiveness, and language understanding** over its predecessors, but it withholds information about the model architecture, including the number of parameters and the makeup of the training dataset. GPT-4's capacity to follow intricate instructions and perform at a level comparable to humans on a variety of academic and professional standards, including standardized tests such as the SAT and the bar exam, is one of its most notable capabilities.

Moreover, in education, a student could upload a picture of a complex diagram from a textbook, such as a circuit board or a biological process, and then ask GPT-4 to explain it or solve an associated problem. The model's ability to interpret the visual data alongside the textual query allows it to provide accurate and detailed explanations, acting as a personal tutor that can bridge the gap between visual and text-based information. This capability is a game-changer for fields such as STEM, where visual learning is critical, enabling more personalized and effective educational tools.

Using methods such as **Reinforcement Learning from Human Feedback (RLHF)**, the report emphasizes how well GPT-4 aligns with human values. In both **zero-shot and few-shot scenarios**, GPT-4 shows better adherence to **user intent, fewer hallucinations, and enhanced factual accuracy**. Its multilingual capabilities are also greatly improved, surpassing previous versions in many languages. Notwithstanding these developments, the article also lists drawbacks, such as sensitivity to input wording and difficulties with factual consistency, which emphasize the necessity of cautious implementation and ongoing improvement. All things considered, GPT-4 is a significant advancement in general-purpose language model creation, opening the door to more sophisticated and dependable AI-powered applications.

Retrieval-Augmented Generation for Large Language Models: A Survey

The study **"Retrieval-Augmented Generation for Large Language Models: A Survey"** provides an in-depth analysis of RAG, a paradigm that integrates external knowledge retrieval systems with large language models (LLMs) to improve their capabilities. Despite their strength, traditional LLMs are limited by their set knowledge bases, which are only available for the data they were trained on. By obtaining pertinent documents or facts from a knowledge corpus during inference time, RAG overcomes this constraint and enables the model to produce more precise, current, and well-founded responses. Based on architecture, retrieval techniques, integration tactics, and application domains, the survey classifies different RAG approaches.

The article explores the **generator and retriever**, which are the two main parts of RAG systems. It talks about various fusion strategies (early versus late fusion), dense and sparse retrieval approaches (such as **BM25 and FAISS**), and how recovered content is integrated into the model's generating pipeline. Evaluation methods, issues such as **latency and hallucinations**, and practical uses such as open-domain inquiry answering, customized chatbots, and scientific research assistants are all covered in the study. The authors also point up new research directions, including enhancing factual consistency and training creation and retrieval simultaneously. The survey offers useful insights for researchers and practitioners aiming to develop more dependable and knowledgeable NLP systems by summarizing developments in the area.

Customer service and enterprise knowledge management provide an interesting real-world application case. Consider a business that has a lot of internal documentation, including product specs, technical manuals, and HR policies.

RAG enables the model to "*look up*" the most recent, pertinent information from a company's own knowledge base in **real-time, eliminating the need to retrain a big, costly LLM each time** a policy changes or a new product is introduced. When an employee asks a question such as "*How do I troubleshoot error code* 748?" or "*What is the updated parental leave policy*?", the RAG system initially pulls the relevant documents. It then "*augments*" the prompt with the gathered data, providing the LLM with the **factual foundation** it needs to provide a **reliable and accurate response**. This method **avoids "hallucinations," guarantees that responses are constantly up to date**, and offers an affordable means of implementing strong, domain-specific AI assistants.

Chain-of-Thought Prompting Elicits Reasoning in LLMs

The paper **"Chain of Thought Prompting Elicits Reasoning in Large Language Models"** explores a novel prompting strategy aimed at enhancing the reasoning capabilities of LLMs. Instead of simply asking for a final answer to a question, Chain of Thought (CoT) prompting guides the model to generate intermediate reasoning steps, mimicking the human approach of thinking aloud before concluding. This method helps models handle complex tasks such as **arithmetic reasoning, common sense inference, and symbolic logic,** where linear or step-by-step problem-solving is essential.

The authors demonstrate that CoT prompting significantly improves performance on reasoning-intensive benchmarks, especially when applied to sufficiently large models such as PaLM. They also show that the effectiveness of CoT increases with model scale, as smaller models often fail to generate meaningful reasoning chains. By including examples that model not just the question and answer but also the thought process in between, CoT enables LLMs to reason more transparently and accurately.

Let us understand a real-world use case in the context of data analysis or problem-solving. **"Analyze the quarterly sales data to identify which product line has the highest growth, and then explain the probable reasons based on recent marketing campaigns and customer feedback"** is an example of a multi-step query that a user (for example, Data Analyst) could use to prompt a model rather than just asking for a conclusion. Using a Chain-of-Thought approach, the model would first describe how it analyzed the sales data before comparing it with data on marketing initiatives and consumer feedback. By clearly demonstrating its process, the LLM not only reaches a **more precise and solid result** but also gives the user an understandable route to that solution, which facilitates verification, debugging, and fostering confidence in the AI's output.

NLP Agents and Automation

AI/NLP agents are autonomous systems powered by natural language processing and machine learning, designed to perform tasks, make decisions, and interact with users or systems using human-like language capabilities. These agents move beyond static question-answer systems by exhibiting dynamic behaviors such as **reasoning, planning, memory recall, and tool usage**. They can understand instructions, decompose them into subtasks, retrieve and utilize information, and execute actions across digital environments. At their core, NLP agents aim to bridge the gap between raw natural language and meaningful autonomous action in real-world or digital tasks.

Components of an NLP Agent

- **Memory**: Memory allows agents to retain and recall context from previous interactions or task progress. It can be:
    - **Short-term memory:** Holds context during a single session.
    - **Long-term memory:** Stores facts, previous results, or historical data for persistent performance. Embedding-based memory retrieval systems (for example, FAISS or ChromaDB) often support memory for NLP agents.
- **Tools**: Tools refer to external functionalities the agent can invoke to complete tasks it cannot perform natively. This may include:
    - Web search APIs
    - Code execution environments
    - Calculators or document parsers

    The ability to invoke tools expands the agent's capabilities, making them adaptable across domains.
- **Planner**: The planner breaks down complex user prompts into manageable subtasks, determines their execution order, and sets goals. For example, in a research task, the planner may first decide to search for papers, then summarize key points, and finally synthesize them.
- **Executor**: The executor carries out the subtasks identified by the planner. It interfaces with tools, interacts with memory, and handles decision-making at

each step. The executor often loops through tool invocation, content parsing, and response construction, creating a coherent workflow.

Tools for Building NLP Agents

- **LangChain**: LangChain is an open-source framework for building applications using LLMs with chains, agents, and tool integrations. It provides abstractions for memory, tools, prompt templates, and agent workflows, making it easier to prototype and scale NLP agents.
- **Auto-GPT**: Auto-GPT is a pioneering project that enables LLMs such as GPT-4 to autonomously complete goals by generating and executing tasks iteratively. It includes internet access, memory, and command execution, demonstrating how LLMs can act with minimal human intervention.
- **AgentVerse**: AgentVerse is a platform focused on multi-agent communication and collaboration. It allows the deployment of multiple AI agents that work together on tasks, simulate human interactions, or explore cooperation and competition in artificial intelligence environments.

Use Cases of NLP Agents

- **Research Assistants**: NLP agents can conduct literature reviews, summarize research papers, extract key information, and generate research outlines. These agents can streamline academic and industrial R&D workflows.
- **Customer Support Bots**: By leveraging tools and memory, agents provide contextual, dynamic, and multi-step assistance–handling FAQs, resolving account issues, or escalating complex queries to human agents.
- **Knowledge Miners**: Agents can be used to crawl, parse, and analyze large volumes of unstructured data from documents, websites, or databases to build knowledge graphs or structured insights.
- **Business Process Automation**: NLP agents can help with email management, report generation, task scheduling, or meeting summarization–automating routine office tasks using language as the interface.

In summary, NLP agents represent the evolution of LLM applications from passive responders to proactive, task-driven, and tool-integrated autonomous systems. By incorporating components such as memory, planning, and tool usage, and using frameworks such as LangChain or Auto-GPT, developers can build agents that not only understand language but also act intelligently upon it. This growing paradigm promises to redefine the future of human-computer interaction and automation.

The Future of NLP

The future of Natural Language Processing (NLP) is evolving at a transformative pace, fueled by the advancements in foundation models, increased computational resources, and growing societal integration of AI. As we look ahead, NLP is moving far beyond sentence classification or chatbot interactions–it is redefining how humans communicate with machines, how businesses operate, and how information is consumed, generated, and acted upon. Below is a comprehensive look at the key pillars shaping the future of NLP.

Major Trends in NLP's Future

Major Trends in NLP's Future reflect a significant shift toward making language models more efficient, intelligent, and accessible. Key trends include the rise of lightweight and energy-efficient models through **quantization and distillation, increased personalization using user-specific data and context-aware interactions, and enhanced reasoning capabilities** through techniques such as **chain-of-thought prompting and multi-agent collaboration**. Additionally, multimodal learning and the emergence of democratic, open-access NLP tools are driving broader adoption and innovation across diverse domains and languages. These trends are reshaping how NLP systems are developed, deployed, and experienced.

- **Efficiency: Doing More with Less**

  With large models demanding massive computation and energy, there is a growing push toward *efficiency-focused* NLP. This trend includes techniques such as:

  - **Quantization:** Reducing model size by representing weights with lower precision.
  - **Distillation:** Creating smaller models that mimic large models.
  - **Sparse Architectures:** Like **Mixture-of-Experts (MoE)**, where only parts of the model activate during inference.
  - **Edge Deployment:** Making NLP models runnable on mobile devices and embedded systems without sacrificing performance.

Efficient NLP is becoming essential not just for sustainability but also for accessibility, bringing powerful models to low-resource environments and users without expensive infrastructure.

- **Hyper-Personalization**

Future NLP systems will deeply understand user preferences, goals, contexts, and interaction histories to deliver personalized outputs. Whether it is tailoring search results, customizing educational content, or creating individualized AI writing assistants, **context-aware and user-specific NLP** will be foundational. Key techniques include:

  - Embedding user history and feedback in the model's memory.
  - Fine-tuning or prompting LLMs with user-specific data.

  - Federated learning to enable on-device personalization without compromising privacy.

- **Advanced Reasoning Capabilities**

Language models are increasingly expected not just to generate fluent text, but to **reason**, **plan**, and **solve complex problems**. Research areas that will dominate include:

  - **Chain of Thought (CoT) prompting:** Explicitly guiding LLMs to generate intermediate reasoning steps.
  - **Self-consistency decoding:** Aggregating multiple reasoning paths to reach consistent answers.
  - **Program synthesis:** Enabling models to write and debug code as part of reasoning workflows.

This transformation is pushing NLP closer to **Artificial General Intelligence (AGI)**, where language is not just communication, but a medium for cognition.

- **Rise of Multi-Agent Systems**

Instead of relying on a single LLM, **multi-agent NLP systems** will become prominent. These systems involve multiple specialized agents communicating and collaborating to solve tasks:

  - A **planner agent** breaks down a task.
  - A **retriever agent** gathers relevant context.
  - A **writer agent** drafts or summarizes information.

This modular architecture will improve reliability, explainability, and performance for complex applications such as research, autonomous business processes, and real-time decision-making.

Democratization of NLP

The democratization of NLP means making powerful language technologies accessible to all—regardless of technical background, geography, or resources.

- **Open-Source Models and Frameworks:** Projects such as Hugging Face's transformers, **EleutherAI's GPT-NeoX, Meta's LLaMA, and BigScience's BLOOM** are ensuring that the foundational layers of NLP are no longer confined to big tech. Developers, researchers, students, and even small organizations can build on cutting-edge LLMs.
- **Low/No-Code Tools:** Frameworks such as **Streamlit, Gradio, and LangChain** allow non-experts to build sophisticated NLP applications using simple

interfaces or minimal code. This accelerates NLP application development across domains like healthcare, education, law, and customer service.

- **Language Inclusion and Accessibility:** Efforts to train models in **low-resource languages** and **multilingual corpora** (for example, IndicNLP, Masakhane, and NLLB by Meta) are expanding NLP's benefits beyond the English-speaking world. Democratization includes both **technological access** and **linguistic inclusiveness**, ensuring that NLP reaches diverse global communities.

The Evolving Role of Developers

The era of foundation models has dramatically altered what it means to "build NLP systems." Instead of training models from scratch, developers now:

- **Design and Engineer Prompt-Based Solutions:** Prompt engineering–crafting effective prompts to elicit the desired behavior from LLMs–has become a key developer skill. Developers must understand context windows, temperature settings, output constraints, and dynamic prompt chaining.
- **Orchestrate Agent Workflows:** NLP developers are increasingly building intelligent systems, not standalone models. This involves chaining LLMs with external tools (for example, databases, APIs), managing memory, and incorporating human feedback into iterative pipelines.
- **Prioritize Ethics and Safety:** Developers today must factor in **bias detection**, **content filtering**, **auditing model behavior**, and ensuring **regulatory compliance** (for example, GDPR, HIPAA) when deploying NLP applications. Responsible AI practices are not optional–they are integral to modern NLP development.
- **Act as Curators, Not Just Coders:** With models such as GPT-4 capable of complex text generation, developers are often curators–guiding, supervising, and refining the output of models rather than handcrafting every line of logic. This calls for **domain expertise**, **judgment**, and **human-AI collaboration skills**.

Conclusion

The future of NLP is not only technologically rich, it is also socially transformative. It promises intelligent systems that reason, interact, and adapt. It promises decentralization, accessibility, and inclusivity. Additionally, it necessitates a new generation of developers who comprehend how models connect with the outside world in addition to how they operate. Whether we are an enthusiast, researcher, or practitioner, this is the moment to take advantage of these developments, make a responsible contribution, and be ready for an intelligent, human-centered, and global future of natural language processing.

This brings an end to the book on NLP Projects using spaCy and Hugging Face. I hope the book readers will find the book informative, resourceful, and equipped enough to build real-life NLP projects and applications from scratch.

References

- https://github.com/doccano/doccano
- https://labelstud.io/
- https://prodi.gy/
- https://research.ibm.com/blog/ai-fairness-360
- https://fairlearn.org/
- https://docs.opendp.org/en/stable/index.html
- https://shap.readthedocs.io/en/latest/
- https://c3.ai/glossary/data-science/lime-local-interpretable-model-agnostic-explanations/
- https://captum.ai/
- https://eli5.readthedocs.io/en/latest/
- https://www.capitalnumbers.com/blog/nlp-trends-use-cases/
- https://www.linkedin.com/pulse/nlp-current-trends-future-directions-bushra-amjad-f9xxf/
- https://savvycomsoftware.com/blog/natural-language-processing-trends/
- https://medium.com/@yashsinha12354/ai-for-natural-language-processing-nlp-in-2024-latest-trends-and-advancements-17da4af13cde
- https://www.shaip.com/blog/nlp-trends-2025/
- https://arxiv.org/pdf/1706.03762
- https://arxiv.org/pdf/1810.04805
- https://arxiv.org/pdf/2303.08774
- https://arxiv.org/pdf/2312.10997
- https://arxiv.org/abs/2201.11903#
- https://github.com/Timothyxxx/Chain-of-ThoughtsPapers
- https://huggingface.co/learn/agents-course/en/unit0/introduction
- https://www.coursera.org/learn/learn-ai-agents
- https://medium.com/@maximilian.vogel/mastering-ai-agents-the-10-best-free-courses-tutorials-learning-tools-46bc380a19d1

- https://learn.microsoft.com/en-us/training/modules/ai-agent-fundamentals/
- https://www.udemy.com/course/ai-agents-course/?srsltid=AfmBOoqXyQusk-tqfzxH0GBAqjnTVCUkIvhlt_ATHNcgwNeBG_QwxOa0&couponCode=LEARNNOWPLANS
- https://medium.com/data-science-collective/the-open-source-stack-for-ai-agents-8ab900e33676
- https://getstream.io/blog/multiagent-ai-frameworks/
- https://medium.com/data-science-collective/the-complete-guide-to-building-your-first-ai-agent-its-easier-than-you-think-c87f376c84b2
- https://www.marketermilk.com/blog/best-ai-agent-platforms
- https://openai.com/index/new-tools-for-building-agents/

Index

Symbols

B

C

M

N

S

T

U

W